DOCTOR · WHO

THE ENCYCLOPEDIA

A Definitive Guide to Time and Space

Gary Russell

BBC
BOOKS

1 3 5 7 9 10 8 6 4 2

Published in 2007 by BBC Books, an imprint of Ebury Publishing.
Ebury Publishing is a division of the Random House Group Ltd.

Doctor Who is a BBC Wales production for BBC One
Executive Producers: Russell T Davies and Julie Gardner
Series Producer: Phil Collinson

The Random House Group Limited Reg. No. 954009.
Addresses for companies within the Random House Group can
be found at www.randomhouse.co.uk

A CIP catalogue record for this book is available from the British
Library.

ISBN 978 1 84607 291 8

The Random House Group Limited makes every effort to ensure that
the papers used in our books are made from trees that have been
legally sourced from well-managed and credibly certified forests. Our
paper procurement policy can be found at www.randomhouse.co.uk

Commissioning Editor: Mathew Clayton
Project Editor: Steve Tribe
Designer: Stuart Manning

Printed and bound in Italy by Graphicom SRL

To buy books by your favourite authors and register for offers,
visit www.rbooks.co.uk

Introduction

It seemed such an easy task – an alphabetical list of everything in televised *Doctor Who* between 2005 and now! More than 1,700 entries and over 90,000 words later and we have it. And I just know that someone – probably you in fact – will go to find your favourite reference and say, 'It's missing!'

But I'd like to think you won't be able to find anything omitted, because I've had sterling help from an amazing team of elves and pixies helping out on this – checking my facts, my grammar, my tenses and querying, more than once, my sanity. So, in no particular order, thanks to Andrew Pixley, Edward Russell, Matt Nicholls, Mark Oliver, John Roulston-Bates, Nicholas Pegg, Barnaby Edwards, Peter Anghelides, Joseph Lidster and, most importantly, Scott Handcock, who so foolishly said one afternoon when I was especially stressed, 'Do you want me to write a couple of entries for you'? So I gave him a dozen of the biggest, most convoluted ones needing the most research – which he did magnificently. Still, bet he won't be asking that again.

Thanks also to the team behind the book, Mathew Clayton at BBC Books, Steve Tribe, wise and wonderful editor, and Stuart Manning, design god. And to Cameron Fitch and Kari Speers for their invaluable help. One day we'll all have longer than 'yesterday'.

Should there be an update of this book in the distant future, here is a list of words and phrases that *might* become entries in that next edition:

Adipose	Gray, Private	Rattigan, Mrs	Skree, Lt.
Bannakaffalatta	ICAPS	Red-Eye	Spartacus
Blyton, Enid	Major Domo	Red Widow, the	Spectre Inspectre
Carravaggio, Daniel	Noble Corporation PLC Limited	Scoles, Mr	Sto
Century House	– Intergalactic	Sense-Sphere	Unicorn
Chandrakala, Miss	Passenger 57	Sibylline Oracles	Vespiform
Foss Street	Peth, Astrid	Silicon Valley	

Thanks as always to Russell T Davies, Julie Gardner and Phil Collinson, without whom…

0207 946000: The phone number for people to call if they had information regarding the whereabouts of Rose Tyler after her disappeance in March 2005. (1.4)

0207 946003: The phone number of the company Rodrigo worked for as a tow-truck driver. (1.13)

0301-566-9155-76544891: Telephone number the presenter of *Crime Crackers* asked viewers to call if they had any information about the disappearances of children from Stratford in 2012. (2.11T)

08081 570980: The freephone number used by the authorities after the Slitheen-augmented pig crashed its spaceship into Big Ben, in case anyone needed information about missing relatives. It was later open to any member of the public to report alien sightings. Jackie Tyler called it to report the Doctor, which set off a Code Nine alert in the Government. (1.4, 1.5)

100,000,000,000,000: The year in which the Doctor and Martha Jones arrived on Malcassairo and discovered Captain Jack Harkness outside the TARDIS – Jack had travelled through the Vortex attached to the outside of the ship, causing it to take them to the end of the universe. They found the last survivors of humanity preparing to board a huge rocket that would transport them to the legendary planet Utopia, hoping to colonise it and start a new life. The Master later took Lucy Saxon even further, arriving at Utopia to find the human survivors had trapped themselves inside spheres, which he named 'Toclafane'. He then used the Doctor's TARDIS to house a paradox machine that enabled the Toclafane to exist both 100,000,000,000,000 years in the future and on 21st-century Earth simultaneously. When the paradox machine was destroyed, time jumped out of synch by one year, backwards, to the point when the Toclafane first arrived en masse. This left the Toclafane trapped on Utopia, in the far future, unable to ever escape. (3.11, 3.12, 3.13)

12,005: The Doctor took Rose Tyler to this year to visit the New Roman Empire during her first TARDIS trip but, in the end, they didn't leave the TARDIS. (1.2)

133 Squadron: The RAF Squadron that Captain Jack Harkness was a volunteer member of. (1.9)

1336: In this year, the Doctor, Rose Tyler and Captain Jack Harkness visited Kyoto when it was still the capital city of Japan, at the beginning of the civil wars of the Yoshino period. The Doctor later explained that they only just escaped. (1.12)

15.39: The scheduled time for Earthdeath. (1.2)

15-10 Barric Fields: Discovered by the mathematician San Chen not San Hazeldine. Rodrick didn't know this when asked by the Anne Droid in *The Weakest Link* aboard the Game Station. (1.12)

1540: The year that a shooting star reportedly crashed into the Glen of St Catherine, carrying with it the original Haemovariform that periodically sought a host from then on. (2.2)

1599: The year the Doctor took Martha to when they encountered William Shakespeare and the alien Carrionites. (3.2)

1727: The year when the Doctor first met the young Jeanne-Antoinette Poisson, aka Reinette. He met her again a few months later in the same year. (2.4)

1730: The year in which the Doctor visited the then occupier of 10 Downing Street, a Mr Chicken. (1.5)

1744: Arthur the Horse went through a time window from this year to the 51st century. The Doctor used the same time window to briefly visit Paris and keep an eye on Reinette Poisson. (2.4)

1753: The year that Rose Tyler visited Reinette (now Madame de Pompadour) to warn her of the Clockwork Robots' plans for her. (2.4)

1758: The year in which Madame de Pompadour turned 37 and the Clockwork Robots made their final assault on Versailles. (2.4)

1764: The Doctor returned to collect Madame de Pompadour in April of this year, six years too late: illness had taken her. He watched as she left Versailles for the last time, in a hearse. (2.4)

1796: By this year, a specific room inside 10 Downing Street had been established as the Cabinet Room, and still was by 2006. In 1991, a three-inch steel protective wall was added to the room. (1.4, 1.5)

1860: The Doctor wanted to take Rose Tyler to Naples in this year. He failed. (1.3)

1869: When the Doctor tried to take Rose Tyler to Naples in 1860, they arrived instead in Victorian Cardiff on Christmas Eve. (1.3) Captain Jack Harkness was later stranded in this year after fleeing the Game Station, burning out his Vortex Manipulator in the process. (3.11)

1879: The TARDIS took the Doctor and Rose to this year, when they met Queen Victoria travelling by coach through the lowlands of Scotland. (2.2)

1883: The year of the Krakatoa eruption. (1.1) At Christmas, a Graske kidnapped a street urchin from London and took him back to the hatchery on Griffoth, replacing him with a malevolent changeling. (AotG)

1892: The year that, after a man shot him on Ellis Island, Captain Jack Harkness realised he couldn't die, thanks to Rose Tyler's use of the Time Vortex to bring him back to life after his extermination by the Daleks. (1.13, 3.11)

1913: The year that the now-human Doctor, living as John Smith, schoolteacher, and Martha Jones, acting as his maid, lived in for nearly three months while avoiding the Family of Blood. The Family finally caught up with the time travellers on the night of 11 November. (3.8, 3.9)

1914: The year of the outbreak of the First World War, which effectively started in June with the assassination of Archduke Ferdinand of Austria.

Son of Mine wondered if all the boys Mr Rocastle had taught to fight in the years beforehand would thank him as they died in the trenches. (3.9)

1915: In the possible future dreamed of by John Smith and Joan Redfern, they married in this year. (3.9)

1916: In John Smith and Joan Redfern's fictional future, they had their first daughter in this year. (3.9)

1920: The year the Weeping Angel sent Kathy Nightingale to; she arrived in Hull on 5 December. (3.10)

1926: In the fictional future dreamed of by John Smith and Joan Redfern, they had had two girls and a younger boy by this year. (3.9)

1930: The Doctor and Martha visited New York on 1 November and discovered the Cult of Skaro working secretly beneath the streets of Manhattan. (3.4, 3.5)

1941: The TARDIS arrived in London on 21 January, shortly before the beginning of an air raid, a regular occurrence during the Blitz. (1.9, 1.10)

1948: The year that the Olympic Games had last been held in Britain before the 30th Olympiad in 2012. The Doctor sat through it twice, he enjoyed it so much. (2.11)

1953: The Coronation of Queen Elizabeth II was on 2 June of this year. The Doctor and Rose Tyler missed the event itself, but went to the street party after defeating the Wire. (2.7)

1956: The year the Doctor was hoping to get Rose Tyler to, so they could watch Elvis Presley perform 'Hound Dog' live on *The Ed Sullivan Show* on 28 October. (2.7)

1963: In John Smith and Joan Redfern's fictional future, John died in 1963, leaving behind Joan, his children and their children, all safe. (3.9)

1969: The year one specific Weeping Angel sent the Doctor, Martha Jones and Billy Shipton back to. Without the TARDIS, the Doctor and Martha were trapped there, and she had to get a job in a shop to support them.

With Billy's help, the Doctor filmed messages for Sally Sparrow and, nearly 40 years later, Billy encoded these onto DVDs for Sally to find. (3.10)

1979: The Doctor dropped Rose Tyler off at Wembley in November of this year to see ABBA, while he chased after the alien Graske. (AotG) The Doctor also planned to take Rose to see Ian Dury and the Blockheads perform in Sheffield on 21 November. (2.2)

1982: Pete Tyler married Jackie Prentice in this year. (1.8) On 'Pete's World', John Lumic established Cybus Industries. (2.5T)

1987: The year Katherine Wainwright, née Nightingale, wrote a letter to Sally Sparrow, asking her grandson to deliver it 20 years later. She died that same year. (3.10)

1989: The Doctor mentioned that heading to Marbella in 1989 would be a good way of avoiding the Dalek Stratagem of 200,100. (1.13)

200,000: The year in which the TARDIS materialised aboard Satellite Five. (1.7)

200,100: The year when the TARDIS was brought to the Game Station by the Controller, who wanted the Doctor to find a way to destroy the Daleks. (1.12, 1.13)

2005: The year Rose Tyler met the Doctor for the first time. She was reported by her mum, Jackie, as having gone missing on 6 March (1.1, 1.4)

20-Point-5: Date on 'Pete's World' used by Ricky Smith to signify when Pete Tyler began working for Cybus Industries. Presumably this was 2005, and related to when Pete sold his Vitex company to John Lumic. (2.6)

2007: The year from which the Doctor and Martha Jones fled the Family of Blood. The Doctor then used the TARDIS's chameleon arch to turn him human for approximately three months, knowing that if the Family hadn't found him by then, they would die. (3.8, 3.9)

2012: The Doctor and Rose arrived in Utah in this year when the TARDIS was drawn there by a stray signal that turned out to be a Dalek distress call. (1.6) Also the year of the Olympic Games in London, which the Doctor took Rose to, so they could see the opening of the event. Arriving in Stratford, they found out that children had been disappearing inexplicably from Dame Kelly Holmes Close. (2.11)

2019: The year in which SMT replaced microprocessors in Earth technology. (1.7)

467-989: The specific DNA-type of the Dalek creatures housed within the armoured shells. (3.4)

5,000,000,023: The year that the Doctor took Rose Tyler to the planet New Earth. (2.1)

5,000,000,029: The year that the mutated Bliss virus wiped out the majority of New New York. (3.3)

5,000,000,053: The year that the Doctor took Martha Jones to the planet New Earth. (3.3)

5.5/apple/26: The year, five billion years in Rose Tyler's future, in which the planet Earth was destroyed when the Sun expanded. The event was called Earthdeath and was witnessed from aboard Platform One. (1.2)

5.6.1.434 sigma 777: The incomplete coordinates of the Dalek fleet from the Game Station, given to the Doctor by the Controller the instant before the Daleks transmatted and exterminated her. (1.12)

5/930167.02: The coordinates of an area within the Rexel planetary configuration known as the Deep Darkness. (3.2)

5006: The year in which the Doctor planned to take Rose Tyler for a visit to the planet Barcelona. Specifically, a Tuesday in October at 6pm. (CiN)

51st century: The era from which both Captain Jack Harkness (1.9) and the 37-year-old SS *Madame de Pompadour* hailed. (2.4)

58.2 North 10.2 East: The coordinates of the *Valiant* when the Doctor, Captain Jack Harkness and Martha Jones teleported aboard, using Jack's Vortex Manipulator. (3.12)

58.5 kiloamperes, transferred charge 510 megajoules: The precise electrical pulse needed to bring down a Toclafane sphere. (3.13)

6879760: Using binary 9, Mickey Smith was able to hack into the Cybus Industries computers on 'Pete's World' and access the code which disabled the Cybermen's emotional inhibitors. Having found the code, he texted it to Rose Tyler's mobile, which the Doctor linked into the Cyber Control mainframe, switching the inhibitors off. (2.6)

761390: The coordinates on Earth of the Globe Theatre to which the portal from the Deep Darkness was trying to connect. (3.2)

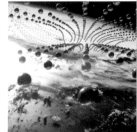

8.02am: The time at which the Paradox Machine attached to the Doctor's TARDIS by the Master activated. This created a rip in time and space, enabling the massed Toclafane to travel from Utopia, at the end of the universe, and destroy humanity, their own ancestors, in the 21st century. This happened seconds after the assassination of President Winters but, when the Paradox Machine was destroyed 12 months later, time jumped out of synch and returned to 8.02am, trapping the Toclafane in the future – their invasion had never happened and, to the majority of humanity, the only Toclafane incursion involved the murder of Winters, after which they vanished completely, as did Harry Saxon. (3.12, 3.13)

ABBA: Swedish pop group that Rose Tyler saw play live at Wembley in November 1979 while the Doctor hunted the Graske. (AotG)

Abbadon: Legendary demon name, one of many attributed to the Beast throughout the galaxies. (2.8, 2.9)

Aberdeen: Queen Victoria was travelling there by coach rather than train as a tree had reportedly been placed on the line, possibly a precursor to an assassination attempt. (2.2) At the time of her original journeys alongside the Doctor, Sarah Jane Smith's home was in South Croydon and that's where the Doctor told her he had brought her to when it was time for them to part ways. After the TARDIS left her, Sarah Jane realised she wasn't in Hillview Road, Croydon at all, but in Aberdeen. (2.3)

Abide With Me: 19th-century Christian anthem, sung by the drivers from the New New York Motorway as they reclaimed the Overcity after the Doctor freed them. (3.3)

Abomination: The Dalek Emperor referred to Rose Tyler as this when she returned to the Game Station, the power of the Time Vortex coursing through her being. She used this power to obliterate him, his Daleks and their fleet from existence. (1.13)

Abzorbaloff, the: The name taken by a creature from the planet Clom, twin world to Raxacoricofallapatorius. Disguised as the human Victor Kennedy, he absorbed humans into his flesh for food, whilst searching for the Doctor so he could steal his TARDIS. He carried a silver-topped claw-shaped cane, which was actually a limitation-field creator that kept him compressed after he had absorbed the humans. When Elton Pope broke the cane, the final four victims, Ursula Blake, Colin Skinner, Bridget and Bliss fought back, and the Abzorbaloff died as he exploded and his remains were in turn absorbed by the earth under the concrete paving stones of London. (2.10) (Played by PETER KAY)

Academy: Ancient seat of learning for Time Lords on Gallifrey. Time Lords entered it at eight years of age, as Novices, after viewing the Untempered Schism. It was destroyed along with the rest of Gallifrey at the end of the Last Great Time War. (3.12)

Acetic acid: A useful defence against the calcium-based Raxacoricofallapatorians who made up the Family Slitheen. Jackie Tyler used vinegar to defeat the Slitheen that threatened her and Mickey Smith. (1.5)

Acorah, Derek: Presenter of the series *Most Haunted*, he bemoaned the fact that, as ghosts were now everywhere, he was out of a job. (2.12)

Adams, Douglas: Author of the *Hitchhiker's Guide to the Galaxy* series of novels. After defeating the Sycorax Leader, the Doctor likened himself to the books' lead character, Arthur Dent, since he was wearing pyjamas and a dressing gown, as Dent did throughout his travels. (2.X)

Adherents of the Repeated Meme: Robotic servants of the Lady Cassandra aboard Platform One, bringing with them the deadly Spider robots. When they arrived in the Manchester Suite, the Steward introduced them as representing the Financial Family Seven, but the Doctor quickly realised this was a ruse and exposed them as frauds, at which point they were all deactivated. (1.2) (Voiced by SILAS CARSON)

Agar, Milton: Wrote the music for 'Happy Days Are Here Again', one of the show tunes used as part of the *New York Revue* at the Laurenzi theatre in 1930s New York. (3.4)

Age of Steel: The Cyber Controller on 'Pete's World' declared that, with its army becoming fully operational, Earth was now in the Age of Steel (2.6)

Agorax: One of the players of *The Weakest Link* aboard the Game Station. When he lost the final round, the Anne Droid appeared to disintegrate him, but in truth he was transmatted over to the Dalek mothership and turned into part of the growing Dalek army created by the Emperor. (1.12) (Played by DOMINIC BURGESS)

Air Force One: Personal aircraft of the President of the United States. It brought President Winters to Britain, along with a cadre of UNIT troops, to discuss the Toclafane with Harry Saxon. (3.12)

Aitchinson Price: Author of a book that was the definitive account of Mafeking, according to John Smith, the history teacher at Farringham School for Boys. (3.8)

Alan: London man who, like his children, had A+ blood and thus was affected by the Sycorax's blood control. (2.X) (Played by SIMON HUGHES)

Albert, Prince of Saxe-Coburg and Gotha: Beloved husband to Queen Victoria, he died in 1861. Foreseeing the danger of the Haemovariform rumoured to exist in the lands around the Torchwood Estate, Albert, along with his friend Sir George MacLeish, built a huge telescope. Linking it to the fabled Koh-I-Noor diamond which he repeatedly had cut down until it was the correct size, they hoped that the beam of moonlight created would be enough to destroy the Haemovariform. They were correct, though neither lived to see their work come to fruition. (2.2)

Albion Hospital: Situated in the City of London, bordering the East End, Albion Hospital was where the augmented pig was taken to be examined by undercover Torchwood scientist Toshiko Sato. (1.4) In 1941, Dr Constantine was the last of the hospital's inhabitants to succumb to the Chula virus that turned people into gas mask zombies but later, along with the patients and staff was returned to a better state of health than they had been in before. (1.9, 1.10)

Alexandra Palace: Originally built in 1873 as North London's answer to the Crystal Palace, in 1936 it ceased being an exhibition centre and became the home for the BBC's first experiments in live television broadcasts – it remained an essential part of the BBC's transmissions until the mid-1960s, although the mast still broadcasts today. The Wire instructed Magpie to go there and hook up a primitive portable television

to the mast. This would enable the Wire to disseminate itself further afield, creating the Time of Manifestation. The Doctor was able to briefly turn the portable TV that Mr Magpie had built from a receiver into a transmitter and beamed the Wire back onto an early Betamax video recorder. (2.7)

Alf: A young boy Nancy agreed to look after on the streets of Blitzed London, brought to her by another lad, Jim. He had been evacuated from London to stay with a family on a farm, but was abused by a man there. Like all the kids now in Nancy's care, he had then fled back home to London. (1.9, 1.10) (Played by BRANDON MILLER)

Algy: British army officer who was with Captain Jack Harkness when the latter spotted Rose Tyler hanging on the mooring rope of a loose barrage balloon while a German air raid was under way in Blitzed London. Later, on duty at the Limehouse Green railway yard where the crashed Chula medical ship was stored, he became infected by the gas-mask illness. He was eventually cured by the Chula nanogenes. (1.9, 1.10) (Played by ROBERT HANDS)

Alien world: A beautiful red-hued planet with massive creatures wheeling in the air, to which the Doctor took Rose Tyler. While there, he asked her how long she would stay with him. For ever was her response. (2.12)

Allhallows Street: Street in Southwark where the crooked house stood that the Carrionites used as their base of operations. (3.2)

Alpha Class: Designation of the type of space station Platform One was – i.e. top of the range. (1.2)

Ambassador of Thrace: Lady Cassandra O'Brien attended a drinks party in his honour one night, when a dying man approached her and told her she was beautiful. She remembered this as being the last time anyone told her that. In truth, the dying man was herself, transplanted into the failing body of Chip. (2.1)

Ambassadors from the City State of Binding Light: Guests aboard Platform One for the Earthdeath spectacle, their oxygen intake required specialised monitoring. (1.2)

Ambrose Hall: A children's home where the orphaned schoolgirl Nina lived. (2.3)

Ancient Britain: Referred to in questions by the Anne Droid aboard the Game Station, during the *Weakest Link* quiz. (1.12)

Andrew: One of the Lever Room operators responsible for bombarding the Wall with particle energy via the giant Levers during a 'ghost shift'. He was killed by Cyberleader One, who arrived to take over Torchwood Tower. (2.12)

Angelica: One of the guests at Donna Noble and Lance Bennett's wedding. She wasn't being particularly helpful during the confusion after Donna vanished on her way to the altar. (3.X)

Angelo, Father: Leader of the Brethren, who worshipped the Haemovariform and brought it to the Torchwood Estate. Having taken over the House and imprisoned its occupants, he forced Sir Robert MacLeish to act as if nothing had changed when Queen Victoria arrived. When he revealed his true motives, Queen Victoria shot him dead. (2.2) (Played by IAN HANMORE)

Annalise: 20-year-old ditzy girl, who had an affair with Clive Jones (she claimed he seduced her) and ultimately set up home with him. She attended Leo Jones's 21st birthday event (although allegedly only bought him a bar of scented soap) and got into an argument with Francine Jones, Clive's wife over Annalise's tanning tones. Annalise then stormed off into the night, pursued by an angry Clive. (3.1) (Played by KIMMI RICHARDS)

Anne Droid: Quizmaster of *The Weakest Link*, a robot with what appeared to be a disintegrator blaster in its mouth, but was in fact a transmat beam, sending losing contestants over to the Dalek mothership, where they were turned into part of the growing Dalek army created by the Emperor. The Anne Droid was later reprogrammed to defend the station against the

Daleks but was exterminated on Floor 495. (1.12, 1.13) (Voiced by ANNE ROBINSON, played by ALAN RUSCOE)

Anne, Princess: Princess Royal in the 21st-century Royal Family. Rose Tyler wondered if she was a werewolf. (2.2)

'Another Rock 'n' Roll Christmas': 1984 hit for Gary Glitter. It was playing in the house where the Graske replaced the parents with changelings. (AotG)

Anti-matter monsters: Sarah Jane Smith told Rose Tyler that during her time travelling with the Doctor, they had fought these creatures. (2.3)

Antiplastic: The Doctor had a vial of this in case he couldn't persuade the Nestene Consciousness to leave Earth voluntarily. Although an Auton stole it from the Doctor, Rose Tyler knocked into the Auton, causing it to drop the antiplastic onto the liquid-plastic form of the Consciousness. (1.1)

Anura: Planet almost entirely covered with water, with only tiny islands just far enough above sea level to require its inhabitants to be amphibious. However, on long journeys away from Anura, the Anurans required portable water tanks to keep them breathing. Ulysses Mergrass, who the Doctor met on Myarr, came from Anura. (TIQ)

Apple Grass: Kind of sweet-smelling grass found on the slopes overlooking the New Atlantic on New Earth. (2.1) Cheen had heard that the air in Brooklyn smelled of apple grass. (3.3)

Appleton, Alistair: Presenter of the television show *Ghostwatch*, which examined the phenomena of the ghosts appearing all over the world. When the ghosts were revealed to be Cybermen, he was killed live on television. (2.12)

Arcadia, the Fall of: One of the last battles, perhaps the actual final battle, in the Great Time War. The Doctor was there and watched as the Daleks fled from it. (2.13)

ARCHANGEL NETWORK:

Communications system in the United Kingdom launched by Harry Saxon. Via its 15 satellites in orbit around Earth, the Master beamed down the four-beat pulsing rhythm with which he hypnotised the population of Britain into voting for him (it was roughly 98 per cent successful). Most of the broadband and mobile phones used in Britain during Saxon's time, including Martha Jones's phone, utilised the Archangel network. The Doctor used the network against the Master, by tuning his mind into it over his year in captivity and linking telepathically all the humans already enslaved by the pulse-beat. Boosted by the empathic chant of 'Doctor' from people across the world, as inspired by Martha Jones, the Doctor was able to use the Archangel network to psychically reverse the ageing process the Master had put him through. With the boost of power this gave him, the Doctor briefly accessed almost preternatural powers, becoming impervious to the Master's laser screwdriver simply by exercising his belief that it wouldn't harm him. The Master's spell over humanity broken, the Doctor and Captain Jack Harkness were able to rid Earth of the Toclafane. (3.12, 3.13)

Archduke Ferdinand: Austrian leader assassinated by a Serb, an event that led directly to the First World War, according to the Doctor. (3.9)

Architect: The architect of the Blaidd Drwg Project died when he was run over in bad weather by the Lord Mayor of Cardiff, Margaret Blaine. (1.11)

Archive Six: Where records were kept aboard the Game Station referring to contestants being transmatted into the game areas. The Female Programmer headed to Archive Six to discover more about the Doctor, but the Controller forbade it, stating that Archive Six was out of bounds. The old Spike Room from which Cathica Santini Khadeni had destroyed the Jagrafess, Archive Six was where the Controller hid the TARDIS from the Dalek monitoring devices. (1.12)

Arctic Desert: Area on Earth that Lady Cassandra O'Brien claimed her mother had been born in. (1.2)

Are You Being Served?: British 1970s sitcom set in a fictional department store. The Doctor quoted the opening lines to the theme song as he exited the elevator at the top of the Empire State Building. (3.5)

'Are you my mummy?': Chilling phrase spoken by the ghostly 'empty' child stalking the streets of East London during the Blitz. The child was actually the corpse of Jamie, a four-year-old boy killed by a falling German bomb and reanimated by confused Chula nanogenes. (1.9, 1.10)

Areas: The SS *Pentallian* was separated into a series of areas, many of which were accessible after a secure closure only by entering a random password set up by the crew after a drunken night of general knowledge quizzes. Area 31 – where the TARDIS materialised. Area 30 – the main area which engineering, medcentre etc spread out from. Erina Lissak was murdered by the sun-possessed Korwin McDonnell there. Area 29 – accessed by entering the date of the SS *Pentallian*'s first flight. Area 28 – accessed by knowing the next in sequence of a set of happy prime numbers. Kath McDonnell used the airlock there to eject herself and the sun-possessed Korwin McDonnell into space. Area 27 – where Lissak was nearly locked into when the secure closure occurred. It was accessed by knowing who had the most pre-download Number One singles in Britain out of The Beatles and Elvis Presley. Area 22 – where the sun-possessed Doctor crawled to after leaving the medcentre, trying to help Martha but instead yelling 'Burn with me'. When the fuel was dumped, he returned to normal there. Area 17 – Martha Jones and Riley Vashtee reached that at the same time as Korwin McDonnell transferred some of his sun-possession to Dev Ashton in engineering. When Ashton went to Area 17, he threatened Martha and Riley and they hid in an escape pod there, which Ashton then jettisoned. The Doctor later left the ship via the Area 17 airlock to remagnetise the outer hull and draw the pod back in. Area 10 – where Kath McDonnell and Orin

Scannell watched the jettisoned pod returning to Area 17 and feared that the Doctor would be crushed if he didn't move from the Area 17 airlock. Area 9 – accessed by knowing Vashtee's favourite colour. Area 4 – where Scannell and Vashtee began to realise they might not get to Area 1 before the ship collided with the sun. Area 2 – where Vashtee and Scannell heard Kath McDonnell's goodbye. Area 1 – where the auxiliary controls for the ship were and where Vashtee and Scannell vented the fuel from, so saving their lives. (3.7)

Arianna: Greek mate of Jackie Tyler's who once successfully sued the local council for suggested she looked Greek. She was Greek. She received £2,000. (1.1)

Arkiphets, the: One of the religions practised in the 42nd century. (2.9)

Armitage: Schoolboy at Farringham School for Boys in 1913, who knew the drill for defending the school when the Family of Blood attacked. (3.9)

Armstrong, Neil: The first man to step onto the Moon. Richard Lazarus estimated that his work with the Genetic Manipulation Device would prove as important to mankind as that achievement. (3.6)

Arthur: A white horse that wandered from 1744 Paris to the 51st-century SS *Madame de Pompadour* via a time window. The Doctor later rode Arthur back to France via the time window overlooking the Ballroom in 1758 Versailles. (2.4)

As You Like It: A play by William Shakespeare. The Doctor uses the phrase 'All the world's a stage' to the writer, thus providing him with part of the play's prologue. (3.2)

Ascension Islands: Henry Van Statten's aide Diana Goddard stated that the Dalek in Van Statten's Vault had come to Earth over 50 years previously, in the early 1960s, and crashed on 'the Ascension Islands'. It is not known if she meant Ascension Island itself or one of its neighbours, St Helena or Tristan da Cunha (which itself is actually five islands). (1.6)

Ascinta: A civilisation lost during the Last Great Time War. (2.3)

Ash, James: Co-writer of Rogue Traders' 'Voodoo Child', which was played by the Master aboard the *Valiant* as the Toclafane began their descent. (3.12)

Ashington: Schoolboy at Farringham School in 1913, who was told to fetch water for the Vickers Gun before the Family of Blood attacked. (3.9)

Ashton, Dev: Oldest crewman aboard the SS *Pentallian*, on his final tour of duty. He was a mechanic and engineer and was caught by Korwin McDonnell. Whereas McDonnell had vaporised his previous victims, with Ashton he transferred a portion of the sun he was consumed by into him, thus creating two agents for the sun amongst the crew. The sun-possessed Ashton then wrecked the ship's systems, meaning that the generators could not be brought back online to jump-start the engines. He then jettisoned an escape pod containing Martha Jones and Riley Vashtee towards the sun, and attacked captain Kath McDonnell in the medcentre. She overpowered him and pushed him into a stasis chamber, activating the cryofreeze unit, destroying the sun parts of him, leaving just his dead body. (3.7) (Played by GARY POWELL)

Asquith, General: Army officer in charge of investigating the Big Ben incident. After seeing the augmented pig at Albion Hospital, he went to 10 Downing Street to discover Joseph Green had been appointed Acting Prime Minister. Convinced the actual Prime Minister had been kidnapped by extraterrestrials, Asquith threatened to remove Green from power – until he was killed and his body used by one of the Slitheen family. The Slitheen version of Asquith then added to the military's confusion rather than aiding it, enabling the Family Slitheen to carry out their audacious plan. Asquith's Slitheen version was later killed when 10 Downing Street was destroyed by a sub-Harpoon missile. (1.4, 1.5) (Played by RUPERT VANSITTART)

Asteroid 7574B: Precise location of the *Infinite*, provided by the datachip possessed by Mergrass. (TIQ)

Astley, Rick: His number one hit 'Never Gonna Give You Up' was playing on Pete Tyler's car radio as he took Rose to St Christopher's Church for the wedding of Stuart Hoskins and Sarah Clark. (1.8)

At the Earth's Core: When Donna Noble realised that there was a tunnel drilled through from the Torchwood base beneath the Thames Barrier she wondered if it led to a world of dinosaurs as in a film she'd seen, most likely this 1976 movie. (3.X)

Atif: Freelance reporter who tried to sell a story about the Torchwood Institute to the editor of *The Examiner* after being given stolen papers by a disgruntled Torchwood employee. The editor, however, betrayed him to Torchwood, who took him away. (2.12T) (Played by SHANE ZAZA)

Atillo, Lieutenant: One of the security officers on the rocket silo base on Malcassairo, charged with ensuring the human refugees there got safely aboard the rocket. When the rocket was about to launch, Atillo joined his fellow humans and headed for Utopia. Whether he or his descendents were turned into the Toclafane by the Master is unknown. (3.11) (Played by NEIL REIDMAN)

Atkins Diet, the: According to Lance Bennett, Donna Noble talked excitedly about this dietary fad. (3.X)

Australasia: The Emperor Dalek's forces bombed this Earth continent in 200,100. (1.13)

Autons: Animated plastic shop-window dummies brought to life by the Nestene Consciousness when it landed on Earth, fleeing from the Time War. They carried lethal energy blasters in their right hands and were responsible for a massacre in the shopping arcade in South London witnessed by Clive Finch and his family, Jackie Tyler (1.1) and Elton Pope (2.10).

Axons: Energy-vampires that the Master had once been forced to bring to Earth. He and the Axons were defeated by the Doctor. The Master reminded the Doctor of this when taunting him over his current defeat. (3.13)

B

Back to the Future: The Doctor used this 1985 movie and it's time-travelling lead character, Marty McFly, to explain to Martha Jones the complexities of the Infinite Temporal Flux. (3.2)

Bailey, Dolly: Cheeky and cheerful host of the Elephant Inn, who provided rooms for William Shakespeare, the Doctor and Martha Jones. She discovers Lilith the Carrionite guiding Shakespeare's hand as he writes the climax of *Love's Labour's Won*, and dies of fright, helped along by Lilith. (3.2) (Played by ANDRÉE BERNARD)

Baines, Jeremy: Unpleasant bullying older boy at Farringham School for Boys, he was a snob and a racist. When he left the school grounds illicitly one night to retrieve beer stashed in a tree in Blackdown Woods, near Cooper's Field, he witnessed the arrival of the Family of Blood's spaceship. He found a way in and was murdered by the Family, who opted to use his body as a vessel for Son of Mine to inhabit. (3.8) (Played by HARRY LLOYD)

Baker, Matt: TV presenter on *Blue Peter*, who demonstrated how to make a cake shaped like the spaceship which had crashed into Big Ben. (1.4)

Balamory: Township which the Doctor pretended he was from when posing as Doctor James McCrimmon upon meeting Queen Victoria in 1879. Balamory is actually a fictional Scottish island created in a television programme for children 123 years later. (2.2)

Balhoon: Planet where the solicitors Jolco and Jolco did business, represented by the Moxx at the Earthdeath event aboard Platform One. (1.2)

Balmoral Castle: Queen Victoria's Scottish home in Aberdeenshire. She was travelling there when her party stopped en route at Sir Robert MacLeish's Torchwood House for a night's rest. (2.2)

Baltazar, Scourge of the Galaxy: A tyrannical despot from the planet Triton. He was about to obliterate Earth in the 40th century when the Doctor

Bad Wolf

Everywhere we go. Two words. Following us. Bad Wolf…

A phrase scattered throughout time and space, written all over the universe after Rose Tyler had looked into the heart of the TARDIS and absorbed the power of the Time Vortex. It followed the Ninth Doctor and Rose across their travels, before Rose realised it was a message from herself in the future, linking the Bad Wolf Corporation to the present day, and proving that she might yet return to the Doctor and save him on board the Game Station.

The phrase first appeared when the Moxx of Balhoon was heard talking about 'the Bad Wolf scenario' on Platform One. (1.2) Gabriel Sneed's psychic Welsh maid, Gwyneth, then spoke of seeing 'the Big Bad Wolf' when she read Rose's mind and glimpsed the future. (1.3) Shortly before the Slitheen attack in London, a young spray painter wrote 'BAD WOLF' onto the side of the TARDIS; the Doctor later made the boy wash it off. (1.4, 1.5) Similarly, in 1987, a street poster was defaced with the words 'Bad Wolf', not far from where Pete Tyler was originally killed (1.8) and, back in 1941, the German bomb due to land on Captain Jack Harkness's Chula ambulance was labelled 'Schlechter Wolf'. (1.10) In the year 200,000, Satellite Five was also responsible for broadcasting several thousand television channels, among them 'Bad WolfTV'. (1.7)

In contemporary Cardiff, Blon Fel Fotch Pasameer-Day Slitheen adopted the Welsh translation, 'Blaidd Drwg', as the name for her nuclear power station, and the Doctor realised for the first time that the phrase had been stalking

them through time, though he dismissed it as coincidence. (1.11) Soon after this, the Doctor and his companions were then abducted from the TARDIS to the Game Station, formerly Satellite Five, and now home to the Bad Wolf Corporation (1.12). It was their logo that Rose had scattered throughout space and time. The words also appeared on a poster in a South East London café

destroyed his ship, which he had grown from the metals on the planet Pheros. After his arrest (he was betrayed by his companion, Caw, for three bars of gold), he was placed in a cell on the prison planet Volag-Noc. There he discovered the story of the *Infinite* and, upon his release many years later, he set about finding the datachips that would create a 3D map to lead him to the legendary vessel. He set in motion a task for the Doctor, sending him on an unwitting quest to collect the chips and planning to relieve him of them later. When they found the location of the *Infinite*, Baltazar left the Doctor on Volag-Noc for three years, while heading to the fabled ship in the TARDIS with Martha Jones. But the *Infinite* was of no real use and the Doctor had Baltazar imprisoned in Volag-Noc once again for the murders of Kaliko, Mergrass and Gurney, the people who originally had the datachips. (TIQ) (Voiced by ANTHONY HEAD)

Banana daiquiri: The Doctor claimed to have invented this cocktail a couple of centuries early, in 18th-century France while drunk at a party with Madame de Pompadour. (2.4)

Bandogge: Mongrel dogs used to guard Bedlam, and which, as a demonstration to visitors, would sometimes be set upon the inmates for sport. The jailer at Bedlam offered to put on such a show for the Doctor and his friends. (3.2)

Banto: Owner of a DVD store where Kathy Nightingale's brother Larry worked. When Sally came in, Banto was watching an episode of the BBC series *Gangsters* and it was his moaning about how characters never go to the police when they're in trouble that sent Sally to the police station where she met DI Billy Shipton. (3.10) (Played by IAN BOLDSWORTH)

Banto's DVD Store: Selling new and second-hand DVDs, this was the shop on Queen Street that Larry Nightingale worked at when Sally Sparrow came to tell him about Kathy's disappearance. Amongst the DVDs on display were *Acid Burn*, *City Justice*, *Candy Kane*, *Angel Smile* and *Shooting the Sun*. While there, Sally also saw more of the recorded message from the Doctor; Larry explained to her that it was on 'Easter eggs' across 17 unrelated DVDs. Later, Sally and Larry bought Banto out and took on the shop for themselves, selling antique books and rare DVDs. (3.10)

and as graffiti on the Powell Estate. (1.13, 2.1) The Host would later associate Rose Tyler with the Wolf upon speaking with her in Scotland, 1879. (2.2)

Elsewhere, Henry Van Statten adopted 'Bad Wolf One' as the call sign for his helicopter, (1.6) whilst the Japanese translation, *akuro*, also appeared on one of the many cars trapped within the New New York Motorway in the year five billion and fifty-three. (3.3) According to Victor Kennedy's research, a Bad Wolf virus was also responsible for corrupting Torchwood's documentation on Rose Tyler. (2.10)

Such is the strength of this link between the Doctor and Rose that, as they said their final farewell across the Void, the Doctor's projection led Rose and her family to Dårlig Ulv Stranden in the 'Pete's World' Norway, otherwise known as Bad Wolf Bay. (2.13)

Barbarella: The Doctor likened the effect Rose's contemporary clothes would have on the people of Naples in 1860 to Jean-Claude Forest's comic-strip heroine, famed for wearing not very much at all. (1.3)

Barcelona: Capital city of Spain. The Doctor was not thinking of taking Rose Tyler there, but instead to the planet Barcelona, where dogs had no noses, on a Tuesday in October of 5006, at 6pm. (1.13, CiN)

Barren Earth Scenario: A study from the 'Pete's World' version of the Torchwood Institute reported that, as male fertility dropped, life spans in the western world were decreasing. (2.5)

Bartock, Daniel: Representative from the Ethics Committee on Sanctuary Base 6 who, according to the Beast, was a liar. He formed something of a flirtatious relationship with Rose Tyler and it was his idea to create a psychic flare that would disable the Ood and perhaps break the hold over them which the Beast had. When that was successful, he, Rose, Toby Zed and Zachary Cross Flane escaped on a shuttleship from Krop Tor as the planet was sucked towards the nearby black hole. (2.8, 2.9) (Played by RONNY JHUTTI)

Basic 5: The telepathic level upon which the Ood operated, communicating with one another. It rose to Basic 30 when the Beast first made contact with them and then, as they attacked the humans on Sanctuary Base 6, peaked at a massive Basic 100, which should have killed them but didn't. (1.8, 1.9)

Bastic bullets: Weaponry that Captain Jack Harkness told the doomed humans aboard the Game Station would be effective against Dalek armour. He knew he was lying to them, and indeed the Bastic Bullets failed. (1.13)

Battersea: Area of South West London, famous for its disused power station. On 'Pete's World', John Lumic's Cybus Industries had converted the power station into a massive Cyber-conversion factory. (2.5, 2.6)

Battery Park: Area of New New York, from where Brannigan and Valerie set out, five miles back from Pharmacytown. They had left it twelve years before the Doctor's arrival. (3.3)

Battle of Canary Wharf: Popular name given to the battle on 21st-century Earth between the Cybermen and the Daleks. (2.12, 2.13) Although the Cybermen were seen by much of the world's population, the Daleks were seen by relatively few (certainly in 2012, no one working for Henry Van Statten knew what a Dalek was, implying that no footage of them existed). (1.6) The Cybermen and Daleks were returned to the Void, although the four-strong Cult of Skaro escaped. (3.4, 3.5). Captain Jack

BBC News 24: The BBC's rolling news channel. Rose watched its coverage of the Henrik's explosion. (1.1) A male BBC News 24 studio newsreader commented on the Big Ben incident. A female newsreader reported on the arrival from Geneva of the UNIT officers. (1.4) It covered the Guinevere One space probe's expedition to Mars and the beginning of the downfall of Harriet Jones. (2.X) Huw Edwards, Bob and Dave were News 24 presenters, commentating on the opening ceremony of the 2012 Olympic Games. (2.11) The Doctor and Martha Jones watched Professor Lazarus announce his GDM process on it from her flat. (3.6) It broadcast Harry Saxon's triumphant first message as Prime Minister, and warned the public that the Doctor, Martha and Captain Jack Harkness were dangerous criminals. (2.12)

Harkness later investigated the lists of the dead or missing and found Rose Tyler's name among them, but was relieved to learn from the Doctor that she, her mum, Jackie, and Mickey Smith were all alive and well, though trapped on the parallel Earth known as 'Pete's World'. (3.11)

Battle of Trafalgar: The Doctor told Rose he could take her to witness this. (2.2)

Battle of Waterloo: The final battle in the war between the British and Napoleon Bonaparte's French army in June 1815. John Smith, the fictional character created by the chameleon arch to exist in Farringham School for Boys in 1913, was teaching the boys in his class about the battle. (3.8)

Baudouin I: King of the Belgians in 1953 – the Doctor's psychic paper convinced a security guard at Alexandra Palace that that was who the Doctor was. (2.7)

Bavaria: Modern name for Saxe-Coburg, as the Doctor explained to Rose Tyler. (2.2)

Baxter: A schoolboy at Farringham School for Boys in 1913, he was popular with the older boys for stashing beer in Blackdown Woods outside the school grounds. (3.8)

Baxter, Geoffrey: UNIT adviser in their Mission Control base beneath the Tower of London. As his blood group was A+, he was hypnotised by the Sycorax. (2.X) (Played by IAN HILDITCH)

Baxters, the: Guests at the wedding of Stuart Hoskins and Sarah Clark. They hadn't arrived. (1.8)

Bazoolium: A ceramic which changes temperature to predict the weather. Rose Tyler obtained a jar constructed from it in a bazaar on an asteroid and gave it to her mum, Jackie, as a gift. (2.12)

Bear With Me: One of the programmes broadcast from the Game Station. Three people had to live with a bear. The Doctor liked the celebrity edition, in which the bear climbed into a bath. (1.12)

Beast, the: A legendary creature of evil, imprisoned beneath the surface of Krop Tor by the Disciples of Light, when our universe didn't exist. Its gaolers placed it there because the planet was in a permanent geo-stationary orbit around the black hole later referred to as K 37 Gem 5. If the Beast freed itself, the planet would crash into the black hole, destroying itself and the Beast. However, the Beast managed to transfer its consciousness into humans, firstly a crewman called Curt, whose mind broke under the strain, then later archaeologist Tobias Zed and a group of Ood, willing to sacrifice its huge demonic body for a chance to spread its evil throughout the universe of the 42nd century. When it was threatened, it placed all of its mind in Toby Zed, leaving the Ood comatose, but Rose Tyler ejected Toby into space where he and the trapped consciousness of the Beast were destroyed for good in the event horizon of the black hole, followed shortly after by its now empty body, which was drawn, along with the planet Krop Tor itself, into the black hole. (2.8, 2.9) (Voiced by GABRIEL WOOLF)

Beatbox Club: South London nightclub, where Sarah Clark had been the night she met Stuart Hoskins. (1.8)

Beatles, The: British pop group of the 1960s and early 1970s. The crew of the SS *Pentallian* had set a trivia question on one of their door seals, asking who had had the most UK number one hits before the download era – Elvis or The Beatles. (The Beatles lost!) (3.7)

Beckham, Victoria: According to Lance Bennett, Donna Noble talked excitedly about this former Spice Girl, known as Posh Spice, and whether she was pregnant. (3.X)

Bedlam: Common name for Bethlem Royal Hospital. (3.2)

Bee: One of Sarah Clark's guests, expected at her wedding, but who hadn't shown up. (1.8)

Beethoven, Ludwig van: 18th-century German composer, often cited as one of the greatest who ever lived, who was tragically deaf by the time he was 30, although he carried on composing. The Doctor reckoned he learnt to play the organ by hanging around with Beethoven. (3.6)

Beijing: Capital of China. Martha Jones claimed to have gone there and collected one of the phials of liquid needed to arm the gun she was allegedly preparing to kill the Master with. (3.13)

Bell family: Florizel Street residents and recent purchasers of a television set on which they could watch the Queen's Coronation. (2.7)

Bell, Alexander Graham: Scottish thinker, generally recognised as the inventor of the telephone in 1876 in America. The very first phone call, made by Bell to his assistant Thomas Watson, bled through onto both Sonny Hoskins' portable phone and Rose Tyler's anachronistic mobile phone in 1987. This was just as a time breach occurred, as a result of Rose saving her father's life earlier. (1.8)

Bell, Doctor Joseph: The Doctor, posing as Doctor James McCrimmon, tells Queen Victoria that he studied under Bell at Edinburgh University. (2.2)

Bennett, Lance: Personnel officer at HC Clements, who made a deal with the Empress of the Racnoss. In exchange for supplying her with a sacrificial victim, who could be imbued with Huon particles and become a key to unlock the ship at the centre of Earth, the Secret Heart, where the Racnoss young were imprisoned, he would get to explore the stars with her. Meeting Donna at work, he faked a relationship with her as he fed her Huon liquid every day, hidden in cups of coffee. He was even willing to go through with marrying her but the hormones in Donna's body, excited by the wedding, caused the Huon particles to react early and she was drawn into the Doctor's TARDIS. Pretending to go along with the returned Donna and the Doctor, Lance betrayed them to the Empress. However, when the Doctor escaped with Donna, the Empress, now knowing exactly how much Huon energy a human body could take, force-fed Lance more Huon particles, turning him into a spare key. Eventually tiring of her plaything, the Empress threw Lance down to the centre of the planet and, as his body hit the Secret Heart, it opened and the Racnoss children escaped, most likely eating Lance's body along the way. (3.X) (Played by DON GILET)

Bennett, Stan & Mrs: Lance Bennett's parents, who were at the church when Donna Noble disappeared during her wedding to their son. They later partied at the reception, and Stan was injured when the Christmas baubles exploded under the direction of the Roboforms. (3.X) (Played by ASH CRONEY, SANDRA SCOTT)

Bering Strait: A strait running between East Russia and Alaska. The Master and the Toclafane had turned Russia into the massive Shipyard Number One, which ran from the Black Sea to the Bering Strait. (3.13)

Bessan: Homeworld of a race who resembled bats. The Krillitane invaded and dominated Bessan, and absorbed the inhabitants' physical characteristics. (2.3)

Betamax: Domestic videotape system available from 1975. The Doctor stored the defeated Wire on a Betamax tape in 1953 and claimed he was going to record over it. (2.7)

Bethlem Royal Hospital: London Institute for the insane, based in Bishopsgate. The Doctor, William Shakespeare and Martha Jones headed

Big Brother: One of the many 'games' being played on the Game Station and broadcast throughout Earth – there were 60 *Big Brother* contests going on simultaneously throughout the Game Station. Like all the games, losing appeared to be instantly fatal, although in fact eviction from the *Big Brother* house involved being transported to the Dalek mothership and turned into part of the growing Dalek army created by the Emperor. (1.12)

Big Brother 504: An earlier *Big Brother* series to the one the Doctor found himself part of aboard the Game Station, in which the contestants had rebelled and walked out. After that, all *Big Brother* studios were locked with a deadlock seal to prevent a repeat of that situation. (1.12)

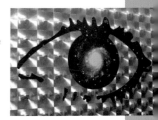

Biggs, Ronald: Great Train Robber from the 1960s, who fled to Brazil and remained there in hiding, because Brazil and Britain had no extradition treaty. The Doctor likened the Plasmavore's hiding on Earth to Biggs in Brazil, as the Judoon could not track it down on Earth. (3.1)

Binary 9: Access to information about John Lumic, including passcodes and logins for Cybus Industries, were found by Pete Tyler and transmitted on wavelength 657 using binary 9, which he then passed to the Preachers in the guise of Gemini. Mickey Smith subsequently used the same path to access the code that disabled the Cybermen's emotional inhibitors on 'Pete's World'. (2.6)

Binary dot tool: A device the Doctor used to construct a portable scanner to help him find the Isolus Podship. (2.11)

there to visit Peter Streete, who had been incarcerated under terrible conditions after talking about witches. (3.2)

Betty, Aunty: Eddie Connolly's sister who, with her husband John and pet terrier, visited Eddie's house to watch the Coronation on his new television set. She suggested that Eddie should beat Tommy Connolly, to stop him growing up a 'mummy's boy'. (2.7) (Played by JEAN CHALLIS)

Bev: Friend of Jackie Tyler's. (1.1) She was in the wedding party at Stuart Hoskins' marriage to Sarah Clark in 1987 when Pete Tyler died. (1.8) Jackie was having a gossip on the phone with her when Rose returned home after being attacked by the Roboform mercenaries. She later called Jackie to tell her it was snowing. (2.X) (Played by EIRLYS BELLIN)

Bexley: South London town on the border with Kent. Martha Jones and Thomas Milligan planned to stay overnight in slave quarters there whilst on their way to a North London UNIT base. Martha found a chance to tell her story about the Doctor there, before she was interrupted by the Master who came to find her. Thomas Milligan tried to protect Martha, but was lasered down on the streets by the Master. (3.13)

Big Ben: Colloquial name for the clock attached to Westminster Palace, home of the British Parliament – Big Ben is actually the bell, the tower structure is St Stephen's Tower. In 1941, Rose Tyler and Captain Jack Harkness danced on his invisible Chula warship in front of the clock face during the Blitz. (1.9) The clock, bell and tower top were destroyed in 2006 when the spaceship piloted by an augmented pig crashed through it before landing in the River Thames. (1.4) Rebuilding work was still going on by the time the Sycorax ship arrived over London the following Christmas. (2.X)

Binyon, Laurence: The poet who wrote 'For the Fallen', which was read at the Remembrance Day service which Tim Latimer attended. (3.9)

Biocattle: The Sisters of Plenitude tried using biocattle to cultivate their cures and vaccines, which failed, so they bred New Humans instead. (2.1)

Biochip: All of the crew of Sanctuary Base 6 had a biochip implanted in them, so their whereabouts could be monitored and they were locatable in an emergency. (2.8, 2.9)

Bio-Convention: On 'Pete's World', the Bio-Convention was a piece of legislature from the Ethical Committee that the Cybus Industries Ultimate Upgrade Project contravened. (2.5)

Biodamper: The Doctor gave one of these to Donna, in the shape of a ring, hoping it would keep her hidden from the Roboform Santas that were pursuing her. However, the Roboforms were were still able to find her at her non-wedding reception, because the Huon particles in her blood were so old that a biodamper could not conceal them. (3.X)

Bishop, Detective Inspector: Baffled policeman in North London, charged with investigating the outbreak of faceless people. He locked the victims in a cage for their own safety and, when he encountered the Doctor, discovered that an alien criminal called the Wire was responsible, shortly before he too fell victim and lost his face. Once the Wire was defeated, his face returned and Bishop was able to resume his duties. (2.7) (Played by SAM COX)

Bishop, the: Local church leader whose son drowned. The body looked a mess but, as a favour, Cardiff undertaker Gabriel Sneed used all his embalming skills to make the body look cherubic. (1.3)

Bistro 10: Cardiff Bay restaurant where the Doctor and Margaret Blaine dined. (1.11)

Black Death, the: Regular pestilence that plagued London, most likely a mutation of the bubonic plague. William Shakespeare's son Hamnet was a victim and it was grief over his death that saw Shakespeare at his lowest ebb, almost incarcerated in Bedlam for a while, enabling the Carrionites to use his words of despair to access Elizabethan England. (3.2)

Black Gold, the: The pirate ship owned by Captain Kaliko. It patrolled Bouken, a desert planet OilCorp were sucking dry of its natural resources in an oil-starved 40th century, then selling them at inflated prices. (TIQ)

Black hole: Deep-space phenomenon. The one designated K 37 Gem 5 was connected by a gravity funnel to the planet Krop Tor, impossibly in orbit around it. When the funnel finally collapsed, Krop Tor was drawn back towards the black hole. The survivors aboard Sanctuary Base 6 tried to use an escape shuttle to flee the black hole but were pulled back after the Beast, in its human host Toby Zed, was sucked into the event horizon. Using the TARDIS, the Doctor drew the shuttle to safety, but Krop Tor was eventually destroyed within the black hole's event horizon. (2.8, 2.9)

Black hole converters: Technology the Master had placed within his 2,000 war rockets, with which he planned to destroy planets and convert them into black holes. With his plans on the verge of failing, he threatened to set the black hole converters off on Earth, but the Doctor pointed out that this would kill him. The Master relented, passing over his wristwatch, which contained the detonator. (3.13)

Black Sea: Inland sea, stretching between Russia and the south-eastern end of Europe. The Master and the Toclafane had turned Russia into the massive Shipyard Number One which ran from the Black Sea to the Bering Strait. (3.13)

Blackbeard: 18th-century English pirate, famed for lighting matches within his huge beard and frightening his foes, who believed he resembled the devil. The Doctor cited him as a great warrior commander to Martha Jones. (TIQ)

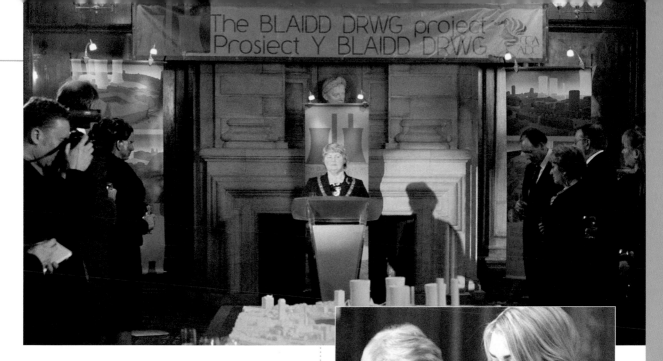

Blackdown Woods: Jeremy Baines, a pupil at Farringham School for Boys was sent there to retrieve beer but became intrigued by a spaceship that landed in Cooper's Field. (3.8)

Blackfriars: Area of London, on the north bank of the Thames, where Mr Crane collected Morris and the other homeless, an act videotaped by Jake Simmonds on 'Pete's World'. (2.5)

Blaidd Drwg: Welsh for 'Bad Wolf'. It was the name selected by Blon Fel Fotch Pasameer-Day Slitheen, posing as Margaret Blaine, for the nuclear power plant she intended to destroy. The resultant energy would have enabled her to open the Rift above Cardiff and escape. (1.11)

Blair, Tony: Former Prime Minister of Great Britain, and possibly the one murdered by the Family Slitheen. (1.4) Mickey Smith commented that 'Pete's World' was perhaps a parallel world where Blair never got elected. (2.5)

Blake, Major Richard: UNIT officer in charge of the Sycorax situation. He briefed Harriet Jones and Daniel Llewellyn on the protocols of dealing with extraterrestrial beings and was with them both when they were teleported aboard the Sycorax ship. After the death of Llewellyn, Blake tried to protect Harriet Jones, but died when the Sycorax Leader struck him with his energy whip. (2.X) (Played by CHU OMAMBALA)

Blake, Ursula: Caught up in the events surrounding the Sycorax invasion on Christmas Day, Ursula had gone to Trafalgar Square in London that night to celebrate being alive. While there, she took a photo of the Doctor, which led to her meeting Colin Skinner and then the other members of a group of Doctor-fans who later became known as LINDA. Ursula was especially drawn to Elton Pope and they started a mild relationship. When Victor Kennedy, in reality the alien Abzorbaloff, infiltrated LINDA, only Ursula and Elton stood up to him, and Ursula was, like Skinner and the other LINDA

BLAINE, MARGARET: An MI5 officer who was murdered by the Family Slitheen and her body used so the Slitheen could infiltrate the British Government after everyone's attention was diverted by the Big Ben incident. She was responsible for the death of the Prime Minister. (1.4, 1.5) She was the only Slitheen to escape the bombing of 10 Downing Street by activating a short-range teleport device concealed in her earrings and brooch. She ended up on the Isle of Dogs in East London and later made her way to Cardiff, where she became the Mayor, pushing through the construction of the Blaidd Drwg nuclear facility. A scale model of the facility was built on the back of a tribophysical waveform macro-kinetic extrapolator. Not having the power to use it herself, she was hoping that a nuclear meltdown would supply the energy she needed to open the space and time Rift running through Cardiff and power up the extrapolator. As it turned out, the arrival of the TARDIS and Captain Jack's wiring up of the extrapolator to the ship's console supplied the very power she needed. Despite the Doctor's best attempts to get Margaret to recognise the error of her ways, she still tried to kill Rose Tyler to ensure the Doctor took her away from Earth. Instead, the extrapolator's power, mixed with that of the Rift and the time machine itself, opened up the heart of the TARDIS. Margaret gazed into the pure energies of the Time Vortex and was reverted back to an egg. The Doctor took the egg back to Raxacoricofallapatorius in the hope that, reborn, Margaret might take a different path. (1.11) (Played by ANNETTE BADLAND)

members before her, absorbed into his skin. When Elton broke the Abzorbaloff's cane, Ursula and the others managed to exert enough pressure internally that the Abzorbaloff exploded. The Doctor was able to restore Ursula's life essence as she had been the last one absorbed, and so she survived as a face embedded in a concrete slab, living in Elton's flat. (2.10) (Played by SHIRLEY HENDERSON)

Blake: One of the soldiers under Captain Reynolds protecting Queen Victoria in 1879. (2.2)

Blazen Scale: Method of monitoring energy in the 42nd century. The energy readings from beneath Krop Tor were over 90 statts, enough energy to fuel the Empire. (2.8)

Bliss [1]: An artistic member of LINDA, Bliss was the first victim of the Abzorbaloff, ending up as part of his posterior, although he told LINDA that she had left to get married. When the absorbed victims fought back to explode the Abzorbaloff, Bliss died alongside her fellow LINDA teammates, Bridget and Colin Skinner (2.10) (Played by KATHRYN DRYSDALE)

Bliss [2]: A new Mood Patch developed in New New York in 5,000,000,029. It mutated quickly into an airborne virus and killed everybody in the Overcity in seven minutes. Only the Face of Boe and Novice Hame, protected by his smoke, survived and set about ensuring those living in the Undercity and on the Motorway could survive. (3.3)

Bloodtide, Mother: One of the Carrionites who had escaped into Elizabethan England, seeking to have William Shakespeare write the words that, when spoken at the end of his play *Love's Labour's Won*, would open a portal in time and space and release the rest of the Carrionites from the Deep Darkness into which the Eternals had cast them at the dawn of time. When William Shakespeare turned their spellcasting back on them, Mother Bloodtide and the other Carrionites were trapped inside their crystal ball for eternity. (3.2) (Played by LINDA CLARK)

Bloxham Road: Street close to the Powell Estate, where the Sycorax teleport sent the Doctor, Mickey Smith, Rose Tyler, Alex Klein and Harriet Jones. (2.X)

Blue Division: A troop of security guards under the command of Bywater, working for Henry Van Statten in his Vault, deep below Utah. (1.6)

Blue Peter: Children's television magazine programme. Presenter Matt Baker demonstrated how to make a cake shaped like the spaceship that had crashed into Big Ben (1.4)

Bob: Huw Edwards' fellow commentator at the Olympic Games Opening Ceremony. Bob was in the Stadium when the Isolus extracted everyone,

Bob included, and placed them in an ionic holding pen. He was later returned when the Isolus left Earth safely. (2.11)

Boemina: The alleged name to be given to the Face of Boe's offspring, according to the *Boewatch* programme on Bad WolfTV. (1.7)

Boer War: More accurately the Second Boer War, fought between the British and the Transvaal allies over the ever-growing British Empire and ownership of the precious jewels and mineral ores in Africa. Joan Redfern's husband Oliver died at the battle of Spion Kop in January 1900. (3.8)

Boeshane Peninsula: A tiny colony, where Captain Jack Harkness grew up and was the colony's first successful applicant to the Time Agency. This achievement got his image on posters and he was referred to as the Face of Boe. (3.13)

Boewatch: A programme about the Face of Boe on Bad WolfTV, which was reporting his pregnancy when the Doctor and Rose Tyler visited Satellite Five. (1.7)

Boléro: 1928 ballet work, composed by Maurice Ravel. Toby Zed listened to this while working on the ancient Veltino inscriptions he had found on the surface of Krop Tor. The music switched off when the Beast contacted his mind. (2.8)

Bonaparte, Napoleon: French general and later his country's Emperor, who was a brilliant strategist and campaigner. He dominated much of Western Europe during the early 19th century. The Doctor cited him as a great warrior commander to Martha Jones. (TIQ)

Bond, James: Fictional spy featured in many popular movies. Martha Jones likened the Doctor to him as they walked to the LazLabs reception because the Doctor was wearing a tuxedo. (3.6)

Bosphorus: Turkish restaurant in Cardiff Bay, where Captain Jack Harkness entertained the Doctor, Rose Tyler and Mickey Smith with his tales of life as a Time Agent. The Doctor's holiday mood was broken when he saw a photograph of Margaret Blaine on the front page of the *Western Mail*. (1.11)

Boston Tea Party: The Doctor told Rose Tyler that he had been present in December 1773 at the start of the American Revolution, actually pushing boxes onto the decks of the British ships ready to have their contents tipped overboard. (1.3)

Boudicca: English queen of Norfolk who led an uprising against the invading Romans in AD 61. She came so close to success that Emperor Nero almost considered withdrawing his garrisons from the British Isles, but ultimately she was defeated in the West Midlands. The Doctor cited her as a great warrior commander to Martha Jones. (TIQ)

Bouken: Desert world overrun by the oil rigs owned by OilCorp, who were sucking the planet dry of its natural resources in an oil-starved 40th century and selling them on at inflated prices. OilCorps' biggest opponents were a number of pirates who would attack the rigs and steal the oil, selling it at low prices to poorer planets. (TIQ)

Bowie, David: Iconic British rock star (real name David Jones). When the Doctor was trying to sneak quietly away from the Tylers' flat on the Powell Estate, Bowie's 1972 top ten hit 'Starman' was being played by one of their neighbours. (1.4)

Boxer: Mate of Leo Jones's, who was visiting Brighton with Leo, Shonara and Keisha when Harry Saxon kidnapped Leo's parents and eldest sister. (3.12)

Boy: Young member of a family whose Christmas was almost ruined when his parents were kidnapped by the Graske and replaced with changelings. But the real parents were swiftly returned, none the wiser. (AotG) (Played by JAMES HARRIS)

Braccatolian space: An area in which the Master planned to open up a rift and launch through it the war rockets containing black hole converters, which would herald the dawn of his New Time Lord Empire. (3.13)

Bradbury, Ray: Author of a sci-fi short story called 'A Sound of Thunder', in which a time traveller crushes a butterfly in prehistoric times and finds his world changed when he returns to the future. Martha Jones asked the Doctor if it was safe to travel through Elizabethan England in case she did something similar. (3.2)

Brakovitch: Someone from Captain Jack Harkness's past, according to one of his amusing anecdotes. (1.11)

'Brand New Key': Originally a hit for Melanie in 1971, Bliss and Ursula of LINDA sang this song together at one of their meetings. (2.10)

Brandon, Joe: A resident living close to Deffry Vale High School who first brought the UFOs to the attention of local newspapers. (2.3T)

Brannigan family: Thomas Kincade Brannigan (played by ARDAL O'HANLAN) was an eccentric Catkind car driver in the Motorway tunnels of New New York who, along with his human wife Valerie (played by JENNIFER HENNESSEY) and their litter of kittens, offered the Doctor a lift. Brannigan initially thought the Doctor was a little bit dim, then quite rude, but after a while gained a great deal of respect for the Time Lord. Valerie was amused by the Doctor at first, but got anxious about his influence when he began insisting that, with three adults aboard, they should head to the Fast Line to find Martha Jones. She was adamant she would not take her kittens down there. The Brannigans' car was one of the first to get out of the Motorway system and up to the Overcity once the Doctor had opened up the roof. (3.3)

Brecon: When the Doctor pointed upwards to indicate where the Gelth had come from, undertaker Gabriel Sneed assumed he meant this picturesque rural area north of Cardiff, famous for the Brecon Beacons. (1.3)

Brethren: The Monks of St Catherine, who worshipped the Haemovariform and brought it to the Torchwood Estate, locked within its current Host. Having taken over Torchwood House and imprisoned Lady Isobel and the staff, the monks' leader, Brother Angelo, forced Sir Robert

MacLeish to act as if nothing had changed when Queen Victoria arrived to stay. (2.2)

Bridge Street: Road in London where the Doctor, Rose Tyler, Pete Tyler and the Preachers planned to meet up after escaping the Cybermen on 'Pete's World'. (2.6)

Bridget: A young single mum, she had come to London to search for her missing daughter, who had got into drugs. Bridget joined the LINDA group to find the Doctor too. She travelled down from the north of England for each meeting but one day stopped coming, shortly after her romance with Colin Skinner had begun to blossom. Victor Kennedy told Skinner that he could help him find her but, in truth, Bridget had already been absorbed by Kennedy's real persona, the Abzorbaloff. When the absorbed victims fought back to explode the Abzorbaloff, brave Bridget died alongside her beloved Skinner. (2.10) (Played by MOYA BRADY)

Brighton: East Sussex city, home of Roedean School, which Lucy Saxon had attended, and where Leo Jones had taken his family for a break when Martha Jones tried to warn him about Harry Saxon. (3.12)

Bringer of Night: Legendary demon name, one of many attributed to the Beast throughout the galaxies. (2.8, 2.9)

British Empire: Part of Yvonne Hartman's ideology for Torchwood was to re-establish the British Empire that had existed during the reign of Torchwood's founder, Queen Victoria. (2.12)

British Rocket Group: Research group from the 1960s whose skills and expertise were still influencing projects such as Guinevere One four decades later. (2.X)

Broadmarsh Street: In the fiction the TARDIS created for the human-Doctor's background, John Smith believed he had grown up on this road in Radford Parade, Nottingham. (3.9)

Broff: One of the players of *The Weakest Link* aboard the Game Station. After Fitch's apparent death, Broff tried to escape the studio so the Anne Droid seemed to disintegrate him. In truth, he was transmatted over to the Dalek mothership and turned into part of the growing Dalek army created by the Emperor. (1.12) (Played by SEBASTIAN ARMESTO)

Brooklyn: Part of New New York where it was said that there were jobs aplenty, wooden houses and air that smelled of apple grass. Access to it was via the Brooklyn Flyover, ten miles from Pharmacytown, a six-year trip (approximately) via the Fast Lane. (3.3)

Brooklyn Turnoffs 1 and 2: Parts of the New New York Motorway which were closed to traffic. (3.3)

Bucknall House: Block of the Powell Estate where the Tyler family lived at number 48.

Budapest: Hungarian capital. Martha Jones claimed to have gone there and collected one of the phials of liquid needed to arm the gun she was supposedly preparing to kill the Master with. (3.13)

Buffalo: Codeword Mickey Smith used to gain access to the UNIT computer system. (1.5)

Bunyan, John: 17th-century poet and preacher. Passages from his work *The Pilgrim's Progress* form the basis of the hymn 'To Be A Pilgrim', sung by the choir at Farringham School for Boys in 1913. (3.8, 3.9)

Burbage, Richard: Actor, of the Lord Chamberlain's Men. In 1599, he played the King of Navarre in both *Love's Labour's Lost* and *Love's Labour's Won* and was due to speak the closing passage which would bring the Carrionites to Earth. (3.2) (Played JALAAL HARTLEY)

'**Burn with me**': Phrase used by the sun-possessed Korwin McDonnell and Dev Ashton before they killed members of the SS *Pentallian* crew. When the Doctor became sun-possessed, he made the same threat to Martha Jones. (3.7)

Bursar: The financial administrator at Farringham School for Boys. The latest, Mr Phillips, was murdered by Son of Mine, who was inhabiting the body of schoolboy Jeremy Baines. (3.8, 3.9)

Businessman: Driver of a car on the New New York Motorway, occupying the final lane before the Fast Lane, a thousand feet below. He gave the exhausted Doctor a glass of water and witnessed the Macra thrashing about in the fumes, and was then surprised by the arrival of Novice Hame. (3.3) (Played by NICHOLAS BOULTON)

Butcher's boy, the: A boy Gwyneth, the maid at Gabriel Sneed's undertakers, had her eye on. (1.3)

Butetown: A district of Cardiff. Madame Mortlock, a medium, was based there when it was the main dockland area for the city during Victorian times. (1.3)

Butler: In service to the Duke of Manhattan, and present when he was cured of Petrifold Regression in the Hospital run by the Sisters of Plenitude. (2.1) Although he survived the attack by the New Humans, it seems almost certain he later died as a victim of the mutated Bliss virus that wiped out the majority of New Earth's population. (3.3) (Played by STUART ASHMAN)

Bywater: Security Commander in the Vault, Henry Van Statten's underground bunker. Charged with overseeing the Dalek on its escape from the Cage, he sent one of his officers, De Maggio, on escort detail, to ensure Rose Tyler and Adam Mitchell's safety, before engaging in combat – and was the first of the Vault staff to be exterminated by the Dalek's re-energised blaster. (1.6) (Played by JOHN SCHWABB)

Caan, Dalek: Former Attack Squad Leader of the Thirtieth Dalek Assault Squad, later one of the Cult of Skaro, who brought the Genesis Ark to Earth in the Void Ship, after the Time War ended. (2.12, 2.13) After fleeing the Battle of Canary Wharf via an emergency temporal shift, along with the rest of the Cult, Caan ended up in Manhattan in 1930, where he was the Cult's go-between with Mr Diagoras, eventually bringing Diagoras to the Transgenic Lab to take part in the Final Experiment. Dalek Caan patrolled the sewers, sometimes alone, sometimes with Thay. Caan led the attack on Hooverville and exterminated its leader, Solomon. After realising that Dalek Sec had betrayed them, the rest of the Cult accepted Caan as their new leader and he wired himself up to their Battle Computer to guide and ultimately exterminate their new Dalek-Human army. When confronted by the Doctor, Caan once again activated an emergency temporal shift and escaped. (3.4, 3.5) (Operated by DAVID HANKINSON (2.12, 2.13), BARNABY EDWARDS, NICHOLAS PEGG (3.4, 3.5), voiced by NICHOLAS BRIGGS)

Caesar, Gaius Julius: The Doctor told Rose he could take her to witness this Roman Emperor crossing the Rubicon. (2.2)

Calcium: One of the main constituents of Raxacoricofallapatorians, the race to which the Family Slitheen belonged. Realising that the compression field they used to wear human skins had weakened their physical bodies, the Doctor suggested acetic acid as a good weapon against them. (1.4, 1.5)

Caledonia Prime: Water riots were in their third day in the Glasgow region of Caledonia Prime, according to Channel McB. (1.7)

California: Western state of America, which was settled in the 19th century around the San Andreas Fault, a geological flaw in the land mass. Many of the earthquakes that have plagued the region are attributable to the fault as the two plates that make up the fault move northwards and southwards. The Doctor likened the Rift threaded through Cardiff to California on the San Andreas Fault. (3.11)

Call My Bluff: One of the programmes broadcast from the Game Station. It used real guns. (1.12)

Calypso, Sally: Holographic news reporter beamed directly into the cars travelling on the New New York Motorway. Most of her reports were of car accidents, car-jackings and current traffic and weather conditions, and they were being generated automatically by the Senate building under the control of the Face of Boe, who wished the inhabitants of the Motorway to believe life above the Motorway was perfectly normal. (3.3) (Played by ERIKA MACLEOD)

Cambridge University: Harry Saxon allegedly attended this university, and had a particular prowess for rugby and athletics. (3.12)

Canary Wharf: Colloquial name for the tower at One Canada Square, although Canary Wharf is actually the business district it sits in. The main tower was taken over by the Torchwood Institute as their London base until the defeat of the Cybermen and Daleks in what became known as the Battle of Canary Wharf. (2.12, 2.13)

Cane: Victor Kennedy/the Abzorbaloff carried this disguised limitation-field creator. When Elton Pope broke it, the Abzorbaloff was destroyed. (2.10)

Cappuccino!: Coffee house where Sally Sparrow read the letter from her old friend Kathy Nightingale, detailing her life in the past. (3.10)

Car 10hot5: Registration details of the car occupied by Ma and Pa before it was destroyed by the Macra living below the Fast Lane, part of the New New York Motorway. (3.2)

Car 465diamond6: The car registered to Milo and Cheen. (3.3)

Cardiff: The capital city of Wales. The Doctor and Rose first visited it on Christmas Eve 1869, when they helped stop a Gelth invasion through the Rift in space and time that crossed the city. (1.3) They returned to the city in late 2006 to enable the TARDIS to ingest some Rift energy and discovered a member of the Slitheen family planning to destroy the city by using an energy extrapolator combined with the destruction of a new nuclear facility to tear open the Rift, enabling her to pilot the extrapolator home. (1.11) Captain Jack Harkness later joined a small Torchwood team to monitor the Rift directly under Millennium Square, where the TARDIS had been parked. He was recovering from injuries alone in the Torchwood Hub when he heard the TARDIS materialise directly above, the energy shaking his base. He raced to the surface, eager to contact the Doctor again. Seeing him on the TARDIS monitor but unwilling to face his old friend, the Doctor tried to leave, but Jack was quicker and he was holding onto the exterior shell of the TARDIS as it dematerialised. (3.11)

Cardiff Gazette: Local newspaper for which Cathy Salt worked as a journalist. (1.11)

Cardiff Heritage Committee: A team who were electrocuted in a swimming pool, ostensibly due to normal wear and tear of pools. (1.11)

CARRIONITES: Female-dominated species which existed when the universe was young, based in the 14 stars of the Rexel Planetary configuration. As a species, they were cast into the Deep Darkness by the Eternals, who, legend had it, used the Rexel stars as a prison door. Three Carrionites escaped back to 16th-century England through the words of a despondent William Shakespeare – Carrionite science being based on sensing emotions such as grief and suffering and using them to manipulate matter via words, shapes, numbers and names. They then had Peter Streete design a 14-sided amphitheatre that would channel their energies back into the Deep Darkness when the correct words were spoken aloud at the epicentre of the structure – a moment the Carrionites referred to as the Hour of Woven Words. Their true form was more akin to a giant skeletal raven or crow but, by using words, the three Carrionites could reshape themselves into more humanoid form, although this required a lot of energy, so they usually appeared aged and ugly. The three Carrionites failed in their attempt to create a Millennium of Blood on Earth by allowing the others out of the Deep Darkness. The portal was sealed once more by William Shakespeare and the Doctor, and the three Earth-based Carrionites were trapped within a crystal ball for eternity. (3.2)

Cartwright, Lucy: Six-year-old girl who was skipping along the lane in her home village of Farringham when she was kidnapped by a Scarecrow, one of the soldiers created by the Family of Blood. Taken back to their invisible ship, she was murdered, her form taken on by Daughter of Mine, who then returned to Lucy's home and killed her parents. (3.8) (Played by LAUREN WILSON)

Casp, Matron: Leader of the Sisters of Plenitude, she controlled the experiments on the humans in the secret Intensive Care Unit beneath the Hospital on New Earth. Fleeing from the infectious patients, Casp fell to her death from a lift shaft when a patient grabbed her ankle, spreading its numerous viruses to her immunity-free body. (2.1) (Played by DONNA CROLL)

Cassandra: See *O'Brien Dot Delta Seventeen, Lady Cassandra.*

Cassini couple: Elderly married ladies, who had been driving on the Motorway for 23 years – theirs was one of the first cars to set off. Although this was a year after the Bliss-mutated Mood Patch had wiped out the Overcity, it is unknown if the earlier drivers were aware of the disaster that had befallen their fellow New New Yorkers. Alice (played by BRIDGET TURNER) was the driver; May (played by GEORGINE ANDERSON) was a car spotter and was able to identify the car that had kidnapped Martha Jones for the Doctor. (3.3)

Catkind: Feline race found in Galaxy M87, many of whom shared the planet New Earth with the variety of humans living there. Amongst the Catkind on New Earth were the Sisters of Plenitude, Brannigan (who married a human) and Javit. (2.1, 3.3)

Catrigan Nova: A planet possessing whirlpools of gold. The Master offered to take Tanya, his masseuse, there after he'd established his New Time Lord Empire. (3.13)

Catrin: Little girl from London who, like her father and brother, had A+ blood, and thus was affected by the Sycorax's blood control. (2.X)

Catullus, Gaius Valerius: Roman poet whose Latin works were the subject of prep for Hutchinson's class at Farringham School for Boys. Unwilling to do it himself, he forced brighter pupil Timothy Latimer to do it for him. (3.8)

Caw: Baltazar's ally, Caw was a gold-eating bird from the planet Pheros. His bio-mechanical race, formed from a living metal, was powered by fusion reactors. He was working for Baltazar and rescued him from his destroyed ship, but later betrayed Baltazar to the authorities for gold bars. Years later, he

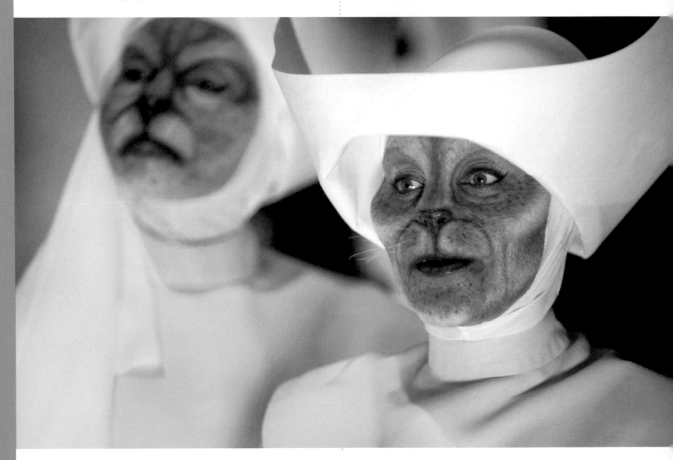

was reunited with a forgiving Baltazar and they set in motion the trap to retrieve the *Infinite*, with Caw charming the Doctor and Martha Jones into going on a quest. Caw also gave Martha a brooch, which was in fact his son, Squawk, who relayed details of where the TARDIS was going back to Caw and thus Baltazar. When the final datachip leading to the location of the *Infinite* had been recovered, Caw flew Baltazar to Volag-Noc, but Caw was shot in the fusion chamber by Gurney, and died, apologising to Martha, on the icy surface of the planet. (TIQ) (Voiced by TOBY LONGWORTH)

Clements, HC: Owner of a security company that was actually a subsidiary of the Torchwood Institute. One of his employees, Lance Bennett, was secretly working for the alien Empress of the Racnoss and, possibly through Lance's duplicity, HC Clements ended up as food, killed and prepared for her children to eat once they emerged from their entombment at the centre of planet Earth. Rather unkindly, due to his distinctive footwear, his employees often referred to him as the Fat Cat in Spats. (3.X)

Central Park: Vast open parkland at the heart of Manhattan's midtown area. It was in the southern end that Solomon presided over the Hooverville that had been erected there. (3.4, 3.5)

Central World Authority: Cyberleader One demanded of Yvonne Hartman that he address such an official body on Earth, but she pointed out there wasn't one. Cyberleader One opted to create one there and then, with himself at its head. (2.13)

Ceres System: Secondary location of the *Infinite*, its whereabouts provided by the datachip possessed by Kaliko. (TIQ)

Chaka Demus 'n' Pliers: American male singing duo (Demus's real name was John Taylor, Pliers' was Everton Bonner), cited by Elton Pope as an example of a good use of 'n' in a phrase, along with fish 'n' chips and rock 'n' roll. Hence LINDA – the London Investigation 'N' Detective Agency. (2.10)

Chambers, Mr: Conductor and leader of the band that played at the dance in the Farringham village hall. He was disintegrated by Father of Mine. (3.8) (Played by PETER BOURKE)

Chambers: The areas in the Cyber-conversion factory in the 'Pete's World' Battersea Power Station, where the humans were either upgraded or incinerated. Chambers 5, 6, 8, 9, 10, 11 and 12 were all cited. (2.6)

Chameleon arch: A device in the Doctor's TARDIS that enabled him to rewrite his biology, every single cell, and become the human, John Smith. The process was painful and his essence was then stored within a special Gallifreyan fob watch. The Master also used one of these to become Professor Yana. (3.8, 3.9, 3.11)

Chan, Bau: Friend of the Tylers and Smiths from the Powell estate. He joined his wife in berating Rose for her year-long absence and the effect it had had on Mickey Smith. (1.4) (Played by BASIL CHUNG)

Chan, Ru: Friend of the Tylers and Smiths from the Powell Estate. She watched the news of the Big Ben incident from the Tylers' living room, berating Rose for her year-long absence at the same time. (1.4) On 'Pete's World', her parallel version told Rita-Anne that Ricky Smith had been seen with the Preachers. (2.5) (Played by FIESTA MEI LING)

Chancellor Street: Street in London where Martha Jones encountered the Doctor for the first time as he removed his tie to prove to her later self that he could travel in time. (3.1)

Changelings: False humans, used by the Graske to replace people they kidnapped, which the Graske would then exploit to create mayhem. (AotG)

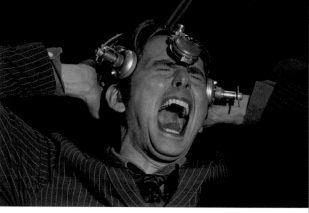

C

Channel 44,000: Channel broadcasting the version of *Big Brother* that the Doctor found himself part of aboard the Game Station. (1.12)

Chantho: Last surviving member of the Malmooth race, which had originally lived in the Conglomeration on Malcassairo. Chantho worked alongside Professor Yana as both his scientific assistant and his friend. However, when she saw him become the Master after he opened his Gallifreyan fob watch, she realised he had to be stopped. The Master instead electrocuted her but, with her dying breath, Chantho shot him, causing him to regenerate inside the Doctor's TARDIS. (3.11) (Played by CHIPO CHUNG)

Chapel of Rest: Room within Gabriel Sneed's undertakers where the recently deceased were laid in their coffins. (1.3)

Charles II: 17th-century English King. The Doctor offered Martha Jones the chance to meet him, but she declined. (3.13)

Charles, Oliver: Transport Liaison Officer at 10 Downing Street, who was murdered and his body used for a few weeks by a member of the Family Slitheen. During this time, he enjoyed a number of sexual liaisons, with Charles's wife, his mistress and a young farmer. However, Oliver Charles wasn't that important to the Slitheen's plan and so, when the opportunity came to get rid of it and wear the body of General Asquith, he took it, discarding Charles's empty skin and dumping it in the cupboard where Harriet Jones was hiding. (1.4) (Played by ERIC POTTS)

Chavic Fice: When the Government there collapsed, many of the non-human races that existed within the Fourth Earth Empire ceased visiting Satellite Five. (1.7)

Cheem: Planet covered in foliage. The Doctor met Jabe, Lute and Coffa, representatives of the Forest of Cheem, aboard Platform One. (1.2)

Cheen: A young woman in New New York, she was heading to Brooklyn with Milo, who was seeking a job in the Foundries there, thus creating a new home for them both and their unborn son away from Pharmacytown. She and Milo kidnapped Martha Jones so that they could legitimately register as having three adults aboard their car and gain access to the Fast Lane. Once down there, the car was attacked by the Macra and Milo switched off everything in the vehicle to avoid attracting the creatures' attention. Realising that they would quickly run out of air, Milo, Cheen and Martha made the decision to reactivate the car and take their chances of getting away from the Macra. When the Doctor reopened the cover of the Motorway, Milo and Cheen were able to return to the Overcity and start a new life up there. (3.3) (Played by LENORA CRICHLOW)

Chen, San: In physics, San Chen, not San Hazeldine, discovered the 15-10 Barric Fields. Rodrick didn't know this when asked by the Anne Droid in *The Weakest Link* aboard the Game Station. (1.12)

Chenna: Young Torchwood Archivist aboard Sanctuary Base 6. She discovered her friend Curt in Captain Walker's quarters, his face bearing strange tattoos, his mind completely destroyed. Exactly what happened to Chenna and Curt after this is unknown but, by the time the Doctor and

Rose Tyler arrived on Sanctuary Base 6, they were no longer present, and no mention was made of Curt's markings when a similar fate befell Toby Zed. (2.9T) (Played by ALYS THOMAS)

Chernobyl: Mr Cleaver indicated in his online comments about the Blaidd Drwg Project that it could end up more devastating than this 1986 Ukrainian nuclear power station disaster. (1.11)

Chez Alison: Shop where Donna Noble got her wedding dress. Unsurprisingly, she didn't ask them to put pockets in the dress. (3.X)

Chicane, Heidi: Singer at the Laurenzi theatre, originally slated to sing the lead number, 'Heaven or Hell', in the New York Revue, but she broke her ankle and Tallulah had to step up and take her place. Tallulah maintained she had had nothing to do with Heidi's accident. (3.4)

Chicken, Mr: The occupier of 10 Downing Street in 1730, visited by the Doctor, who recalled him as 'a nice man'. Two years later, the building was officially declared the Prime Minister's residence, although it was another three years before Mr Chicken moved out and Robert Walpole became the first Prime Minister to live there. (1.5)

Chieftain: Leader of the cannibalistic Futurekind, who started the hunt for Padra Fet Shafe Cane. After the humans had left Malcassairo, he took his people into the empty Silo base and, although there was a brief hunt for the Doctor's party, once they too had gone the Futurekind were left alone on the planet to starve. (3.11, 3.12) (Played by PAUL MARC DAVIES)

Child Princess: Young member of the Royal family on Padrivole Regency Nine who, with her blonde curls, pink cheeks and simpering voice, had been a target for a Plasmavore, who drained her blood. The Plasmavore was later executed for the murder. (3.1)

Children of Skaro: Dalek Caan described the Cult of Skaro by this name to the Doctor and Martha Jones in the Transgenic Lab, whilst waiting for the results of Dalek Sec's attempt to combine his body with that of the human, Mr Diagoras. (3.4)

Children of the Motorway: Name given to those kittens and babies born while their parents drove along the New New York Motorway. (3.3)

China: Listing things of importance that happened in 1979, the Doctor told Rose Tyler that China invaded Vietnam. (2.2) Martha Jones walked across the Earth telling her story about the Doctor, preparing people for the right moment to chant his name. Amongst the places she went to were the Fusion Mills of China. She also told Professor Docherty she had been to Beijing, to collect part of the weapon she wanted to kill the Master with, knowing the Professor would betray her to the Master. (3.13)

Chip Type: The Nurse on Satellite Five initially offered a Type One Chip to Adam Mitchell. It would be implanted into the back of his skull and costs 100 credits. He opted for the Type Two, implanted into his forehead and giving full access to the information spikes and thus the entire history of the human race, which was activated at the click of his fingers. It cost 10,000 credits, but the Doctor had arranged unlimited funds for him. The procedure took a picosurgeon just ten minutes. (1.7)

Chip: A force-grown clone (possibly grown from the cells of Lady Cassandra O'Brien). He served Cassandra loyally and, when she was exposed as being behind the events on Platform One and her skin burst, Chip rescued her brain and frame and recreated her using salvaged skin from her posterior. With his henna tattoos and limited life span, Chip's devotion annoyed Cassandra until she realised that he was willing to sacrifice his life to keep her alive by donating his body to her mind. After she entered his body, the Doctor took her back in time to meet her original human self and Chip/Cassandra died in the original's arms. (2.1) (Played by SEAN GALLAGHER)

Chiswick: Area in West London where Donna Noble and Lance Bennett were due to get married. (3.X)

Cholet, Madame: Fictional cook, one of the Wombles and featured in the novels by Elizabeth Beresford before transferring to television in the 1970s. The Doctor referred to her as one of the greatest chefs on Earth. (TIQ)

Chosen Scholars: From Class 55, out of the University of Rago Rago 5 6 Rago. They were guests aboard Platform One to see the Earthdeath spectacle. (1.2)

Chrissie: One of Jake Simmonds' troopers, brought over from 'Pete's World' to Rose's Earth to fight the Cybermen, and then the Daleks. He ordered her to monitor the Cybermen's communications from the Lever Room. (2.13)

Christianity: One of the many religions practised in the 42nd century. (2.9)

Christie, Agatha Mary Clarissa: Twentieth-century writer of crime fiction. The Doctor offered Martha Jones the chance to meet her, but she declined. (3.13)

Christmas Carol in Prose, Being a Ghost Story of Christmas, A: Published in 1843 by Charles Dickens, this was one of his most successful

CHULA: Advanced warrior race, one of whose ships Captain Jack Harkness had commandeered from a Chula woman, reprogramming its onboard computer (played by DIAN PERRY) to consider him as its owner. It had a powerful tractor beam, and could become invisible, as camouflage. Like all Chula ships, its internal air was saturated by nanogenes, intelligent subatomic robots which could repair living tissue. Jack, a conman, had also stolen a Chula medical ship and sent it ahead to crash on Earth, hoping to draw out Time Agents, convince them it was valuable and sell it to them before a German bomb destroyed it, but not before he'd fled with their payment (he had calculated exactly when it was due to strike). Unknown to Jack, the medical ship leaked on impact and the nanogenes escaped into the air there. Those particular nanogenes had not been programmed to recognise human beings, and the first contact they made was with a recently deceased child, Jamie, wearing a gas mask. Assuming all humans were 'empty' of life, they reanimated him, the gas mask now blended into his flesh, and proceeded to make contact with other humans, making flesh-and-bone gas masks and scars identical to Jamie's grow on their bodies. When the nanogenes encountered the DNA of both dead Jamie and his living mother, they recombined to bring Jamie back to full health. The Doctor was then able to programme the nanogenes to bring all the other affected humans back to perfect health, which included making a lot of them fitter than they were before. Jack's ship was destroyed when he used the tractor beam to capture the detonating German bomb and hold it in a deteriorating stasis. He was then rescued by the Doctor's TARDIS. (1.9, 1.10)

novels, originally written as a means to pay off debts. Dickens travelled to Cardiff in 1869 to give a charity reading of the story. (1.3)

Church of the Tin Vagabond: One of the many religions practised in the 42nd century. (2.9)

Churchill, Winston: Conservative Prime Minister of Great Britain, the Queen's Coronation took place in 1953 during his third term of office. The Doctor was appalled to see the British police operating clandestinely on the streets of Muswell Hill, surprised that such things could happen in Churchill's Britain. (2.7) Vivien Rook likened Harry Saxon to Churchill. (3.12)

'Circle of Life': Oscar-nominated song from the movie *The Lion King*, written by Tim Rice and Elton John. The Doctor quoted the opening lyrics to the Sycorax Leader. (2.X)

City of Binding Light, the: Remarkable place that sent Ambassadors to Platform One to witness Earthdeath. (1.2)

Clancy's Garage: Car-repair shop where Mickey Smith worked. (2.X)

Clark, Farmer: Slightly pompous man who ran Oakham Farm in the village of Farringham. He spotted a Scarecrow in one of his fields that seemed to wave at him. Investigating, he was set upon by a horde of Scarecrows, which took him to the Family of Blood's invisible spaceship. There he was murdered, and his body inhabited by Father of Mine. (3.8) (Played by GERARD HORAN)

Clark, Sarah: It was on the way to pregnant Sarah's wedding to Stuart Hoskins that Pete Tyler was killed in a hit-and-run car accident. However, when Rose Tyler saved her father's life, time was disturbed, enabling the antibody-like wraiths, the Reapers, to spill into the world of 1987, wiping people out of time and feeding off the resultant chronal energy. Stuart and Sarah had met when she had lost her purse outside the Beatbox Club and couldn't get a cab home. After Pete Tyler sacrificed his life, thus mending the wound in time, the wedding took place, with no one recollecting any of what had occurred other than the unfortunate death of Pete outside the church. (1.8) (Played by NATALIE JONES)

Classic Earth: The National Trust rearranged the continents of Earth prior to Earthdeath, so it once again resembled what was known as 'Classic Earth' to observers from space. (1.2)

Clavadoe: In the Pan Traffic Calendar, the month of Hoob is followed by Pandoff, not Clavadoe. Fitch didn't know this when asked by the Anne Droid in *The Weakest Link* aboard the Game Station. (1.12)

Cleaver, Mr: Welsh nuclear adviser, charged by the Government with investigating the Blaidd Drwg Power Station Project. He realised that the power station was badly designed, fearing that the suppression pool would cause the hydrogen recombiners to fail. Thus the containment isolation system would collapse, resulting in a meltdown – a potential nuclear explosion which would take most of South Wales with it. After posting some of his fears on Clive Finch's internet site, by then run by Mickey Smith, he reported his findings to the Mayor of Cardiff, former MI5 operative Margaret Blaine, only to discover as she decapitated him that she was actually Blon Fel Fotch Pasameer-Day Slitheen, a member of the alien Family Slitheen. (1.11) (Played by WILLIAM THOMAS)

Cleopatra: Mickey Smith and Rose Tyler discussed the fact that the Doctor once mentioned he knew, and clearly got on well with, the legendary Queen of the Nile. He referred to her as Cleo. (2.4)

Clifton's Parade: Road in South East London where Mickey Smith was when he heard the TARDIS materialisation sound as it brought Rose Tyler home after Emergency Programme 1 had been activated. (1.13) Mickey's dad, Jackson, used to work at a key-cutter's there before he went to Spain. (2.5)

Clive: A footman in the service of the MacLeish family in Torchwood House. He was killed by the Haemovariform. (2.2)

Clockwork Robots: Repair androids aboard the SS *Madame de Pompadour*, who were following their programming and trying to repair the ship after it was caught in an ion storm. Their programming slightly corrupted, they had already used the bodies of the human crew to try and operate the ship, but to no avail. They reasoned that they required the brain of the original Madame de Pompadour, and used time-window technology aboard the ship and localised teleports to access different times in French history until they found her. The Doctor broke the time-window connections to the 51st century and, after deactivating themselves, the Robots stayed inert in 18th-century Versailles. (2.4)

Cloister Bell: The TARDIS's internal alarm system, which rings when the ship is in imminent danger. When the newly regenerated Doctor accidentally programmed the TARDIS to crash in the Powell Estate, it rang. (CiN, 3.12)

Clom: Twin world to Raxacoricofallapatorius and home to the vile Abzorbaloff. (2.10)

Clonemeat: The Sisters of Plenitude tried using clonemeat to cultivate their cures and vaccines, but it failed, so they bred the New Humans instead. (2.1)

Clovis, Frau: Fastidious PA to the Duke of Manhattan, present when he was cured of Petrifold Regression in the Hospital run by the Sisters of Plenitude in New New York. (2.1) Although she survived the attack by the New Humans, it seems almost certain she later died as a victim of the mutated Bliss virus that wiped out the majority of New Earth's population. (3.3) (Played by LUCY ROBINSON)

Code Nine: The emergency codeword used by the Government to acknowledge that the Doctor has been sighted. When Jackie Tyler called to let the authorities know the Doctor was in South East London, Indra Ganesh, a junior secretary for the Ministry of Defence, told General Asquith that a Code Nine was confirmed, unaware that Asquith was by then an alien. (1.4) Harriet Jones asked Major Blake of UNIT if a Code Nine had indicated the presence of the Doctor as the Sycorax ship approached Earth. (2.X)

Coffa: One of Jabe's associates from the Forest of Cheem aboard Platform One. He was distressed to hear of Jabe's death from the Doctor. (1.2) (Played by PAUL CASEY)

Colleen: One of the strongest players of *The Weakest Link* aboard the Game Station, who banked loads of money. When she lost a round, the Anne Droid appeared to disintegrate her but, in truth, she was transmatted over to the Dalek mothership and turned into part of the growing Dalek army created by the Emperor. (1.12) (Played by KATE LOUSTAU)

Collins, Jackie: Author of the novel *Lucky*. Rodrick didn't know this when asked by the Anne Droid in *The Weakest Link* aboard the Game Station. (1.12)

Commander: Troop commander in the Weapons Testing Area of the Vault, he tried to stop the Dalek getting any further out of the complex. He died, along with all his men, plus countless lab technicians and office workers when the Dalek electrocuted them after setting off the water sprinkler system. (1.6) (Played by JOE MONTANA)

Communards, The: Pop-synth duo whose top-five single 'Never Can Say Goodbye' was heard when the TARDIS materialised in 1987 to see Pete Tyler's death in a hit-and-run accident. (1.8)

Compact Laser Deluxe: Weapon used by Captain Jack Harkness to destroy Trine-E and Zu-Zana aboard the Game Station. No one wanted to ask where it was concealed, as he was naked when he produced it. (1.12)

Condensate Wilderness: One of the furthermost explored regions of the universe. It was believed that Utopia was far beyond it. (3.11)

Condition Red [1]: An alert status that enabled an Earth Empire Security Commander to shoot dead anyone he or she felt compromised a situation. Mr Jefferson threatened to shoot Toby Zed on Sanctuary Base 6 under the terms of such an alert. (2.8)

Condition Red [2]: Codeword within the Saxon administration to imply a plan had gone wrong. The Sinister Woman referred to Clive Jones warning Martha Jones to stay away from the family home as a Condition Red. (3.12) When the Jones family and Captain Jack Harkness, aboard the *Valiant*, tried to stage an assassination attempt on the Master's life, a Condition Red alert went out. (3.13)

Conglomeration: The city on Malcassairo in which the Malmooth had lived before their virtual extinction. (3.11)

Connie: Child at the reception for Donna Noble and Lance Bennett's non-wedding. Donna checked up on her after the attack by the Roboform Santas. (3.X)

Connolly, Eddie: Husband to Rita and father to Tommy, who lived with them and his mother-in-law in Florizel Street, Muswell Hill, North London. An ex-serviceman since the Second World War, Eddie's pride and patriotism bordered on extremism. He was scared by the changes occurring in 1950s Britain, realising they didn't fit his view of the world, which manifested itself as bullying towards his wife and son. When the Doctor visited his home and embarrassed him before his family, he got worse and had the faceless Grandma (who actually owned the house) removed by the police. When Rita discovered that Eddie had done this to her mother, and other friends and neighbours, she threw him out of the house in front of other members of their family. (2.7) (Played by JAMIE FOREMAN)

Connolly, Rita: Downtrodden wife to the bullish Eddie Connolly, who insisted that Rita prepared for a party to celebrate the Coronation, putting up decorations and flags as well as preparing food and drink for Eddie's family. During the Coronation party, Rita finally decided she had taken enough from Eddie and threw him out of their house when she realised it had been her husband who had shopped their neighbours and friends and her mother to the police after they had lost their faces to the power of the Wire. (2.7) (Played by DEBRA GILLETT)

Connolly, Tommy: Teenaged son of the bullying Eddie Connolly, closer to his mum, Rita, and his grandmother than Eddie would have liked. Tommy realised that the Doctor might be able to explain what had happened to his grandmother, who had lost her face, and joined him on his trip to Alexandra Palace to defeat the Wire. After Rita threw Eddie out of their home, Rose Tyler persuaded Tommy that, whatever Eddie's faults, he was still his father, and so the boy helped carry his dad's bags to wherever he ended up. (2.7) (Played by RORY JENNINGS)

Control and Application of Gunpowder, The: A book in Sir Robert MacLeish's library. (2.2)

Control Voice: One of the military commanders of the Earth Empire, contacted by Pilot Kelvin on Myarr. (TIQ) (Voiced by BARNEY HARWOOD)

Controller [1]: Young unnamed woman plugged directly into the Game Station who monitored all its broadcasts. She had been sent insane by the demands of her job – having been doing it since the age of five. However, she had also been planning the downfall of the Daleks ever since she had learned of the Doctor's existence, and she was responsible for transporting him, Rose Tyler and Captain Jack Harkness to the Game Station. The Male and Female Programmers believed she would not recognise the Doctor's existence as he was not a member of staff, but in fact the Controller had been watching him for years. When solar flares disrupted the Station's transmissions, the Daleks could not monitor events there, and she was able to explain to the Doctor what was going on. Although the disruption then ended, she gave the Doctor the coordinates for the Dalek fleet, knowing that the Daleks could now hear her – which they did. They transported her to their ship and exterminated her. (1.12) (Played by MARTHA COPE)

Controller [2]: The role assumed by Dalek Caan after the Cult had deemed Dalek Sec no longer capable of leading them. As such, he wired himself into the machinery in the Transgenic Lab and monitored the results of the Final Experiment. From there he was able to send a massive mental pulse of energy into the brains of every single Dalek Human hybrid and kill them instantly after they had destroyed Daleks Thay and Jast. (3.5)

Cook [1]: One of the household of Lady Isobel MacLeish, she survived the Werewolf attack on Torchwood House. (2.2) (Played by SUZANNE DOWNS)

CONSTANTINE, DR: The last person in Albion Hospital to be affected by the gas-mask virus created by the Chula nanogenes, he was able to show the Doctor that the seemingly dead patients were just immobile until triggered by something. Like the four-year-old boy they were now based upon, the only question in their minds was 'Are you my mummy?' Constantine had done some experimental therapy with the 'empty' child in room 802 and recorded it – his empathy existing perhaps due to the fact he had lost his own children and grandchildren to the war. Eventually Constantine succumbed and became a gas mask zombie like the others, threatening the Doctor, Rose Tyler and Captain Jack Harkness. When the nanogenes later recognised the correct human DNA, they repaired all those who had been infected, restoring Constantine, who was then able to carry on his good work at the hospital. (1.9, 1.10) (Played by RICHARD WILSON)

Cook [2]: In charge of feeding the boys and staff at Farringham School for Boys. (3.8)

Cooper, Miss: Villager at the dance in Farringham when the Family of Blood attacked, killing Mr Chambers and demanding the Doctor hand himself over to them. She may well have been the daughter of the man who owned Cooper's Field. (3.9)

Cooper's Field: Area of Farringham where the Family of Blood landed their invisible spaceship, just on the border of Blackdown Woods. (3.8, 3.9)

Copacabana Beach: Popular resort in Rio de Janeiro, Brazil, which Martha Jones randomly elected to go to in the TARDIS. (TIQ)

Corporation, the: The company that owned various space stations such as Platform One and were responsible for programming the Control Computers which ran them. (1.2)

Corvin, Sister: One of the Catkind Sisters of Plenitude. She wrote a thesis about the migration of sentience, referring to the process as the Echo of Life. (2.1)

Costard: Character from *Love's Labour's Lost* and later *Love's Labour's Won*, played by William Kempe, a member of Shakespeare's company. (3.2)

Costello, Elvis: Irish rock star (real name Declan McManus) who wrote the song 'Pump It Up', which donated its rhythm riff to Rogue Traders' 'Voodoo Child', as played by the Master aboard the *Valiant* as the Toclafane began their descent. (3.12)

Countdown: One of the programmes broadcast from the Game Station. Contestants had 30 seconds to stop a bomb detonating. (1.12) It was an updated version of a British quiz show broadcast by Channel 4; in the erased 2009 timeline that followed the Toclafane domination of Earth, Professor Docherty reminisced that she used to enjoy *Countdown*, presented by either of the Des's (Lynam or O'Connor) (3.13)

Crabtree: Thuggish plain-clothed policeman who assisted Detective Inspector Bishop in taking away the faceless people of Muswell Hill in 1953. (2.7) (Played by IEUAN RHYS)

Craddock, Phyllis 'Fanny': British television cook from the 1950s to the 1970s, whom the Doctor referred to as one of the greatest chefs on Earth. (TIQ)

Crane, Matt: Torchwood operative based in the Lever Room in the Torchwood Tower. He spotted the TARDIS at the Powell Estate, much to the delight of Torchwood's CEO, Yvonne Hartman. Matt was later led to the upper floors of the Tower, where he was killed by the Cybermen and reanimated via a Cybus Industries ear pod that was connected directly into his cerebral cortex. When the Doctor discovered this, he jammed the signal to the ear pods and the already dead Matt died once again. (2.12)

Crane, Mr: John Lumic's right-hand man on 'Pete's World'. He had worked alongside Lumic for many years and knew how ruthless his boss could be. He had no conscience when it came to fooling London's homeless that he could give them food, instead having them converted into Cybermen. However, when Lumic activated the ear-pod signal that would blank everyone's mind, Mr Crane realised it was meant to include him. He confronted Lumic and tried to kill him, but a Cyberman electrocuted him. (2.5, 2.6) (Played by COLIN SPAULL)

Credit Five: Form of currency, resembling thin metal strips, on Satellite Five. (1.7)

Creet: Orphaned refugee child who assisted Lieutenant Atillo in the Silo base on Malcassairo. He helped reunite the Shafe Cane family and later went aboard the rocket to Utopia, telling Martha Jones that his mother believed the skies above Utopia were full of diamonds. When Martha Jones heard this phrase repeated by one of the inhabitants of a Toclafane sphere, she realised who the Toclafane really were. (3.11) (Played by JOHN BELL)

Crespallions: Blue-skinned race charged with running Platform One. Some Crespallions were of average humanoid height, others no taller than human children. (1.2)

Crimean War: 19th-century war fought by Britain and her allies against the Russians. The doorman at the village hall in Farringham was a veteran of the war. (3.8)

Crime Crackers: Television programme that alerted the public to the disappearances of the children from Stratford in 2012. (2.11T)

Croft, David: Co-producer of British TV sitcom *Are You Being Served?* who also wrote the lyrics to its theme song, quoted by the Doctor as he exited the elevator at the top of the Empire State Building. (3.5)

Crofter: Travelling through the moorlands of Scotland in 1840, he was killed by the original werewolf that had crashlanded on Earth 300 years earlier. (2.2T) (Played by ALAN DORRINTON)

Croot, Billy: Local man who asked Jackie Tyler out while Rose was missing for a year. (1.4)

Croot, Mrs: Resident of South East London, who Elton Pope met and she told him where Jackie Tyler lived. Presumably the mother of Billy. (2.10) (Played by BELLA EMBERG)

Crosbie: Housemate alongside Strood and Lynda in the *Big Brother* house when the Doctor was transported in. Shortly after, she was the eighth housemate to be evicted. A great cook, she apologised for stealing Lynda Moss's soap and, although apparently disintegrated, she was in fact transmatted over to the Dalek mothership and turned into part of the growing Dalek army created by the Emperor. (1.12) (Played by ABI ENIOLA)

Cross Flane, Zachary: Second-in-command of the Torchwood Archive's Sanctuary Base 6, he took charge after the death of Captain Walker when their ship crashed on Krop Tor after encountering the black hole which the planet was orbiting. Not really wanting the command, he nevertheless successfully dealt with the attack by the Beast imprisoned beneath the planet's surface and took the survivors away in a shuttle ship. Just when they thought they were safe, they found themselves drawn towards the black hole, but were saved by the Doctor using the TARDIS's force fields to protect the ship and drag it away. (2.8, 2.9) (Played by SHAUN PARKES)

Crossgate Cabs: London taxi firm. The Doctor, Martha Jones and Captain Jack Harkness watched a television in its window and realised the Master had set them up as public enemies. (3.12)

Croydon: At the time of her original journeys alongside the Doctor, Sarah Jane Smith's home was in South Croydon and that's where the Doctor told her he had brought her to when it was time for them to part ways. After the TARDIS left her, Sarah Jane realised she wasn't in Hillview Road, Croydon at all, but in Aberdeen.

Cruciform: When the Dalek Emperor took possession of this towards the end of the Time War, the Master realised his people, the Time Lords, were defeated and fled, turning himself human via a chameleon arch and becoming Professor Yana. (3.12)

Cryofreeze: Part of the stasis chamber in the medcentre aboard the SS *Pentallian*. Kath McDonnell used it to kill Dev Ashton when he was sun-possessed, and the Doctor made Martha Jones use it to try and freeze the sun out of him when he too became sun-possessed. (3.7)

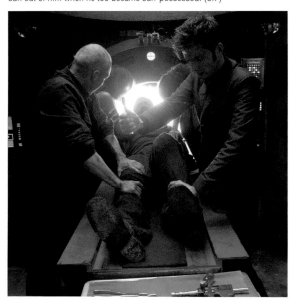

CULT OF SKARO, THE: Legendary group of four Daleks, appointed by the Emperor during the Time War to think and plan, each having a degree of individuality and emotion denied most rank-and-file Daleks. They gave themselves names, Caan, Jast, Thay, and their leader, a Black Dalek, was Sec. They fled the end of the Time War, a limited time-travel capability built into each of them, unaware that the Emperor had survived, and they hid, along with the Genesis Ark containing millions of Dalek prisoners, in the Void, waiting for the chance to ease themselves into reality. Once this had been achieved, Sec released the Dalek prisoners and began a war against both humans and Cybermen. However, when the Doctor reopened the Void, all the Daleks were in danger of being drawn back in. Ultimately every Dalek, plus the empty Ark, was returned to the Void apart from the four members of the Cult, who used an emergency temporal shift to escape the carnage. (2.12, 2.13) They ended up trapped in 1930, in Manhattan, with no supplies and little energy. Realising that their future might lie in genetic experimentation to create a new race of Daleks, they oversaw the construction of the Empire State Building, intending to use it as a conductor for gamma radiation caused by a solar flare. The radiation would then carry the Dalek Factor into nearly a thousand specially prepared unconscious humans. This Final Experiment would provide the Cult with a new army. However, they had not foreseen that Dalek Sec's desire to merge his consciousness with a human body, creating the Dalek Sec Hybrid, would in turn give him a conscience and a degree of humanity. Sec turned against his fellow Daleks and they exterminated him. Not long after, their Dalek-Human army, influenced by the addition of Time Lord DNA courtesy of the Doctor, turned on the Cult – both Thay and Jast were destroyed before Caan exterminated all the Dalek-Humans. The Doctor tried to appeal to Caan, now probably the last Dalek in the universe, but Caan activated an emergency temporal shift and vanished. (3.4, 3.5) (Operated by BARNABY EDWARDS, NICHOLAS PEGG, DAVID HANKINSON, ANTHONY SPARGO, DAN BARRATT, voiced by NICHOLAS BRIGGS)

Curt: Young Torchwood Archivist aboard Sanctuary Base 6 who was charged with going through Captain Walker's personal belongings after his death. Amongst them, he found the book of hieroglyphs and maps Walker had been given by McMillan on Earth. As soon as he touched it, he heard the Beast speak to him. The book then burst into flames and Curt tried to escape. He was found moments later by fellow crewmember Chenna, his face covered in alien tattoos, identical to the ones from the destroyed book, his mind completely broken. It is unknown what Curt's final fate was but he was presumably no longer alive by the time the Doctor and Rose Tyler arrived on Sanctuary Base 6 and no mention was made of Curt's markings when a similar fate befell Toby Zed. (2.8T, 2.9T) (Played by KENON MANN)

Cyber Control: The heart of the Cyber-conversion factory on 'Pete's World', where the Doctor, Rose and Pete Tyler met the Cyber Controller, who had once been John Lumic. It was destroyed in a massive explosion that obliterated the factory and the Controller itself. (2.6)

Cyber Controller: Advanced Cyberform on 'Pete's World', powered via a massive energy throne it sat in, akin to the one John Lumic, its creator, had used. Lumic's brain was placed inside the Controller, but even that wasn't enough to outwit the Doctor. After the rest of the Cyberforms had their emotional inhibitors switched off, they went insane and rampaged through Cyber Control, destroying everything. The Controller eventually left its throne and pursued the Doctor, Rose Tyler and Pete Tyler up a rope ladder to the Cybus Industries zeppelin. Pete used the Doctor's sonic screwdriver to cut the rope ladder and the Controller plummeted to its destruction amidst the exploding Cyber-conversion factory below. (2.6) (Played by PAUL KASEY, voiced by ROGER LLOYD PACK)

Cyberleader One: The Cyberleader responsible for taking over Torchwood Tower. He was later destroyed by Jake Simmonds' troopers from 'Pete's World', but downloaded all his knowledge into another Cyberman, who became Cyberleader Two. (2.12, 2.13) (Played by PAUL KASEY, voiced by NICHOLAS BRIGGS)

Cyberleader Two: When Cyberleader One was destroyed, one of the Cybermen charged with converting Jackie Tyler was immediately upgraded to Cyberleader, and Jackie Tyler was able to escape in the momentary confusion. (2.13) (Played by PAUL KASEY, voiced by NICHOLAS BRIGGS)

Cyberman: The head of a non-Cybus Industries Cyberman was in the exhibit room in Henry Van Statten's base deep under the surface of Utah. (1.6)

Cyberpunk Girls: A couple of teenaged Japanese drivers on the New New York Motorway. When the Doctor entered their car, he borrowed a blue scarf to keep the exhaust fumes from choking him. (3.3) (Played by NAOMI HAYAMA, KAMAN CHAN)

Cybus Industries: Established in 'Pete's World' in 1982. By 2001 it had estimated profits of $78 billion. (2.5T) It had almost complete control of the communications market, and it was via the Cybus ear pods worn by most of society, that Cybus was able to bring people to their factories for the Ultimate Upgrade – to become Cybermen. Among the other sub-companies that Cybus Industries owned or ran were Vitex, International Electromatics, IE24, Cybus Finance, Cybus Properties and Cybus Network. The latter was the primary communications provider on 'Pete's World', providing access to communications, the internet and countless other forms of information. (2.5, 2.6)

Cynaps: One of Cybus Industries' technological advances on 'Pete's World'. It was the process by which the human brain, once placed in the Cyberform head, could interact with the steel exoskeleton – referred to as the Ultimate Upgrade. (2.5)

its entirety by a direct bazooka blast. In the event of a Cyberman's destruction, their knowledge was retained within a central consciousness, and could be downloaded into another drone if necessary.

By transmitting a signal via the Cybus Industries ear pods, Lumic was able to lure the entire population of London into Battersea Power Station, where they were then subjected to the Upgrade process. Reject stock was incinerated

The Cybermen

You are inferior. Man will be reborn as Cyberman, but you will perish under maximum deletion…

Intended as the next level of mankind, the Cybermen were created on 'Pete's World' by John Lumic, who was investigating means of prolonging his own degenerating life span. The result of the Cybus Industries Ultimate Upgrade

project, these Cybermen consisted of a human brain welded directly into a steel exoskeleton, suspended within a cradle of copyrighted chemicals. Beneath the chest plate, metal gears and servos were intertwined with human flesh, threaded throughout the suit with strings of tissue to serve as a central nervous system. Emotions were inhibited, and all humanity removed, turning the Cyberform into a simple drone, although the suits themselves could also function without a human subject.

Immensely strong and invulnerable to attack, the Cybermen were able to dispense a lethal electrical charge through their hands, and later developed laser weaponry, which they concealed in their forearms. Although impervious to bullets, a Cyber suit could be rendered inoperative by means of an electromagnetic bomb or Dalek gun, and could be destroyed in

on site, and pre-converted Cybermen were kept suspended in Deepcold storage tunnels until required. The Doctor and his companions were later able to deactivate the signal transmitting to the emotional inhibitors, and destroyed the factory, freeing the surviving humans and driving the Cybermen mad in the process. However, with Cybus factories still in operation over seven continents, Mickey Smith remained on 'Pete's World' to help Pete Tyler and Jake Simmonds combat the remaining Cyber threat. (2.5, 2.6)

Although Pete Tyler eventually managed to assert a degree of control, Earth's new Golden Age under the auspices of President Harriet Jones meant that many people opted not to destroy the surviving Cybermen, arguing they had rights as living beings. Three years later, the Cybermen had vanished – heading into the Void and crossing over into the 'real'

Earth, initially appearing as 'ghosts', and successfully transposing five million Cybermen across the planet, before revealing their true form to the world.

Following their arrival en masse, Cyberleader One took control of operations, using a camera located in a Cyberform's forearm to transmit a message of triumph to the world. Basing themselves in the Torchwood Institute at Canary Wharf, the Cybermen went out onto the streets, taking people away for upgrading. They then encountered the Daleks, offering them an alliance, which the Daleks rejected, thus beginning a war between the two alien races, with humanity caught in the middle. As the Cyberman fatalities mounted, they began the emergency upgrading of Torchwood personnel, and attempted a retreat through the Void, but were stopped by Yvonne Hartman's Cyberform. The Doctor and Rose Tyler managed to reopen the Void, drawing nearly all the Cybermen and Daleks back inside, sealing them inside the Void, unable to enter any other world for all eternity. (2.12, 2.13)

Back in our universe, the Cybermen presumably live on. They started life on an ordinary world like Earth, spawned from the best of intentions, then swarmed across the galaxy like a plague, converting all those who weren't already like them. (2.6) By 2012, the head of one of these Cybermen was part of Van Statten's museum in Utah. (1.6)

(Voiced by NICHOLAS BRIGGS)

D

d'Étoiles, Madame: Jeanne-Antoinette ('Reinette') Poisson married Charles-Guillaume d'Étoiles in 1741 but divorced him four years later when she became the King's consort and moved into Versailles as Madame de Pompadour. The Doctor referred to her as Madame d'Étoiles as he worked out who Reinette was. (2.4)

Dad: A London man kidnapped by the Graske at Christmas, and replaced with a changeling. He was eventually returned home with no memory of his experiences. (AotG) (Played by NICHOLAS BEVENEY)

Daemos: Civilisation which had the concept of evil represented by a horned beast in its culture. (2.9)

Dagmar Cluster: Location of the SS *Madame de Pompadour* in the 51st century, two and a half galaxies away from Earth. (2.4)

Daily Contemplation: Every day at the same time, the drivers of the cars on the New New York Motorway took a few moments to sing together, as one voice, a hymn to celebrate their lives. (3.3)

Daily Download: On 'Pete's World', Cybus Industries regularly downloaded information such as news, weather, sport, TV schedules, lottery numbers and a daily joke directly into people's ear pods. (2.5)

Daily Telegraph: British daily broadsheet newspaper, read by the Abzorbaloff before it revealed its true self to Elton Pope and Ursula Blake. (2.10)

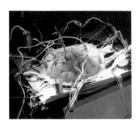

Dalek embryo: An early aborted experiment in creating new Daleks by the Cult of Skaro resulted in failed Dalek embryos being flushed into the Manhattan sewer system in 1930. The Doctor found one and, after discovering its DNA type was 467-989, realised that he was facing his old foes. (3.4)

Dalek Stratagem: The Dalek Emperor's plan for humanity in 200,100. Having set the Jagrafess up in Satellite Five 191 years previously, the Daleks had been manipulating mankind, first through news broadcasts, later through the quiz and game shows, gradually building up a new army harvested from the 'losing' contestants, transported there illegally by the Controller. The Daleks had been waiting just on the edge of Earth's solar system – 200 ships, containing almost half a million new Daleks, ready to dominate the galaxy. As the plan neared completion, Rose Tyler absorbed the Time Vortex from the heart of the TARDIS and was able to erase the Daleks, their ships and the Emperor himself from all existence, and the galaxy was saved. (1.12, 1.13)

Dalekanium: The metal which laces a Dalek's polycarbide armoured shell. Slats of this were attached to the mooring mast atop the Empire State Building so that, when struck by a bolt of gamma radiation, they would conduct the pulse precisely into the bodies of the comatose humans in the Transgenic Lab. (3.4, 3.5)

Damascus Road: North London street where Mr Magpie abandoned the faceless Rose Tyler in 1953. (2.7)

Dame Kelly Holmes Close: A residential street in Stratford, East London from which children had been disappearing inexplicably in 2012. (2.11)

'Daniel': A 1973 top five hit for Elton John – possibly the record that inspired Elton Pope's parents to name him after their favourite singer. (2.10)

Daniels Family: Southampton-based family that the Doctor befriended, apparently stopping them from boarding the RMS *Titanic* before its fateful voyage in 1912. (1.1)

'Danny Boy': The Nurse on Satellite Five tells Adam Mitchell that one recipient of the Type Two information spike chip used to whistle this 20th-century Celtic song, written by Frederick Weatherly, to activate his chip. (1.7)

Dark Matter Reefs: An area of space, most likely unexplored, towards the edge of the known universe. Utopia wasn't quite as far as the Dark Matter Reefs, nor the Wildlands. (3.11)

Dark Times: Period of Gallifreyan history, about 4.6 billion years ago. According to the Doctor, the Nestenes, the Racnoss and the Great Vampyres rampaged through space back then, as did the legendary Great Old Ones. The Fledgling Empires, amongst which were the Gallifreyans, banded together to fight these foes. (3.X, TIQ)

Dårlig Ulv Stranden: The beach in Norway in 'Pete's World' where the Doctor, as a hologram, and Rose, were reunited for two minutes, able to say a final, heartfelt goodbye. It translates into English as Bad Wolf Bay. (2.13)

Daughter of Mine: One of the Family of Blood, who took on the form of Lucy Cartwright and murdered her parents and, later, the headmaster of the local school, Mr Rocastle. Once the Doctor had regained his Time Lord form, he tricked the Family and blew their spaceship up. The Doctor trapped Daughter of Mine – still in Lucy's form – within the refractive index of a mirror. She was to inhabit the dark recesses of a mirror, all mirrors, for eternity, the Doctor returning to visit her once a year, every year. (3.8, 3.9) (Played by LAUREN WILSON)

Dave [1]: One of Sarah Clark's guests due at her wedding, who hadn't shown up. (1.8)

Dave [2]: Dave was Huw Edwards' fellow commentator at the Olympic Games Opening Ceremony, observing the Torch-bearer's route. (2.11)

Davinadroid: Robotic voice that controlled the *Big Brother* house aboard the Game Station. (1.12) (Voiced by DAVINA McCALL)

Davis, Steve: Co-writer of Rogue Traders' 'Voodoo Child', which was played by the Master aboard the *Valiant* as the Toclafane began their descent. (3.12)

de Chateauroux, Madame: Mistress of King Louis XV of France, whose death in 1744 enabled Jeanne-Antoinette Poisson to become his new consort. (2.4)

De Maggio: An officer in Bywater's security detail in the Vault, in Henry Van Statten's underground base. She was charged with getting Rose Tyler and Adam Mitchell to safety after the Dalek broke free. Having slaughtered her comrades, the Dalek caught up with the fleeing trio in a stairwell. Relieved, assuming the Dalek couldn't climb after them, they were astonished when it began to elevate. De Maggio sent the youngsters on, trying to negotiate with the Dalek, to no avail. Finally, she opened fire, and it exterminated her. (1.6) (Played by JANA CARPENTER)

De Niro, Robert: Mickey Smith mimicked De Niro as Travis Bickle, quoting his 'You lookin' at me' moment from *Taxi Driver* while aboard the SS *Madame de Pompadour*. (2.4)

Deathless Prince: Legendary demon name, one of many attributed to the Beast throughout the galaxies. (2.8, 2.9)

The Daleks

You are superior in only one respect … You are better at dying.

Secured within tank-like life-support machines, the Daleks were genetically engineered on the planet Skaro to be impulsive, emotionless killers, with a primary order to simply conquer and destroy all other life across the universe and to ensure the survival and purity of the Dalek race. Bred as soldiers, the Daleks lived for commands, and elected designated controllers to coordinate units via a military computer.

Protected by a polycarbide outer shell, with a force field capable of melting bullets on impact, the Daleks were almost completely invulnerable. They were armed with a projected energy weapon that scrambled internal organs and killed on impact, fitted to a midsection that could rotate 360 degrees, and their only weaknesses were concentrated gunfire aimed at their eyepieces and an assault using their own weaponry.

Most Daleks were also equipped with a multi-functional sucker arm, capable of manipulating computer equipment, reading brainwaves, detecting pulses and performing intelligence scans. It could also be used as a rudimentary weapon, suffocating victims and collapsing their skulls when otherwise low on energy. Although Daleks were equipped with these basic appendages, others could also be fitted, such as more advanced weaponry or assault claws capable of cutting through doors.

Designed for survival, the Dalek casing formed the perfect life-support system, capable of moving across any terrain, in space, or underwater, and affording visual contact between units. Within this shell sat the Dalek itself – fundamental DNA type 467-989 – secured into position by a series of metal clamps and pistons cut into the flesh, surrounded by a series of controls. Daleks could draw back these casings, exposing themselves to the world outside, or pulling other beings inside. As part of their organic nature, the Daleks were also capable

of basic telepathy, harnessing their wills to manipulate the feelings of those around them, and could project ideas across space into the minds of potential allies.

They were said to have disappeared from space following the Tenth Dalek Occupation, but went to fight against the Time Lords in the Last Great Time War. The Time War ended when the Doctor – known in the legends of Skaro as 'the Oncoming Storm' – destroyed both civilisations.

A single Dalek survived, however, insane and alone in 2012. It fell through time, crashing into the Ascension Islands in the middle of the 20th century, and burning in a crater for three days before it was rescued. For 50 years it was sold at private auction from one collector to another, before coming to the attention of billionaire Henry Van Statten, who imprisoned it in chains as the prize of his collection and named it the 'Metaltron'. It was tortured in an attempt to make it talk, and so shielded itself from the humans, causing men to burst into flames on contact. Transmitting a distress signal, the Dalek slowly discovered itself to be the last survivor of its race, and manipulated Rose Tyler into rejuvenating its physical form, the Daleks having evolved an ability to use temporal radiation as a power supply during the Time War. Contaminated with Rose's human DNA, however, this Dalek then began mutating, eventually opting to exterminate itself through fear of what it might otherwise become.

Far into the future, the Dalek Emperor had also survived, hiding in the depths of space. Although crippled, its ship remained alive, and the Emperor shaped the development of Earth through its news and television output, guiding humanity's progress for centuries. It waited patiently, then infiltrated the systems of Earth, harvesting dispossessed humans and nurturing them in Dalek form: a new army of Daleks and a fleet of 200 ships. The Emperor soon proclaimed himself to be God, creating new life in his image, claiming Earth as a Dalek Paradise. It then perished alongside every other Dalek in the universe when

Rose Tyler absorbed the power of the Time Vortex and reduced them to atoms.

Although every Dalek in the universe had now been destroyed, shortly before the Daleks' initial defeat a secret order had escaped: the Cult of Skaro. Above and beyond the Emperor, who had established the Cult to think and reason outside the Dalek norm, these four Daleks had fled into the Void between different realities. They emerged from their Void ship in Earth's Torchwood Institute in 2007, just as Cybermen from a parallel world had taken over the planet. The Cult promptly declared war. They primed the Genesis Ark and unlocked it over the London skies, releasing millions of Daleks from within. These were later all drawn back into the Void, however, when the Doctor briefly reopened the breach between realities.

The Cult of Skaro performed an emergency temporal shift to escape the Doctor's trap, and relocated themselves to 1930s New York, draining their power cells in the process. The Cult's leader, Dalek Sec, then initiated research into the conception of Dalek-Human hybrids, and sacrificed his own existence in an attempt to ensure the survival of Dalek-kind. Daleks Jast and Thay were later exterminated by their own Dalek-Human hybrids, and Dalek Caan performed an emergency temporal shift in order to escape.

Just one Dalek, in the whole of the universe…

(Operated by DAN BARRATT, STUART CROSSMAN, BARNABY EDWARDS, DAVID HANKINSON, NICHOLAS PEGG and ANTHONY SPARGO, voiced by NICHOLAS BRIGGS)

Debbie: Friend of Jackie Tyler's who lived on the Powell Estate and had a friend on the *Mirror* newspaper. (1.1)

Deep Darkness: Prison dimension into which the Eternals cast the Carrionites within the Rexel planetary configuration. (3.2)

Deep Realms: Area of space where the Isolus began their journey thousands of years ago. (2.11)

Deepcold 6: Underground area leading to the Cyber-conversion factory in Battersea Power Station on 'Pete's World'. The Doctor and Mrs Moore entered the factory via this area and found it full of immobile Cybermen. (2.6)

Defabricator: A device operated by the robots, Zu-Zana and Trine-E aboard the Game Station as part of their *What Not to Wear* programme. It literally disintegrated fabrics and saved time disrobing. Captain Jack Harkness later used it as a weapon to destroy a Dalek. (1.12, 1.13)

Deffry Vale High School: Selected by Brother Lassar of the Krillitanes to be the base for their plan to solve the Skasas Paradigm. Mickey Smith drew the Doctor and Rose Tyler's attention to it after reports in the press of UFO activity in the area three months earlier. The Krillitanes used Krillitane Oil to improve the mental capacity of the students, but the building was blown up by a self-sacrificing K-9, to destroy the alien invaders. (2.3) A web page about the school was seen by the Doctor when he accessed a mobile phone with his sonic screwdriver to search for HC Clements. (3.X)

Delaney, Trisha: Shop assistant who Mickey Smith tells Rose Tyler he's dating to make her jealous. Rose knows her brother, Rob, and also believes Mickey is lying, as Trisha is not his type. (1.11)

Delta Wave: Trapped on the Game Station, facing half a million Daleks, the Doctor opted to use the station's resources as a huge transmitter, and created a Delta Wave, using Van Cassadyne energy. The Wave would fry anything in its path. The Emperor foresaw this and reminded the Doctor that using the Delta Wave would indeed wipe out the Daleks, but it would first kill everything between them, including the population of Earth. In the end, faced with the choice of using the Delta Wave or not, the Doctor resigned himself to failing, and the Wave was never activated. (1.13)

Dent, Arthur: Fictional character from Douglas Adams' *Hitchhiker's Guide to the Galaxy* series of novels. The Doctor likened himself to Dent after defeating the Sycorax Leader, because he was wearing pyjamas and a dressing gown, as Arthur Dent had throughout his travels. (2.X)

Derek: A mate of Rose's at Henrik's, she assumed he was responsible for setting up a prank to trap her in the basement of the store. (1.1)

Desk Sergeant: Police officer at the station Sally went to, who wasn't too interested until, when she mentioned Wester Drumlins, he asked her to wait while he fetched DI Billy Shipton. (3.10) (Played by RAY SAWYER)

DICKENS, CHARLES JOHN HUFFAM: Foremost novelist of Victorian England, he was giving a charitable seasonal reading of his novel *A Christmas Carol* in Cardiff when one of his audience, Mrs Peace, appeared to die, exhaling a translucent spirit as she did so. The tired and jaded Dickens then met the Doctor and became embroiled in the fight against the alien Gelth. Indeed, it was Dickens who realised the Gelth could be drawn out of the corpses they had reanimated if overloaded with gas. He returned to London, revitalised and ready to finish his latest novel, which he elected to name 'The Mystery of Edwin Drood and the Blue Elementals'. The Doctor sadly told Rose Tyler that this would never happen — Dickens was destined to die the next year and would leave the story of Edwin Drood unfinished. (1.3) (Played by SIMON CALLOW)

Diagoras, Mr: Former soldier and building foreman, the Cult of Skaro offered Diagoras a chance to improve his position in life, and they gave him the opportunity to prove himself by overseeing the construction of the top floors of the Empire State Building, including the fixing of Dalek Thay's Dalekanium armour to the mooring mast. Dalek Sec, impressed by Diagoras, realised he now had the last component he needed for the Final Experiment and had Diagoras brought to him. Opening his casing, Sec drew Diagoras into himself, physically merging their two bodies, resulting in Sec's Dalek form gaining mobility via Diagoras's body, creating a template for the Cult's Dalek-Human army. However, in absorbing Diagoras, Sec also gained a rudimentary conscience and began to question exactly what Daleks were. If there was anything left of Diagoras himself after this process, apart from his torso, it was lost for ever when Dalek Sec was betrayed by his fellow Daleks and exterminated. (3.4, 3.5) (Played by ERIC LORENS)

Diary Room: Area of the *Big Brother* house aboard the Game Station where the contestants could talk freely without their fellow housemates hearing. (1.12)

Didcot: Pete Tyler won the third prize in a bowling competition before his death. The winner and runner-up got to go to the Berkshire town of Didcot. (1.8)

Digihumans: One of the names used by the humans of five billion years in Rose Tyler's future to describe themselves. It implied they were different from the then-extinct (bar Lady Cassandra) humans originating from Earth itself. (1.2) This was probably the same stage of human evolution as that referred to by the Doctor in the Silo base on Malcassairo, when he noted that humanity had spent time as 'digital downloads' before reverting to their basic physical shape. (3.11)

Dillane, Sylvia: One of the arrivals at 10 Downing Street after the Big Ben incident. Chair of the North Sea Boating Club, she was actually a disguised Slitheen, the real Dillane having already been killed. (1.5)

'Ding Dong Merrily On High': Traditional Christmas Carol being sung by carollers in the London streets of 1883 when the Graske kidnapped a street urchin. (AotG)

Dinner Lady: A Krillitane who had taken human form and worked at Deffry Vale High School. She was killed when K-9 heated up the drums of Krillitane Oil in the school kitchen and blew the Dinner Lady, the school and himself to pieces. (2.3) (Played by CAROLINE BERRY)

Dinosaurs: Sarah Jane Smith told Rose Tyler that, during her time travelling with the Doctor, they had encountered real dinosaurs. (2.3)

Disciples of Light: The beings credited with imprisoning the Beast below the surface of Krop Tor, in a pit, before the creation of the universe. They left behind a pictorial representation of the Beast's imprisonment, in a form that resembled prehistoric cave paintings on Earth. (2.9)

'Disco Inferno': Lady Cassandra quoted the refrain 'Burn baby, burn' from this hit for the Trammps when she gloated that everyone would burn to death aboard Platform One as she teleported away. (1.2)

DJ: Played records such as 'Love Don't Roam' and 'Merry Xmas Everybody!' at the reception to celebrate the non-wedding of Donna Noble and Lance Bennett. His equipment, boosted by the Doctor's sonic screwdriver, destroyed the Roboform Santas that then attacked. (3.X) (Played by MARK HASTE)

Doctor Who?: Website about the Doctor that leads Rose and Mickey to Clive Finch's house. (1.1) After Clive's death, Mickey Smith takes it over, eventually renaming it 'Defending the Earth', until he leaves Earth to travel full-time in the TARDIS. (2.3)

Dolls: The Carrionites, especially Lilith, used tiny cloth or straw dolls, with the hair or skin of their victim attached to it to control his body. The Doctor described these as basic DNA Replication Modules. (3.2)

'Don't Bring Me Down': The Electric Light Orchestra's most successful single, reaching number three in 1979 (although a year later they'd have their only number one, with 'Xanadu', on which they shared the credit with Olivia Newton-John). Elton Pope and his LINDA friends used to do a cover version in the basement meeting room at Macateer Street (2.10)

'Don't you think she looks tired?': Six words spoken quietly to Harriet Jones's right-hand man, Alex Klein, after she had had the Sycorax ship destroyed despite the Sycorax surrender and retreat. Her premiership crumbled because those words began a chain reaction leading to her downfall. (2.X)

'Don't Mug Yourself': A 2002 single by The Streets which broke through onto Pete Tyler's car radio in 1987 as the time breach occurred, as a result of Rose Tyler saving her father's life earlier. This disturbed Rose, who recognised the song and knew something was wrong. (1.8)

DNA Replication Module: The Doctor's scientific rationale for the technology behind the dolls which the Carrionites use to make puppets of menfolk. (3.2)

Docherty, Professor Allison: Scientist engaged in work for the Master in Nuclear Plant Seven in southern England. Although the Resistance seemed to count her as a major player in their ranks, she was, in fact, loyal to the Master and betrayed Martha Jones and the Resistance, though only because the Master's people held her son captive, and she was never sure if he was truly alive or dead. When Martha gave Docherty the correct frequency to disable a Toclafane sphere, she and Tom Milligan helped Martha do this, only to discover that the Toclafane were really the last humans, from the far future. After time jumped out of synch and erased the previous year, Martha sought out Docherty at the university where she worked and gave the bemused professor flowers, explaining that she didn't blame her. None the wiser, Docherty accepted the flowers and went on to work. (3.13) (Played by ELLIE HADDINGTON)

Dock Worker: Dalek prisoner captured by the Pig Slaves and inspected by Daleks Thay and Jast in the sewers of Manhattan. They decided he was of low intellect and ordered him to be turned into a Pig Slave. (3.4) (Played by MEL TAYLOR)

Doctor of TARDIS, Sir: The title bestowed upon the Doctor by Queen Victoria after he destroyed the Haemovariform that threatened her life at Torchwood House. Victoria then exiled him from the British Empire. (2.2)

Doomfinger, Mother: One of the Carrionites who had escaped into Elizabethan England, seeking to have William Shakespeare write the words that, when spoken at the end of his play *Love's Labour's Won*, would open a portal in time and space and release the rest of the Carrionites from the Deep Darkness into which the Eternals had cast them at the dawn of time. Mother Doomfinger could kill people with a touch but, when William Shakespeare turned their spellcasting back on them, Mother Doomfinger and the other Carrionites were trapped inside their crystal ball for eternity. (3.2) (Played by AMANDA LAWRENCE)

Doorman: Crimean war veteran, who was greeted guests at the village dance in Farringham. He was disintegrated by Son of Mine's gun. (3.8) (Played by DEREK SMITH)

Doors, The: American rock band which broke up after the death of their charismatic singer Jim Morrison. They were mentioned by the Doctor when he realised that the Graske's hatchery had, he reckoned, more doors than Jim Morrison. (AotG)

Dorsal tubercle: The Doctor had a weak one in his right wrist. (CiN) When his right hand was cut off in a swordfight with the Sycorax Leader, he was able to grow a new and presumably far stronger one. (2.X) The weakened hand was found by Captain Jack Harkness, who kept it in a jar as a Doctor-detector. (3.11) When the Master stole the hand, he was able to programme his laser screwdriver with its DNA, using technology from Professor Lazarus's GMD, to age the Doctor, initially by 100 years, (3.12) and then to suspend his regenerative capabilities and age his body to its full 900-plus years. (3.13)

Dougal: A farmer who drove the Doctor and Rose Tyler back to the TARDIS in his cart after Queen Victoria had exiled them from the British Empire. (2.2)

Downing Street, Number 10: The residence and office of the Prime Minister of the United Kingdom of Great Britain and Northern Ireland. The Doctor and Rose Tyler went there and met and befriended Harriet Jones MP. Trapped in its Cabinet Room, they helped stop the Family Slitheen destroying Earth. When a missile strike hit the building, it was destroyed, wiping out most of the Slitheen present, but the Doctor, Rose and Harriet sheltered in a small reinforced box room which survived the blast. (1.4, 1.5) Downing Street had been rebuilt by the time the Master, posing as Harry Saxon, became Prime Minister. (3.12)

Draconia: Civilisation which had the concept of evil represented by a horned beast in its culture. (2.9)

Dravidia: A planet in the Rexel planetary configuration. (3.2)

The Doctor

This is who I am, right here, right now, all right? All that counts is here and now, and this is me!

The Last of the Time Lords and sole survivor of the planet Gallifrey, the Doctor fought on the front line of the Last Great Time War and was ultimately responsible for the destruction of the Daleks and of his own kind. He had tried every other option beforehand, but was unable to save a number of worlds in the process, and was present at the Fall of Arcadia – something he never came to terms with. With no alternative available, the Doctor's brother, children, family and friends all perished along with his planet, and he was left to wander the universe alone in his TARDIS. He could never go back to save them.

A lonely child, when he was eight years old the Doctor was entered into the Academy, where he became childhood friends with the Master, was taught recreational mathematics and chose his own name. He later claimed to have run from the sight of the Untempered Schism during his initiation ceremony and, years later, began roaming the universe in a TARDIS.

The Doctor's travels to Earth eventually resulted in him attracting the attention of UNIT, a top-secret intelligence organisation, for whom he worked occasionally, and who considered him to be the ultimate expert in extraterrestrial affairs. He often used the alias 'John Smith' when on Earth, and, on occasion, 'Doctor James McCrimmon' (2.2) and 'Sir Doctor of TARDIS' (3.2), while on the planet Myarr he called himself

Doctor Vile. (TIQ) He was also known as 'the Oncoming Storm' in the Dalek legends on Skaro. (1.13)

Although he was initially reluctant to travel with company again after the Time War, the Doctor's companions included Rose Tyler, Adam Mitchell and Captain Jack Harkness, although only Rose was present at the time of his next regeneration. The regenerated Doctor then continued to travel with Rose until the Battle of Canary Wharf, for a while alongside Mickey Smith, and had a brief reunion with former companions Sarah Jane Smith and K-9. Following Rose's departure, the Doctor met Donna Noble and Martha Jones, and was later reunited with Captain Jack Harkness. He also inadvertently visited Madame de Pompadour at various points throughout her life, whilst his John Smith alter ego could have lived a long and happy life with his soul mate, Joan Redfern.

As the last remaining Time Lord in existence, the Doctor is unique, and is therefore easily tracked across time and space. Although his physical form appears human, he actually has two hearts and the ability to regenerate upon death. Essentially immortal, the Doctor has on occasion survived a lightning strike, (3.5) and freezing (3.7) and proved able to absorb Roentgen radiation safely. (3.1) His capacity to regenerate was also suspended by the Master, and he survived a year of torment, living as a 900-year-old man. (3.13)

In times of severe stress, a Time Lord could survive with a single heart beating (2.X, 3.2) and, within the first fifteen hours of a regeneration cycle, could draw upon the process's residual energy to form new limbs, which the Doctor demonstrated when his hand was cut off by the Sycorax Leader on Christmas Day. (2.X) Able to donate this energy to his surroundings, the Doctor once gave up ten years of his life in order to revive the TARDIS in a parallel universe. (2.5) Similarly, the Doctor was able to draw upon the psychic energy of the Earth's population to rejuvenate himself and defeat the Master following a year of humiliation at his hands. (3.13)

Having spent 900 years travelling through time and space, the Doctor has never lived a normal life, and things have frequently happened to him in the wrong order. He is equipped with over five billion languages, is able to identify substances through taste and has identified beings such as the Slitheen and Carrionites simply by narrowing down a series of facts relating to their species. (1.5, 3.2) Whilst on Volag-Noc, he was also discovered to have 3,005 outstanding convictions, earning him two billion years in prison. These charges included 1,400 minor traffic violations, 250 counts of evading library fines and 18 counts of planetary demolition, with 6,000 further charges to be taken into consideration at that time. (TIQ) He would never choose to kill, however, nor ask another to kill for him, and even made himself human in an attempt to spare the Family of Blood in 1913. (3.8, 3.9) Now alone once more, his adventures continue…

(Played by CHRISTOPHER ECCLESTON, DAVID TENNANT)

terminal illness Petrifold Regression. (2.1) Although he was cured, it seems almost certain he later died as a victim of the mutated Bliss virus that wiped out the majority of New Earth's population. (3.3) (Played by MICHAEL FITZGERALD)

Dumfries, Albert: Member of Harry Saxon's Cabinet, originally allied to another political party, but who shifted allegiance when he saw Saxon was the most likely winner. Saxon, really the Master, killed Dumfries, along with the rest of the Cabinet, using cyanide gas. (3.12) (Played by NICHOLAS GECKS)

Dreadlock Man: The Doctor spotted him tapping out the rhythm of the Master's hypnotic signal, being beamed down from the Archangel satellites, in a street in London. (3.12) (Played by JAMES BRYNE)

Driver [1]: A coach driver took the Doctor and Charles Dickens to Gabriel Sneed's undertakers on Christmas Eve, 1869. (1.3) (Played by MEIC POVEY)

Driver [2]: Mini-owner whose car, despite being recently serviced, ceased working as it drove down Dame Kelly Holmes Close – in fact, right over the Isolus ship buried beneath the Tarmac. Council worker Kel and Rose Tyler gave it a push and, once it was free of that immediate area, it roared back into life. (2.11) (Played by RICHARD NICHOLS)

Dunkerque: Northern French port which, whilst under German occupation in 1940, saw an astonishing 338,000 British and French soldiers successfully evacuated due to a determination not to give up, despite the odds. The Doctor cites the 'Dunkirk spirit' to Orin Scannell while aboard the SS *Pentallian*, to convince him to keep trying to find a way out of their predicament. (3.7)

Dury, Ian: Actor and singer who, with his band The Blockheads, had a number one hit with 'Hit Me With Your Rhythm Stick', which the Doctor was playing to Rose Tyler in the TARDIS when he suggested they could go to one of Dury's concerts. (2.2)

Dynamite: The Master arranged to have sticks of this attached to the back of the television set in Martha Jones's flat, primed to go off on a timer. (3.12)

Drumming, the: The sound in the Master's head, ever since he was eight years old and looked into the Untempered Schism on Gallifrey. He held it responsible for making him what he was, and it only stopped when, after being shot by Lucy Saxon, he refused to regenerate and died. (3.11, 3.12, 3.13)

Drunk: A victim of the Reapers as they broke into the world after Rose Tyler saved her dad's life and created a breach in time. (1.8) (Played by COLIN GALTON)

Duck Soup: Marx Brothers film (the last to feature all four of the brothers). The film used the fictitious island of Freedonia as part of the narrative and the Doctor borrowed the name to explain Martha Jones's origins to William Shakespeare. (3.2)

Duke of Manhattan: Charitable patron of New New York's social elite, he was taken to the Hospital and treated by the Sisters of Plenitude for the

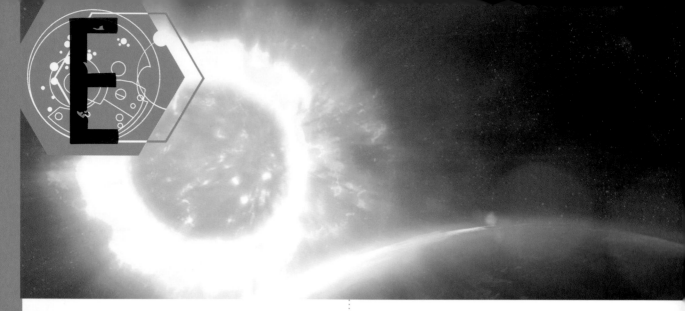

Ear pods: Communications device worn by the majority of the population of 'Pete's World', developed, like most domestic electronics, by Cybus Industries. In fact, they contained the ability to blank the wearer's mind, enabling Lumic to guide them into his Cyber-conversion factories. Mrs Moore and the Preachers had fake ear pods that could get them past Cybus staff without raising suspicion. (2.5, 2.6)

Earth Command: The military strategy centre of the Earth Empire in the 40th century. The Doctor spoke to Earth Command from Myarr, pretending to be Doctor Vile and claiming the war between Earth and the Mantasphids was his fault. Earth Command then circulated Doctor Vile's image across the Empire, demanding he be located, which he was, on Volag-Noc. (TIQ)

Earthdeath: The moment when the planet Earth was consumed as the Sun expanded, after the gravity satellites that had held the moment in check for hundreds of years had been removed. (1.2)

East London Constabulary: Local police force in Stratford trying to ascertain the whereabouts of the children who had been disappearing from the area in 2012. (2.11)

EastEnders: BBC Television primetime soap opera, set in the fictional London borough of Walford. The Doctor made a passing reference to disasters that seemed to befall Walford each Christmas, (2.8) while the ghost of former bad guy Den Watts returned to plague Queen Vic landlady Peggy Mitchell. (2.12)

Ectoshine: A special ghost-inspired household cleaner. (2.12)

Eczema: Skin disorder affecting humans. Posing as Victor Kennedy, the Abzorbaloff claimed that the condition he suffered from was much more extreme – 'x-zeema' – which was why no one could make physical contact with him. (2.10)

Edinburgh: Capital city of Scotland. Sir Robert MacLeish lied to Queen Victoria and said his wife, Lady Isobel, and her household were holidaying there, when they were in fact prisoners in the stables, watched over by the Host. (2.2)

Editor, the: Human in charge of Satellite Five, the broadcasting station that didn't just disseminate the news, it created it, deciding what people did or didn't need to know. Whether the Editor was a corpse reanimated by his true master, the Jagrafess, using Dalek technology, or whether he could simply cope with the subzero temperatures on Floor 500 is unknown. He believed he was in the employ of a consortium of bankers (in truth, the future Bad Wolf Corporation) and willingly betrayed the Earth Empire to the Jagrafess. He discovered the truth about the Doctor's origins, and hoped to gain access to the TARDIS, but when one of the journalists, Cathica, increased the heat levels on Floor 500, the Jagrafess exploded. The Editor tried to resign and escape in the chaos but one of his drones, the reanimated corpse of an anarchist called Eva Saint Julienne, grabbed hold of him and they were destroyed together in the conflagration. (1.7) (Played by SIMON PEGG)

Editor-in-Chief: See *Mighty Jagrafess of the Holy Hadrojassic Maxarodenfoe.*

Edwards, Daniel: One of the children drawn by Chloe Webber, who thus disappeared from Dame Kelly Holmes Close to become a friend for the Isolus. He later returned to the street after the Isolus left Earth and was given a celebratory piggyback by his overjoyed dad. (2.11) (Played by LEON GREGORY)

Edwards, Huw: BBC commentator, reporting on the events of the opening-night ceremonies for the Olympic Games in 2012. (2.11)

Eiffel Tower: Major Parisian landmark, which the 'ghosts' (really Cybermen) materialised around, though they were later drawn back into the Void. (2.12, 2.13)

Eileen: A guest on Trisha Goddard's talk show, sho had married a ghost. (2.12) (Played by RACHEL WEBSTER)

Election Day: May 2008 – and Harry Saxon became Britain's new Prime Minister. (3.12)

Electric Light Orchestra: British rock group from the Midlands who fused traditional rock 'n' roll with classical instrumentation and structure. Elton Pope was a massive fan, often dancing along to their 1978 top ten hit 'Mr Blue Sky'. The members of LINDA sometimes got together as a tribute band, knocking out versions of other hits such as 1979's 'Don't Bring Me Down'. (2.10)

Electricity beds: The power system on New Earth which had fallen into disrepair after everyone in the New New York Overcity had been wiped out by the Bliss virus. The Face of Boe had managed to maintain some power by drawing off his own life energies, but not enough to sustain the electricity beds. The Doctor rerouted the power through the Senate computer banks and used the electricity beds to repower the covers over the Motorway, opening them and enabling those trapped down there to reclaim the Overcity. (3.3)

Electromagnetic bomb: Mrs Moore, one of the Preachers on 'Pete's World', built these as a defensive weapon. She realised they might be useful in combating Cybermen too, and successfully stopped one, which the Doctor inspected, discovering it had once been Sally Phelan. (2.6)

Elephant Inn: The place of lodgings in Southwark where William Shakespeare and latterly the Doctor and Martha Jones stayed, run by Dolly Bailey. (3.2)

Elephant Man: The Doctor joked to Queen Victoria that he'd had the choice of buying either Rose Tyler or the disfigured John Merrick for sixpence. (2.2)

Eliot, TS: Both the Doctor and Richard Lazarus quoted Eliot's poem 'The Hollow Men' to make their points about the benefits and negatives of the GMD that Lazarus had built. (3.6)

Elizabeth I, Queen: Ruler of England when the Doctor and Martha Jones encountered William Shakespeare. The Doctor was looking forward to meeting her but, when she arrived at the Globe Theatre, she immediately sentenced him to death – clearly the result of a prior meeting between them that the Doctor had yet to experience. (3.2) (Played by ANGELA PLEASENCE)

Elizabeth II, Queen: The monarch being crowned on the day that the Wire planned to unleash the full extent of its plasmic powers, feeding off the energy from the Queen's subjects viewing the Coronation on their television sets. (2.7)

Ellis Island: Island in New York's Hudson Bay, through which, from 1892 onwards, immigrants hoping to make a new life in New York had to pass. During that first year, Captain Jack Harkness got into an argument with a man on Ellis Island, who shot him through the heart. (3.11)

Emergency Programme 1: When the Doctor tricked Rose Tyler into getting back into the TARDIS before he activated the Delta Wave aboard the Game Station, this emergency protocol, in the shape of a hologrammatic message, automatically switched on. The protocol explained his likely death and that the TARDIS was programmed to return to Earth, which it did. The ship would then die, ensuring that no one could ever get their hands on Time Lord technology or any of the other secrets therein. (1.13)

**Emergency Protocol
417:** Captain Jack Harkness instructed his onboard Chula computer to activate this protocol when he was about to die. A hyper-vodka was promptly delivered to him. (1.10)

Emergency Protocols: Government documents that detailed the actions to be taken by the British Government in the event of an alien invasion. Indra Ganesh gave them to the Slitheen posing as Joseph Green, the Acting Prime Minister. Under Section Five, General Asquith had the authority to remove Green from power – a decision that led to Asquith's death and subsequent resurrection as a Slitheen. Under the Protocols, communications were monitored for specific words and phrases, including 'blue box', 'TARDIS' and 'Doctor', which triggered a Code Nine alert. (1.4)

Emergency temporal shift: Process by which the four members of the Cult of Skaro fled the Battle of Canary Wharf as they realised it was lost. (2.13) Dalek Caan, the eventual sole survivor of the Cult, repeated this action to escape 1930s Manhattan. (3.5)

Emotional inhibitor: A part of the Cynaps artificial nervous system threaded through John Lumic's Cybermen on 'Pete's World'. When activated, the inhibitor prevented the human brain operating the Cyberform suit from experiencing emotions. When the emotional inhibitors were switched off en masse the Cybermen were driven insane as they realised what had happened to them. (2.6)

Empire House: Building in Wembley outside which, in 1883, the Graske kidnapped a street urchin, replacing him with a changeling. (AotG)

Empire of the Wolf: The era the Host wished to see dawn in 1879 Scotland when he unleashed the werewolf from within himself. It had the potential to lead to a Victorian Age of starships and missiles fuelled by coal and driven by steam. (2.2)

Empire State Building: Art deco skyscraper built between 1929 and 1931 in Manhattan, New York. Motivating the speed of its construction was the Cult of Skaro, operating from a Transgenic Laboratory, secretly built beneath the building. The Cult needed the mooring mast at the top to be completed by November 1930, when they knew a solar flare would create a ball of gamma radiation. Using Dalekanium from the body of one of their number, Dalek Thay, they intended to draw lightning caused by the gamma radiation down through the mast, through the building and into their lab,

where it would be used to transmit Dalek DNA from the hybrid Dalek Sec into the thousand-strong army of comatose humans they had there, as part of their Final Experiment. This would create a hybrid Dalek-Human army, enabling the Daleks to conquer first America, then the world and thus rebuild their empire. Overseeing the construction work was foreman-turned-businessman, Mr Diagoras, whose body Dalek Sec later mutated into a hybrid with his Dalek form on Diagoras's shoulders. (3.4, 3.5)

Empress of the Racnoss: Believed to be the last of her ancient race, legendary foes of and destroyed by the Time Lords. A ship of Racnoss children escaped but was entombed in the Secret Heart, a Webstar ship around which the planet Earth formed millions of years ago. The Empress needed an organic key full of Huon particles to free her children and, as the Torchwood Institute had already drawn her attention, she recreated Huon particles artificially in its secret labs. She convinced Lance Bennett, an employee of a Torchwood subsidiary company, to force-feed a co-worker, Donna Noble, with potentially fatal doses of Huon particles, thus creating the key she required. When Donna escaped, the Empress had her Roboform mercenaries force-feed Lance, thus creating a spare key. The Doctor realised that he had to stop these old foes once and for all and destroyed the children using small bombs to flood the chamber beneath the Thames Barrier, into which they were crawling. As her children died, the Empress escaped back to her Webstar, swearing revenge, but a British army tank, acting on the orders of Minister of Defence Harold Saxon, blew the Webstar to pieces, presumably killing the Empress too. (3.X) (Played by SARAH PARISH)

Endothermic vaporisation: Precise description of the power of the sun-possessed Korwin McDonnell, according to the Doctor after finding the remains of Abi Lerner aboard the SS *Pentallian*. (3.7)

Endtime: 100,000,000,000,000 years in the future, when the universe was nearly at its death. Few races survived, but one was humanity, which believed salvation was to be found on a planet called Utopia. (3.11) When the Doctor defeated the Master's scheme to repopulate 21st-century Earth with the Toclafane, the spheres remained trapped at the Endtime. (3.13)

Endtime Gravity Mechanics: The theory behind the system that Professor Yana had come up with, to power the rocket that would take the human refugees from Malcassairo to Utopia. (3.11)

English, Dame Eve: A member of the Kings Lynn players, whose music was heard on the episode of *What's My Line* playing on a television in Mr Magpie's shop when the Wire first appeared to him. (2.7)

Ernie: One of the young boys Nancy looked after on the streets of Blitzed London. He was evacuated to a family out of London but had experiences similar to another lad, Jim, and fled back home to London. (1.9, 1.10) (Played by JORDAN MURPHY)

EMPEROR DALEK: Giant immobile Dalek, the mutant suspended in a secure glass casing below the strutted body, protected by an inner cadre of black-helmeted Imperial Guard Daleks. He created the Cult of Skaro (2.13) during the Time War and took control of the Cruciform. (3.12) Absolutely despotic and insane, as a survivor of the Time War he believed himself not just the Daleks' Emperor but also their god, with all the immortality, omnipotence and arrogance such a belief could instil. He put in motion the Dalek Stratagem: he set the Jagrafess up in power on Satellite Five around the year 199,909, and manipulated mankind, first through news broadcasts, later though quiz and game shows, and gradually built up a new Dalek army harvested from the 'losing' contestants, transported there illegally by a series of Controllers, creating, in his warped mind, life from nothing – a talent only a god could possess. Over the next 191 years, he built a fleet of 200 ships, and almost half a million new Daleks, ready to dominate the galaxy. However, as the plan neared completion, the Emperor did not foresee that Rose Tyler would absorb the Time Vortex from the heart of the TARDIS and use that power to erase his Daleks, ships and finally himself from existence. (1.13)

Eternals, the: Legendary cosmic beings who existed outside of time and space completely, considering the inhabitants of the universe to be ephemerals, little more than playthings to amuse them. They left the universe for good after the Last Great Time War, distraught at the destruction wrought upon space and time. They referred to the Void as the Howling. (2.12) The Eternals were responsible for banishing the Carrionites to the Deep Darkness soon after the Universe was created. (3.2)

Ethical Committee: Geneva-based organisation on 'Pete's World' from which John Lumic should have gained approval for the Ultimate Upgrade. Dr Kendrick threatened to report Lumic to them, and was killed. Later, Lumic told the President of Great Britain that he had prepared a paper for the Committee, but the President was not interested. (2.5)

Europa: The Emperor Dalek's forces bombed this Earth continent in 200,100. (1.13)

European Safety Inspectors: A group of French experts unfortunately killed, apparently because they couldn't read the sign in Welsh warning them that they were investigating items marked 'Danger Explosives'. (1.11)

Evans, Gareth: An operative at the Torchwood Institute, based in the Lever Room in the Torchwood Tower. He and his colleague Adeola Oshodi went to the upper floors for an illicit snog, only to find that the area still under construction was in fact the new conversion site for the Cybermen. Like Adeola, Gareth was killed and reanimated via a Cybus Industries ear pod that was connected directly into his cerebral cortex. When the Doctor discovered this, he jammed the signal to all the converted ear pods, and the already dead Gareth died once again. (2.12) (Played by HADLEY FRASER)

Evening Standard: London newspaper that told its readers that the Big Ben-Slitheen incident had all been one big hoax. Mickey Smith was appalled, but the Doctor was unsurprised, saying that humanity wasn't ready to accept the idea of alien invaders. (1.5) It was also available on 'Pete's World'. (2.5)

Examiner, The: Daily newspaper. John Smith, the schoolteacher the Doctor became for a few weeks in 1913, read it regularly. (3.8) Nearly 60 years later, its then editor (played by NICKY RAINSFORD) was offered a piece telling the inside story of the Torchwood Institute by a freelancer called Atif. She betrayed him to Torchwood, whose operatives removed him from the newspaper's offices and provided a replacement front-page story for the next day's edition. (2.12T)

Exoglass: The glass aboard Platform One was shattered when the sunfilters were lowered. Exoglass had a self-repair system and once the filters went back up, the Exoglass was renewed. (1.2) According to Lynda Moss, the Exoglass that was used on the Game Station (and, by default, Satellite Five) would require a nuclear bomb to break, although she was proven fatally wrong when a Dalek hovering in space used its blaster to shatter it, killing her. (1.12, 1.13)

Expelliarmus: Martha Jones suggested this word from the Harry Potter books by JK Rowling would help William Shakespeare send the Carrionites back into the Deep Darkness. It did. (3.2)

FAMILY OF BLOOD, THE: Short-lived family of murderous aliens who sought the Doctor, his time-travel capabilities and his Time Lord life essence so that one of the Family, Son of Mine, could live forever. They had never seen the Doctor's face, just his TARDIS, so they had no idea what he looked like but, using a stolen Vortex Manipulator, they were able to pilot their invisible ship to the village of Farringham in Herefordshire in 1913, where they would try to sniff him out with their acute olfactory senses. There, to escape them, the Doctor had taken on the physical form of a fictitious human, John Smith, a teacher at the local boys' school. One by one, the Family found bodies to inhabit – Mother of Mine taking on the body of Jenny, a maid, Son of Mine taking schoolboy Jeremy Baines's life, Daughter of Mine usurping the body of Lucy Cartwright, and Father of Mine becoming Farmer Clark. They attacked the village, killing and maiming at random, until eventually the Doctor came out of hiding. He tricked them, making them believe he was still human, and set their ship to blow up. Fleeing the ship as it did so, the Doctor then, one by one, gave the Family exactly what they wanted – eternity, but in individual prisons of his choosing. (3.8, 3.9)

Family: A family held hostage by the Cybermen, but who were eventually freed when the Cyberman guarding them was recalled to fight the Daleks. The family consisted of Dad (SIMON CORNISH), Mum (LIZ EDNE), a son (FINNIAN COHEN-ENNIS) and a daughter (CIARA COHEN-ENNIS). (2.12, 2.13)

Farringham: Village in Herefordshire which came under attack from the Family of Blood on Tuesday 11 November 1913. A number of its inhabitants died, before John Smith accepted he really was the Doctor and changed back into the Time Lord. (3.8, 3.9)

Farringham School for Boys: The Doctor, having turned himself human to escape the Family of Blood, taught history there as John Smith, with Martha Jones acting as his maid. Smith's colleagues included the Headmaster, Mr Rocastle, the Bursar, Mr Phillips, and the school's nurse, Joan Redfern, who he began a romance with. Amongst the pupils were the gifted Timothy Latimer, Hutchinson the school captain and Jeremy Baines. The Family eventually attacked with their Scarecrow army, but all the boys survived, although neither Rocastle nor Phillips was so lucky. (3.8, 3.9)

Fast Lane: The legendary bottom lane of the Motorway, only accessible with three adults aboard a car. It was rumoured that speeds of up to 30 miles per hour were achievable down there, although Cheen's friend Kate said there were legends of monsters beneath the Fast Lane. Kate was correct – the Macra which had escaped from the New New York Zoo years before had settled there, living off the exhaust fumes, and swatting any cars that disturbed them. (3.3)

Father of Mine: Leader of the Family of Blood, who sought out a Time Lord body to enable Son of Mine to live for eternity. He brought the Family in their invisible spaceship to Earth, where they believed the Doctor was hiding in the village of Farringham. The Doctor had in fact turned himself wholly human, to avoid being sniffed out by the Family. Father of Mine took on the body of a local farmer, Mr Clark, and was responsible for tracking down the Doctor's TARDIS, as well as the murder of bandleader Mr Chambers. Once the Doctor had regained his Time Lord form, he tricked the Family and blew up their spaceship. The Doctor threw Father of Mine, trapped in Clark's form, into an underground chamber for eternity, binding him in unbreakable chains forged in a dwarf star. (3.8, 3.9) (Played by GERARD HORAN)

Female Crewmember: Realising that the *Madame de Pompadour* was about to be caught up in an ion storm, she and her fellow crewman sent a mayday back to Earth. When the storm struck, she survived and was momentarily relieved when a Clockwork Robot appeared on the bridge to help her. Then she realised the Robot was looking for spare parts... (2.4T) (Played by LIZ ARMON-LLOYD)

Female Programmer: One of the administrators of the Game Station, alongside her male counterpart Davitch Pavale. They answered to the

Controller but, when the Doctor exposed the Game Station as a fraud and the Controller was transmatted aboard the Dalek mothership and exterminated, the two programmers joined forces against their foes. They joined Captain Jack Harkness on Floor 499 and were still flirting outrageously with one another when they were both exterminated. (1.12, 1.13) (Played by NISHA NYAR)

Feng Shui: According to Lance Bennett, Donna Noble talked excitedly about this Chinese concept of harmonically spacing furniture and other household items. (3.X)

Fenning, Sir Roderick: Musical arranger for the episode of *What's My Line* playing on a television in Mr Magpie's shop when the Wire first appeared to him. (2.7)

Final Experiment: Audacious plan by Dalek Sec and the Cult of Skaro, trapped in 1930s New York. They intended to create a new form for themselves, realising that humanity now vastly outnumbered them. As humans had the advantage of mobility, Sec reasoned that if the human form could be imprinted with Dalek mentality, the Cult would have the ultimate army. As a precursor to this, Sec experimented on his own form, physically merging his Dalek body with that of a human – Mr Diagoras – via a special chromatin solution and thus became the genetic template for the Dalek-Human army. The Final Experiment required a thousand comatose humans, each of whom would receive a pulse of DNA-rewriting gamma radiation, imbued with Sec's new DNA. This was foiled when the Doctor placed his own DNA into the mix, diluting the hybridisation process and the Dalek-Human army questioned their orders and engaged in a battle with the Daleks. After they had destroyed Daleks Thay and Jast, Dalek Caan wiped out the entire species with a mental bolt that fried their brains. (3.4, 3.5)

The Face of Boe

A five-foot alien head, suspended in a glass tank and wreathed in smoke, the Face of Boe was the oldest inhabitant of the Isop galaxy, and apparently the last member of Boekind. Believed to be millions of years old, legends stated that the Face of Boe had watched the universe grow old, and that before his death he would impart a great secret to a homeless wanderer like himself, a lonely god. Although he was reported to be pregnant with Boemina by the *Boewatch*

programme on Bad WolfTV in 200,000, (1.7) the Face of Boe was alone again in the year five billion, by which time he had based himself on the Silver Devastation, and acted as sponsor of the Earthdeath spectacle on Platform One, when the Lady Cassandra attempted to stage her fraudulent hostage situation. (1.2) Twenty-three years later, the Face of Boe summoned the Doctor to meet him in Ward 26 of the New New York Hospital, where he was dying of old age. Here, he was under the care of Novice Hame, a Catkind nurse with whom he would communicate telepathically as he slept, singing songs in her mind whilst she kept him company and maintained his smoke. When the Doctor eventually came to hear Boe's final secret, the Face willed himself away using pure mental power, keeping his secret until their next, and final, encounter. (2.1) He then remained on New Earth, in the city of New New York, where the Bliss virus wiped out the population of the Overcity. The Face of Boe then ensured Hame's protection from the virus by shrouding her in his smoke,

before wiring himself into the city's mainframe, giving his life force to maintain the Motorway and its inhabitants until the Doctor returned. He gave the last of his energy to help release the population from the Undercity, and was released from his tank by the Doctor and Hame one final time before he perished. (3.3) His dying words – 'You Are Not Alone' – were later revealed to be a warning of the Master's presence at the end of the universe. (3.11) The Doctor's occasional travelling companion, the immortal Captain Jack Harkness, fondly remembered being nicknamed the Face of Boe, leading to speculation that he would live to become the Doctor's other old friend. (3.13)

(Voiced by STRUAN RODGER)

Financial Family Seven: Origin of the Adherents of the Repeated Meme, who travelled to Platform One to witness Earthdeath. However, as the Adherents were later exposed as robot servants to Cassandra, the true existence of the 'Financial Family Seven' is in some doubt. (1.2)

Finch, Caroline: Clive's wife, who put up with his obsession about the Doctor. She and her son (played by ADAM McCOY) later witnessed Clive's death at the hands of the Autons. (1.1) (Played by ELLI GARNETT)

Finch, Clive: Enthusiastic website-runner, who was obsessed with sightings of the Doctor. Rose visited him for more information but wasn't sure if he was completely sane. He was killed in front of his family when the Autons rampaged through a London shopping arcade. (1.1) (Played by MARK BENTON)

Finch, Hector: Assumed name of Brother Lassar of the Krillitanes, who adopted human form. He posed as the headmaster of Deffry Vale High School, using Krillitane Oil in the food to enhance the minds of his pupils, so that they could solve the Skasas Paradigm. He was killed when K-9 heated up the drums of Krillitane Oil in the school kitchen and blew Finch, the school and himself to pieces. (2.3) (Played by ANTHONY HEAD)

Finch's: Butcher's shop in South East London. Jackie Tyler suggested to Rose she should get a job there. (1.1)

Finnegan, Florence: Elderly patient admitted to the Royal Hope Hospital apparently suffering from a salt deficiency. In fact, the real Florence Finnegan was probably dead, killed by a shape-shifting Plasmavore who had stolen her identity and entered the hospital, hoping to source a rich supply of blood, off which it lived. This Plasmavore was always accompanied by two Slabs to do its strong-arm work and was in hiding because it had murdered the Child Princess of Padrivole Regency Nine, and thus was hiding from the Judoon Platoon sent to execute it. Because the Judoon were forbidden to land on Earth, the Plasmavore believed itself safe, until the Judoon transported the hospital to the Moon. The Plasmavore then absorbed as much blood as it could, including blood corrupted by fat, alcohol and rich foodstuffs, to disguise itself as a human when the Judoon scanned everyone's physiognomy. When it drank the Doctor's blood, it registered as a non-human and was swiftly executed by the Judoon. (3.1) (Played by ANNE REID)

Fire extinguisher: Needing to disable a Clockwork Robot aboard the SS *Madame de Pompadour*, the Doctor used what Mickey Smith thought was an ice gun, but was in fact a fire extinguisher, although it proved very effective at freezing the repair androids. (2.4)

FLOORS: Satellite Five had 501 floors. Floor 016 was the Medical area, which staff such as Cathica Santini Khadeni first attended when they arrived. Adam Mitchell also visited this floor, where a Nurse implanted him with a chip so he could access the information he required via a Spike Room. Floor 139 was where the TARDIS landed. The top floor, which all the workers believed to be lined with gold, was Floor 500. This was actually occupied by the true master of Satellite Five, the Jagrafess, and his minion, the Editor. Unlike the rest of Satellite Five, the temperature on Floor 500 was barely above freezing, and the humans manning it were all in fact dead journalists, just corpses being manipulated by the power of the Jagrafess via their implants. (1.7) One hundred years later, Satellite Five had been renamed the Game Station. Floor 000 was where the staff and game players that had not been evacuated aboard the shuttles gathered. There, Captain Jack Harkness tried to enlist them in the defence of the station against the Daleks. Those that refused were cornered and massacred by the Daleks. Floor 056 was where the *Big Brother* house that the Doctor was transmatted to was positioned – the house had once been a Spike Room (ten floors were occupied by *Big Brother* houses). It also housed an Observation Deck, protected by a door made from Hydra Combination. Lynda Moss died there when the Observation Deck's Exoglass was shattered by a Dalek blast. Floor 229 was where Captain Jack Harkness was transported to take part in *What Not to Wear*. Floor 407 housed the *Weakest Link* studio. Floor 494 was where the first wave of invading Daleks entered the Game Station and overrode the internal laser defences. The *Weakest Link* Floor Manager and her team tried to defend this floor but were massacred. On Floor 495, the Daleks encountered the Anne Droid and destroyed it. They then proceeded to Floor 496 via the ventilation shafts. Floor 499 was where Captain Jack Harkness set up the final line of defence against the Daleks, who used the Western Ducts to get there, and where he, the Female Programmer and Davitch Pavale were all exterminated. Floor 500 was where the programmers worked, overseen by the Controller. On this floor, the Doctor constructed a Delta Wave to stop the invading Daleks, but could not bring himself to use it – instead, Rose Tyler returned to Floor 500 of the Station and erased the Daleks from existence from there. (1.12, 1.13)

Fire Island: The Brannigans driving on the New New York Motorway were heading to Fire Island, hoping to find work in the laundries. (3.3)

Firing Stock 15: Bullets used by the humans on Sanctuary Base 6, not powerful enough to pierce the hull of the station, but lethally effective on organics, such as the Ood. (2.8, 2.9)

First Antigravity Olympics: The Doctor told Rose Tyler that he could take her to witness this. (2.2)

First Contact Policy: An agreement ratified by the UN in 1968, regarding protocol surrounding contact with alien species. Harry Saxon ignored it, gaining the contempt of US President Winters. (3.12)

Fitch: One of the players of *The Weakest Link* aboard the Game Station. When she lost a round, the Anne Droid appeared to disintegrate her but, in truth, she was transmatted over to the Dalek mothership and turned into part of the growing Dalek army created by the Emperor. (1.12) (Played by KATE WINCHESTER)

Fledgling Empires: A grouping of planetary empires from the Dark Times. The Empires included Gallifrey, which fought a war against the Racnoss, and won. (3.X)

Fletcher, Tom: Member of pop group McFly, who endorsed Harry Saxon's campaign to become Prime Minister. (3.12)

Floor Manager: Part of the production team making *The Weakest Link* aboard the Game Station in 200,100. When the Daleks attacked the Station, she joined Captain Jack Harkness's team and led the defence of Floor 494, but the Bastic bullets in her gun had no effect on the invaders and she was exterminated. (1.12, 1.13) (Played by JENNA RUSSELL)

Flora: 15-year-old maid to Lady Isobel MacLeish, she avoided being captured in the initial attack by the Brethren upon Torchwood House but, after meeting Rose Tyler, they were both captured and chained up to face the Host as he transformed into a werewolf. Flora later helped her mistress prepare mistletoe as a defence against the creature and was still present when Rose was invested by Queen Victoria and then exiled. (2.2) (Played by RUTHIE MILNE)

Florida: Southern American state, famous for good weather, and where Mr Stoker had hoped to retire to before being murdered by the Plasmavore disguised as Florence Finnegan in the Royal Hope Hospital. (3.1)

Florizel Street: North London street and home to the Connolly family, the Gallaghers and the Bells amongst many others in 1953. After the Queen's Coronation, it was decked out for a massive street party. (2.7)

Flydale North: The constituency for which Harriet Jones was MP, campaigning for Cottage Hospitals to be considered as Centres of Excellence. (1.4) As Prime Minister, she successfully implemented her New Cottage Hospital Scheme. (2.X)

Footprint Impeller System: Part of the system that Professor Yana had come up with to power the rocket that would take the human refugees from Malcassairo to Utopia. (3.11)

'For the Fallen': Poem by Laurence Binyon, read at the Remembrance Day service Tim Latimer attended as an old man, where he saw the Doctor and Martha Jones for the first time since he had been a schoolboy at

Farringham School for Boys in Herefordshire. (3.9)

Foreman: Mr Diagoras, charged with overseeing the construction of the upper floors of the Empire State Building by the Cult of Skaro, demanded of the workers' foreman that his men work harder. The foreman pointed out that this was impossible and, if need be, he'd happily tell Diagoras's masters that too. He was horrified when he met Dalek Caan and was taken down to the Transgenic Laboratory beneath the streets of Manhattan. He became part of the Final Experiment, leading the Dalek-Humans to the Laurenzi theatre, but asked why he had to obey without question, only to be exterminated by Dalek Jast. (Played by IAN PORTER)

Forest of Cheem: Collective name for the revered tree-people of Cheem. They distrusted machines and found the Time War terrifying and saddening. Made entirely of wood, they were understandably frightened of fire. (1.2)

FOB WATCH: Escaping from the Family of Blood, who wanted his body so they would have access to all of time and space, the Doctor used a chameleon arch in the TARDIS to turn himself human for approximately three months, knowing that, if the Family hadn't found him by then, they would die. The fob watch, decorated with Gallifreyan symbols but otherwise looking like a common-or-garden Earth fob watch, was a special vessel, containing the very essence of his Time Lord existence. When the now-human John Smith was exposed to the interior of the watch, the cells of his body would once more be rearranged and he would become his old self, literally. The fob watch was briefly in the possession of Tim Latimer, a pupil at the school where John Smith taught, and some of the Time Lord energy leaked out, giving him a glimpse of the Doctor and Martha Jones's real lives. Realising that the Family of Blood would happily slaughter everyone in the village of Farringham, John Smith opened the watch and became the Doctor once more. (3.8, 3.9) On the planet Malcassairo, the Doctor and Martha met the human scientist Professor Yana. He had an identical watch, which Martha spotted and warned the Doctor about. The Professor's close proximity to both the Doctor and his TARDIS reawakened something in Yana, and he unconsciously found himself opening the watch – whereupon his Time Lord personality re-established itself, and the Doctor's old foe the Master was reborn. (3.11)

Forget: Coming in varying strengths, this was one of the Mood Patches on sale in Pharmacytown in the Undercity of New New York. A patch was bought by the Pale Woman so that she could forget the disappearance of her parents on the Motorway. (3.3)

Fortes: British café where people watched firstly the murder of President Winters by the Toclafane and then, on leaving the café, were slaughtered by the invading Toclafane spheres. (3.12)

Foundries: Industrial units in the Brooklyn area of New New York, where Milo had learnt there were jobs going. (3.3)

Fourth Great and Bountiful Human Empire, the: The era in which the Doctor, Rose Tyler and Adam Mitchell landed on Satellite Five. (1.7)

France: The European country where Rose had been working as an au pair for a year, or so Jackie Tyler had told Rose's grandmother. (1.5) The Doctor, Rose and Mickey Smith visited it – both Paris and Versailles – on a few occasions while dealing with the Clockwork Robots' hunt for Madame de Pompadour. (2.4)

Frane, Hoshbin: Rodrick knew that this was the President of the Red Velvets when asked by the Anne Droid in *The Weakest Link* aboard the Game Station. (1.12)

Frank: Eighteen-year-old from Tennessee who took the railroad to find enough work in New York to feed his family after his father died. He ended up living in Hooverville and joined the Doctor, Martha Jones and Hooverville's de facto leader Solomon in their exploration of the Manhattan sewers. Frank was captured by the Pig Slaves and, along with Martha Jones, selected to become part of the Final Experiment but, due to the Doctor's

interference, they were able to escape back to Hooverville. The Daleks pursued them, and Frank was traumatised when Solomon, brokering peace, was murdered. Frank later helped Martha defend the Empire State Building against the Pig Slaves and was present in the Laurenzi theatre when the Dalek Human army destroyed the two Cult of Skaro Daleks there. Frank stayed on in Hooverville, negotiating with the survivors for the semi-Pig Man Laszlo to live among them. (3.4, 3.5) (Played by ANDREW GARFIELD)

Franklin, Benjamin: American inventor (as well as acclaimed politician, abolitionist and diplomat), who conducted early experiments into electricity, aided by the Doctor, who got burned. (3.1)

Franzetta, Johnny: Character in Colin Skinner's unpublished novel, 'Ghost Train', as read by Skinner to the other members of LINDA. (2.10)

Freedom Fifteen: Anarchist group dedicated to exposing Satellite Five as corrupt and working against the interests of the Earth Empire. Their last surviving member was Eva Saint Julienne, who disguised herself as Suki Macrae Cantrell and reached Floor 500, intending to destroy what she found there. (1.7)

Freedonia: The Doctor tells William Shakespeare that Martha Jones is from Freedonia, borrowing the fictitious name from the Marx Brothers' film, *Duck Soup* (3.2)

Friends List: Inter-car networking system used by the likes of the Brannigans and the Cassinis to stay in touch with one another as they drove the Motorways of New New York. (3.3)

Friends of the Ood: Movement throughout the Earth Empire of

the 42nd century that objected on ethical and moral grounds to the enslavement, however willingly, of the Ood. (2.8)

Frost, Muriel: UNIT Colonel killed, alongside many other experts on alien incursion, at the 10 Downing Street briefing by the Family Slitheen. (1.4)

Fusion Mills: Martha Jones walked across the Earth telling her story about the Doctor, preparing people for the right moment to chant his name. Amongst the places she went to were the Fusion Mills of China. (3.13)

Futurekind: Mutated humans living on Malcassairo who had become cannibals, living a nomadic existence on the plains near the old Coral City of the Malmooth and hunting any humans foolish enough to venture there. To many, the Futurekind represented everything humanity might become if they allowed themselves to. Human guards at the rocket silo would check approaching humans for pointed teeth – if they had fangs, they were Futurekind and were refused admission. After the rocket launched, taking the humans to Utopia, the Futurekind Chieftain realised the power was off and his people could get into the base and ransack it. The Doctor, Martha Jones and Captain Jack Harkness were still in the silo base and the Futurekind hunted them, still trying to get at them even as they teleported back to 21st-century Earth. (3.11, 3.12)

Gaffabeque: A dish which originated on the planet Lucifer, not Mars. Rose Tyler didn't know this when asked by the Anne Droid in *The Weakest Link* aboard the Game Station. (1.12)

Galaxy M87: Location of New Earth. (2.1)

Gallagher, Edward: Television-owning resident of Florizel Street, who lost his face to the power of the Wire and was reported to the police by Eddie Connolly. Ted was taken away one night by Detective Inspector Bishop and his officers, but returned home after the Wire was defeated and his face had returned to normal. (2.7)

Gallagher, Mrs: Anxious neighbour whose husband was taken away by the police after losing his face to the Wire. (2.7) (Played by MARIE LEWIS)

GALLIFREY: Not a town in Ireland, as Joan Redfern assumed (3.8) but the home world of the Doctor, and the Time Lords. It was known to some as the Shining World of the Seven Systems. Destroyed in the Last Great Time War, which only the Doctor and the Master survived, the Doctor recalled it as having fields of deep red grass, silver-leafed trees and a burnt orange sky. It had two suns, one of which rose in the south, causing the snow-capped mountains to shine. The Citadel of the Time Lords was enclosed in a transparent dome and was situated on the continent of Wild Endeavour, between the mountains of Solace and Solitude. Outside the Citadel could be found the Untempered Schism, which was a tear in the fabric of reality. Time Lord children would be forced to gaze through this before they could enter the Academy – the experience caused some Novice Time Lords to flee, while others were driven mad. (3.X, 3.3, 3.11, 3.12, 3.13)

Game Room 6: The studio on Floor 407 where *The Weakest Link* was being made on the Game Station. (1.12)

Game Station: Formerly Satellite Five but, under the Bad Wolf Corporation, the space station became a huge complex broadcasting 10,000 lethal entertainment shows to Earth – a development brought about directly by the Doctor's interference aboard Satellite Five 100 years earlier. The Game Station was really a front for the Daleks, who swarmed

throughout the Station, slaughtering everyone until Rose Tyler, having absorbed the power of the Vortex, erased the Daleks from existence. When the Doctor and Rose left in the TARDIS, the only other living being was Captain Jack Harkness, who had to use his faulty Vortex Manipulator to try and find his companions, but ended up on 19th-century Earth instead. (1.12, 1.13, 3.11)

Game Station Syndicate: The authority under which the Doctor was arrested aboard the Game Station. (1.12)

Gamma radiation: Electromagnetic radiation known to be able to damage or rewrite human DNA. The Daleks trapped in 1930s New York planned to attract a massive bolt of gamma radiation to Earth after a solar flare, via the mooring mast atop the Empire State Building. Dalek DNA would then be bled into the comatose humans who formed part of the Final Experiment. The DNA-corrupting gamma pulse would rewrite the humans' DNA, imprinting Dalek DNA as well, thus creating a mobile Dalek-Human hybrid army – with the physical freedom of humans but the unquestioning amorality and obedience of rank-and-file Daleks. The Doctor placed himself in the path of the lightning bolt, so, as well as Dalek Sec's already mutated DNA, a fragment of Time Lord DNA went into every Dalek-Human hybrid, leading them to turn on their masters. (3.4, 3.5)

Gandalf: Fictional aged wizard in the *Lord of the Rings* trilogy of books. The Master called the Doctor this after ageing him by 100 years. (3.13)

Ganesh, Indra: A junior secretary with the Ministry of Defence, working at 10 Downing Street during the Big Ben incident. There he met Joseph Green MP and briefed him on the situation, informing him that he was now Acting Prime Minister. He supplied Green with the Emergency Protocols and later, along with Harriet Jones and Rose Tyler, discovered the dead body of the Prime Minister. The Slitheen posing as Margaret Blaine then killed him. (1.4) (Played by NAVIN CHOWDRY)

Gangsters: A 1970s BBC drama series about Birmingham's underworld. DVD store-owner Banto was watching Episode 6 when Sally Sparrow came to see Larry Nightingale (3.10)

Gardener: The first victim of the Reapers as they broke into the world after Rose Tyler saved her dad's life and created a breach in time. (1.8) (Played by KEN TEALE)

Gareth: Husband-to-be of Sally Phelan on 'Pete's World'. Sally was converted to a Cyberman and died the night before their wedding. (2.6)

Gas mask zombies: Nanogenes, subatomic robots leaking from a crashed Chula medical ship in 1941, which were programmed to seek out damaged life forms and aid their recoveries. What they found first in London was a recently deceased child victim of an air raid, Jamie, who had been wearing a gas mask when he died. Assuming all humans were 'empty' of life in the same way, they reanimated him, the gas mask now blended into his flesh, and proceeded to make contact with other humans at the local Albion Hospital, making gas masks and scars identical to Jamie's appear on their bodies – within a week everyone in the hospital bar one consultant, Dr Constantine, had been affected and completely transformed. When the nanogenes later saw the DNA of both dead Jamie and his living mother, they recombined to bring Jamie back to full health. The Doctor then programmed them to revert all the other affected humans back to perfect health, which included making a lot of them fitter than they had been before. (1.9, 1.10)

Gates, III, William Henry: American entrepreneur and co-founder of Microsoft, the world's largest and most proliferate computer software company. Professor Docherty rued his death at the hands of the Toclafane when her computers wouldn't work properly. (3.13)

Gedes: The Torchwood Archive sent and lost an expedition there. Amongst the things that were found was a book of hieroglyphs, maps and drawings which inspired the Empire to instigate a mission to the legendary impossible planet, known as Krop Tor. (2.8T)

Gelth: An alien non-corporeal life form, who were in this state due to the Time War. They arrived on Earth in Victorian times via the space and time Rift which existed across Cardiff. As gaseous creatures, they used the gas from recently deceased humans, as well as the gas in the lighting and heating pipes that were threaded through local housing, to exist in. They convinced the Doctor to let them use a local psychically gifted maid, Gwyneth, to enable them to inhabit dead bodies until they could establish a new form. In truth, they were an invasion force and Gwyneth had to ignite the gas and blow them, and herself, up. (1.3) (Voiced by ZOË THORNE) Rose Tyler pretended to have authority granted to her by the Gelth Confederacy to demand the Sycorax leave Earth. (2.X) Rose wondered if the ghosts breaking through on Earth could be the Gelth,

but the Doctor was convinced they weren't as they were all over the planet rather than just around the Cardiff Rift. (2.12)

Gemini: Codename for the mole in Cybus Industries on 'Pete's World' who fed the Preachers with their information. It was in fact Pete Tyler. (2.5, 2.6)

Genesis Ark: Conical device the Daleks had stored inside their Void ship. It was stolen Time Lord technology from the Time War, although the Doctor didn't recognise it. It required the cellular imprint of a time traveller to activate it and, when Mickey Smith fell against it, his touch was enough. When it opened, the Doctor discovered that it was a Gallifreyan prison, dimensionally transcendental like the TARDIS, and it stored millions of Daleks that the Time Lords had been unable to bring themselves to destroy. The Cult of Skaro immediately sought to get it free of Torchwood Tower, raising it into the sky as it needed a clear radius of 30 square miles, and let the captive Daleks loose to begin a pitched battle with both Cybermen and humans. When the Doctor was able to breach the Wall for one last time and rip open the Void, all the Ark and all its Daleks were sent back into the Void, for ever. (2.13) (Operated by STUART CROSSMAN)

Genetic Manipulation Device: The GMD was a sonic micro-field manipulator, using hypersonic sound waves to create a state of resonance that would destabilise the cell structure of someone's DNA and enable them to literally hack into their genes and, with a metagenic program, instruct

them to change. This is exactly what it did to its creator, Richard Lazarus. Its main effect was shaving 40 years off Lazarus's age, but the side effect was to unleash previously dormant cells within his DNA that caused him to change into a primordial beast that lived off the life forces of others. The Doctor reversed the polarity of its flow of neutrons, which wrecked the machine with one final pulse of hypersonic waves, with which he believed he had reversed Lazarus's DNA changes. However, this was only temporary and the Lazarus Creature rose again. (3.6)

Geneva: Swiss city and home to many United Nations departments. A flight from Geneva, containing recognised experts in extraterrestrial affairs arrived in the aftermath of the Big Ben incident. (1.4) On 'Pete's World', Geneva was where Dr Kendrick threatened to report back to, as the Ultimate Upgrade project contravened the Ethical Committee's Bio-Convention. (2.5) UNIT Control in Geneva was attacked by the Toclafane; when those events were erased, UNIT Control contacted the Valiant, demanding to know what was going on following the assassination of President Winters. (3.12, 3.13)

Genghis Khan: 13th-century Mongolian warlord who created the Mongol Empire. His warriors once tried to break into the TARDIS but failed. (1.1)

 **Geocomtex:** Henry Van Statten's software and hardware company that had made him a billionaire, most probably through his use of illicit alien tech he had acquired. A web page about Geocomtex was seen by the Doctor when he accessed a mobile phone with his sonic screwdriver to search for HC Clements. (3.X)

George IV, King: English monarch for whom the Coronation Coach used by Elizabeth II was built. (2.7)

George, the: A pub on 'Pete's World' where Jackie Tyler had celebrated her 21st birthday. (2.5)

Germany: European country which, according to Lance Bennett, Donna Noble couldn't even find on a map. (3.X)

Ghost Energy: Form of energy that Torchwood monitored each time a Ghost Shift occurred. (2.12)

Ghost Field: The area of distortion around one of the 'ghosts' as they broke through into the world from the Void. The Torchwood Institute believed they were responsible for creating the ghost fields, whereas all they were doing was enhancing a pre-existing gap in reality. (2.12)

Ghost Shift: Term used by the Torchwood Institute when they activated the Lever Room to bring the ghosts into the world, hoping to utilise them, little realising what they were actually doing was giving the Cybermen the energy they needed to cross the Void from 'Pete's World'. (2.12)

'Ghost Train': Title of Colin Skinner's unpublished novel, which he read in chapters to the other members of LINDA. (2.10)

Ghostbusters: The Doctor quoted the theme song, written and performed by former Raydio frontman Ray Parker Jnr, to this 1984 movie when building the ghost triangulator that he used on the Powell Estate to try and entrap a ghost, and learn the source of its emergence. (2.12)

Ghosts: Friendly spirits that began appearing all over planet Earth, much to the delight of its inhabitants. In truth, they were Cybermen, breaking through the Void as a means of travelling to Earth from 'Pete's World', with the unwitting help of Yvonne Hartman and the Torchwood Institute. (2.12)

Ghostwatch: Television show, which examined the phenomena of the ghosts appearing all over the world, presented by Alistair Appleton. (2.12)

Girl: Young member of a family whose Christmas was almost ruined when her parents were kidnapped by the Graske and replaced with changelings. But the real parents were swiftly returned, none the wiser. (AotG) (Played by MOLLY KABIA)

Glasgow Water Riots: These were in their third day on Caledonia Prime, according to Channel McB, when the TARDIS first visited Satellite Five. (1.7)

Glass Pyramid of San Kaloon: The landmark that makes San Kaloon famous. (1.11)

Glen of St Catherine: Area of Scotland where an alien Haemovariform crashed in 1560. The Monks in the local monastery worshipped the creature from then on. (2.2)

Glitter, Gary: British glam rock star (real name Paul Gadd) whose 1984 hit 'Another Rock 'n' Roll Christmas' was playing in the house where the Graske replaced the parents with changelings. (AotG)

Globe Theatre: Designed by Peter Streete, working under the influence of the Carrionites, as a tetradecagon, 14 being an important number in Carrionite science. The Lord Chamberlain's Men performed William Shakespeare's works there and, on the opening night of *Love's Labour's Won*, the Carrionites' plan came together as their Tide of Blood opened a portal to the Deep Darkness, allowing the rest of the Carrionites to descend to Earth. From the stage Shakespeare himself came up with the right words to seal the portal, exiling the Carrionites for ever. (3.2)

'God Rest Ye Merry Gentlemen': Traditional Christmas Carol being sung by carollers in the Cardiff streets of 1869 when Charles Dickens was giving a reading. (1.3) It was heard on the streets of London in 1883 when the Graske kidnapped a street urchin, (AotG) and the Santa Roboforms were playing it when they atttacked Rose Tyler and Mickey Smith (2.X) and again a year later, when one of them kidnapped Donna Noble. (3.X)

'God Save The Queen': National Anthem for Great Britain. Magpie heard it after the closedown moments on his television set shortly before he was visited by the Wire. (2.7)

Goddard, Diana: Polkowski's replacement as chief aide to Henry Van Statten, the American billionaire. Goddard initially supported Van Statten's

Golden Age: An era of prosperity and peace that the Doctor believed would be ushered in for Britain when Harriet Jones became Prime Minister. (1.5) In fact, he was later directly responsible for her downfall after she murdered the Sycorax by having Torchwood destroy their retreating spaceship. (2.X) On 'Pete's World', as Britain's President, she did indeed bring forth a Golden Age, but one marred by climatic disaster. (2.13)

Golden Locust: When Elton Pope stood up to the man he believed to be Victor Kennedy, bemoaning the fact that Victor had stopped LINDA being fun, he announced that he was walking out, along with Colin Skinner and Ursula Blake. Elton and Ursula would then head for a Chinese dinner at the Golden Locust. Before they could get there, both Skinner and Ursula were absorbed by the Abzorbaloff. (2.10)

Gooding Jnr, Cuba: American actor who shared a birthday with Jackie Tyler on 'Pete's World' – 1 February. On Rose Tyler's version of Earth, although Jackie's birthday was still 1 February, Cuba Gooding Jnr's wasn't (it was 2 January). This was just one of many minor differences between the two versions of Earth. (2.5)

Gran [1]: Jackie Tyler hoped that after the defeat of the Family Slitheen she and Rose could go and visit Rose's grandmother. Jackie had told her that Rose had been in France, working as an au pair, for the twelve months when she was actually missing. (1.5)

Gran [2]: Senior member of a family whose Christmas was almost ruined when her daughter and son-in-law were kidnapped by the Graske and replaced with changelings. But the real couple were swiftly returned, none the wiser. (AotG) (Played by GWENYTH PETTY)

Grand Central Ravine: This is named after the Ancient British city of Sheffield, not York. Rose Tyler didn't know this when asked by the Anne Droid in *The Weakest Link* aboard the Game Station. (1.12)

Grandad: Senior member of a family whose Christmas was almost ruined when his daughter and son-in-law were kidnapped by the Graske and replaced with changelings. But the real couple were swiftly returned, none the wiser. (AotG) (Played by ROBIN MEREDITH)

Grandma: Rita Connolly's mother, who lived with Rita and her husband, Eddie, and their son Tommy in a home that Grandma actually owned. She was excited at the prospect of seeing the Queen's Coronation on television, and was present when the TV set was delivered from Magpie Electricals. However, it was playing up and the Wire appeared and stole her face. (2.7T) Eddie Connolly, unbeknownst to his family, then reported Grandma to the police, who took her faceless body away and stored it in a lock-up with all the other locals who had suffered a similar fate. When the Wire was defeated, Grandma's face returned and she went home. (2.7) (Played by MARGARET JOHN)

actions, until the Dalek he was keeping prisoner broke free and systematically slaughtered over 200 staff. After the Dalek was destroyed, Goddard had Van Statten mind-wiped and left to live his life as a brainless junkie on the streets of a random American city. (1.6) (Played by ANNA-LOUISE PLOWMAN)

Goddard, Trisha: The presenter of her own TV chat show, she interviewed a woman called Eileen in an episode entitled 'I Married a Dead Man'. (2.12)

Goffle: The measurement of length defined by Emperor Jate as being from his nose to his fingertip is a paab, not a goffle. Rodrick didn't know this when asked by the Anne Droid in *The Weakest Link* aboard the Game Station. (1.12)

Gold, Murray: Composer of 'Love Don't Roam', one of the songs played at Donna Noble's non-wedding reception. (3.X) Also the composer of 'Heaven or Hell', the number at the heart of the New York Revue at the Laurenzi theatre in Manhattan during November 1930, which was sung by Tallulah after the original singer, Heidi Chicane, broke her ankle. (3.4)

G

Graphite: Principal material within a standard pencil. The Scribble Creature that Chloe Webber created, which attacked Rose Tyler in London in 2012, was made of this, as the Doctor demonstrated by rubbing some of it out with an ordinary eraser. (2.11)

Graske: Diminutive aliens from the planet Griffoth, they either worked for themselves or, more often than not, were employed to do a specific job. Amongst their technology was the ability to kidnap creatures from different times and space and replace them with changelings. These were then controlled by the Graske and used to abduct further victims. (AotG) (Played by JIMMY VEE)

Gravitissimal Accelerator: Part of the system that Professor Yana had come up with to power the rocket that would take the human refugees from Malcassairo to Utopia. (3.11)

Gravity Pockets: Familiar disturbance in space, they are rarely threatening but can cause starships and space stations to judder if hit by one. (1.2)

Gravity Satellites: Devices placed around the Sun to hold it back as it expanded, slowing the destruction of Earth and other planets in the Solar System. (1.2)

Great Atlantic Smog Storm: According to Lynda Moss, this pollution cloud had been raging for 20 years by 200,100. (1.12)

Great Colbalt Pyramid: Built on the remains of the Torchwood Institute on Old Earth. Broff didn't know this when asked by the Anne Droid in *The Weakest Link* aboard the Game Station. He thought it was built on the remains of Touchdown. (1.12)

Great Expectations: A book cited by the Doctor as one of Charles Dickens' canon that he'd read. (1.3)

Great Exterminator: The Dalek Emperor taunted the Doctor while he battled with his conscience over using the Delta Wave, which would destroy Earth as well as the Dalek fleet, by calling him the Great Exterminator. (1.13)

Great Old Ones: According to the Doctor, the legendary Great Old Ones existed from the creation of the universe right up to and including the Dark Times, about 4.6 billion years ago. One of the Great Old Ones had a spaceship, the *Infinite*, and used its great powers to grant the Heart's Desire of anyone who boarded the ship. By the 40th century, the *Infinite* was just a crumbling wreck, with only an echo of the long-dead Great Old Ones' power left in it. (TIQ)

Great Vampyres: One of the legendary races from the Dark Times, mentioned by the Doctor. (TIQ)

Green Crescent: The emblem of medicine by the year 5,000,000,000. It was seen on the side of the Hospital on New Earth and on posters and Mood Patches in New New York. (2.1, 3.3)

Green Mile, The: Elton Pope misquoted a passage from this Stephen King novel when summing up his new outlook on life after meeting the Doctor. (2.10)

Green, Joseph: The MP for Hartley Dale, and chairman of the Parliamentary Commission on the Monitoring of Sugar Standards in Exported Confectionary. The real Green had been murdered and replaced by a member of the Family Slitheen, Jocrassa Fel Fotch Pasameer-Day Slitheen. As Green, he was the most senior Member of Parliament in London and assumed the temporary role of Acting Prime Minister as the

real one had been killed. Jocrassa Fel Fotch Pasameer-Day Slitheen died when a sub-Harpoon missile struck 10 Downing Street. (1.4, 1.5) (Played by DAVID VERREY)

Grexnik: A married character from the holovid series *Jupiter Rising*. (1.12)

Griffoth: Home world of the Graske. (AotG)

Ground Force: One of the programmes broadcast from the Game Station. Losing contestants get turned into compost. (1.12)

Guard: In charge of keeping the Futurekind out of the Silo base on Malcassairo, he let the Doctor, Martha Jones, Captain Jack Harkness and Padra Fet Shafe Cane in, but only after checking they didn't have fangs. He and his men later left on the rocket to Utopia. Whether he or his descendents were turned into Toclafane by the Master is unknown. (3.11) (Played by ROBERT FORKNALL)

Guinevere One: A British space probe sent to Mars, financed by the Government under Harriet Jones and overseen by Daniel Llewellyn. It was taken aboard the Sycorax ship en route, and they used its transmitters to make contact with Earth. (2.X)

Gurney, Constantine Ethelred: He claimed to be the Governor of the prison on Volag-Noc but was actually an impostor. Previously a prisoner on the planet, after he was freed, his old enemies still wanted him dead, so he returned to prison and, with the help of technology he acquired from Ulysses Mergrass, rewired the Governor and Warders, so the Warders saw him as Locke and Locke as Gurney and imprisoned the real governor. When the Doctor brought an end to Gurney's new lifestyle after releasing Governor Locke, Gurney fled to the surface, taking with him the final datachip the Doctor and Martha Jones needed to locate the *Infinite*. Gurney was then attacked and killed by Baltazar after he shot and mortally wounded Baltazar's companion, Caw. (TIQ) (Voiced by STEPHEN GRIEF)

Gwyneth: Orphaned maid in the service of Gabriel Sneed, she was gifted with the ability to contact what she believed were departed human spirits – a natural talent enhanced by her growing up close to the space and time Rift that crossed Cardiff. In fact, the spirits were an alien species who called themselves the Gelth. They sought bodies to inhabit as they crossed to Earth via the Rift, before beginning their intended conquest of the planet. Pretending to be angels, they tricked both Gwyneth and the Doctor into allowing her to act as a conduit for them. As they emerged, they revealed their true forms, killing Gwyneth but leaving enough of her spirit intact that she was able to strike a match and ignite the Gelth's gaseous forms so they, along with her, were destroyed in a massive explosion. (1.3) (Played by EVE MYLES)

H2O Scoop: Colloquial name for the Judoon device that enabled them to take the Royal Hope Hospital from Earth (where they had no jurisdiction) to the Moon. The scoop, in breaking through the atmosphere, created meteorological disturbances and then, as it activated, it drew all the moisture upwards, followed by the instant transmission of the Hospital. The scoop was reversed by the pedantic Judoon to avoid any complaints, and the Hospital was returned (with the rain) to exactly where it had come from. The Judoon used plasma coils that they had, two days previously, placed around the hospital to power the scoop. (3.1)

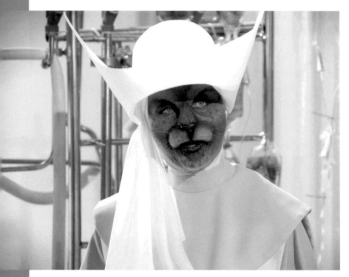

Hame, Novice: A young nun, a member of the Sisters of Plenitude, who was seen in advertisements for the Hospital on New Earth saving a human suffering from Hawtrey's Syndrome. (2.1T) She was charged with looking after the Face of Boe in Ward 26. When the Sisters' plan was exposed, Hame was arrested and taken away. (2.1) Her penance was to be returned to the Face of Boe to minister to him for the rest of their lives, and he protected her from the mutated Bliss mood that eradicated the Senate and everyone else in the Overcity of New New York. She found the Doctor on the Motorway and brought him back to the Senate Building to save New New York and restore those trapped on the Motorway to the City now the danger had passed. When Boe died, the Doctor and Martha Jones left Hame in charge of the city. (3.3) (Played by ANNA HOPE)

Hamilton Colt: Maker of radios in the 1930s. The Doctor used a Hamilton Colt radio Solomon found in the basement of the Laurenzi theatre to cannibalise and make a DNA scanner, which

revealed that his old enemies the Daleks were at work. He then converted it back to a radio receiver, switching it on in the Daleks' Transgenic Lab. The noise temporarily disabled the Daleks, the Dalek Sec Hybrid and the Pig Slaves, so he, Martha Jones and the captured humans could escape. (3.4, 3.5)

Hamlet: *The Tragedy of Hamlet, Prince of Denmark*, a play by William Shakespeare. Shakespeare considered writing it after defeating the Carrionites, as a way to honour his dead son, Hamnet. He also got a line for the play from the Doctor – 'The play's the thing' – although he didn't realise it at the time. (3.2)

Hamnet: William Shakespeare's only son who died, while Shakespeare was away from home, from the Black Death. His grief at the loss caused him such despair, bordering on madenss, that it enabled the Carrionites to gain a foothold on Earth. The defeat of the Carrionites prompted Shakespeare to consider honouring his dead son with a new play, which would later become *Hamlet*. (3.2)

Händel, Georg Friedrich: Composer of 'Zadok the Priest', the anthem heard at the Coronation of Queen Elizabeth II, watched by millions in 1953, while the Wire schemed to steal their life energies and renew itself. (2.7)

Hannibal: Carthaginian military commander whose legendary exploits included taking his troops to face the Romans over the Alps. Legend has it that to get through difficult rocky terrain with his troops and elephants, he used vinegar to corrode the calcium-based boulders. Harriet Jones MP was reminded of this when the Doctor was trying to devise a means to defeat the calcium-based Raxacoricofallapatorians. (1.5)

Hannon, Neil: Singer of 'Love Don't Roam', played at Donna Noble and Lance Bennett's reception to celebrate their non-wedding, which made the Doctor think of Rose Tyler. (3.X)

Happy: Coming in varying strengths, this was one of the Mood Patches available in Pharmacytown in the Undercity of New New York. (3.3)

'Happy Days Are Here Again': One of the show tunes used as part of the New York Revue at the Laurenzi theatre in 1930s New York, when it was still a new song to most people. (3.4)

Happy Prime Numbers: One of the passwords Martha Jones and Riley Vashtee needed to gain access to the next area aboard the SS *Pentallian* was the next in a sequence of numbers which the Doctor realised was a series of happy primes, the number required being 379. Happy numbers are any number which reduces to 1 when you take the sum of the squares of its digits and continue iterating until it yields 1. A happy prime is any number that's both a happy number and a prime number. (3.7)

Harcourt, Mrs: A patient at Albion Hospital who was transformed into a gas mask zombie by the Chula nanogenes. Her DNA was rewritten properly

by the reprogrammed nanogenes, returning to normal, but also replacing the leg she had lost that put her in the hospital in the first place. (1.10) (Played by VILMA HOLLINGBERY)

Harrison, George: British guitarist and singer who, when a member of The Beatles, wrote and sang 'Here Comes The Sun' for the *Abbey Road* album. The Doctor quoted it as the SS *Pentallian* headed towards the sun in the Torajii system. (3.7)

Harry: One of the inhabitants of Hooverville in 1930s Manhattan. Solomon told him to stay with the rest of the people there when they were attacked by the Pig Slaves. (3.5)

Harry Potter and the Deathly Hallows: Final book in the seven-novel run by British author JK Rowling. The Doctor had read this, although Martha Jones hadn't, and it made him cry. Martha used a word from the Harry Potter books – 'Expelliarmus' – to help William Shakespeare send the Carrionites back into the Deep Darkness. (3.2)

Hartley Dale: Constituency for which Joseph Green was MP until he was murdered by Jocrassa Fel Fotch Pasameer-Day Slitheen, and his body used as a disguise. (1.4, 1.5)

Hartman, Yvonne: CEO of the Torchwood Institute, fiercely patriotic and loyal to Queen and Country. Arrogant and self-assured, Yvonne made the mistake of assuming that she understood all the alien tech that Torchwood had accumulated over the years, but had no real idea of what exactly her Ghost Shifts were doing to the fabric of reality. Nor did she understand the Void ship Torchwood had secreted in one of their research labs. When the 'ghosts' revealed themselves to be Cybermen, and Daleks emerged from the Void ship, she was hopelessly out of her depth and unable to resist when taken away for the Ultimate Upgrade. However, even in her Cyberform, Yvonne's duty took precedence, and she turned on the Cybermen and began shooting them down. It is likely that, along with the rest of the Cybermen, she was drawn into the Void for ever. (2.12, 2.13) (Played by TRACY-ANN OBERMAN)

Hartnell, Norman: Designer of the dress worn by the future Queen Elizabeth II on her Coronation day.

Haven Road: Street in Chiswick in which St Mary's Church stood. The church was where Donna Noble and Lance Bennett were getting married when Donna vanished. (3.X)

Haverstock, Mr: London butcher who was having an illicit affair with Arthur Lloyd, and also supplying him with meat to feed his family. (1.10)

Hawking, Professor Stephen William: British theoretical physicist and author of *A Brief History of Time*, confined to a wheelchair due to ALS and only able to speak via a voice synthesizer. Mickey Smith commented on the similarity between Hawking's speaking voice and that of a Dalek. (2.13)

Captain Jack Harkness

Wish I'd never met you, Doctor. I was much better off as a coward.

Originally a Time Agent from the Boeshane Peninsula in the 51st century, Captain Jack Harkness woke one morning to find that two years of his memories had been stolen by his employers, leaving him with no knowledge of what had happened to him during this period. On account of this, Jack set himself up as a freelance conman, travelling to locations such as first-century Pompeii and Second World War London, salvaging alien space junk and selling it back to the Time Agency before pre-known and natural causes resulted in their destruction.

Basing himself in Westminster in 1941, Jack served as an American volunteer for the Royal Air Force, having assumed the identity of the real Captain Jack Harkness. Having previously stolen a Chula vessel for himself from a gorgeous female life form, Jack projected a Chula ambulance at the TARDIS whilst it was travelling through the Time Vortex, with the intention of conning the Doctor and Rose into believing it was actually a warship. A German bomb was scheduled to destroy it soon after. Jack later prevented the bomb from falling on the crash site by suspending it in stasis on board his own ship, but was unable to jettison it. He was then rescued from his ship's destruction by the Doctor and Rose Tyler, who invited him aboard the TARDIS as their travelling companion, even giving him his own TARDIS key. (1.9, 1.10)

The trio's travels then included brief visits to Cardiff, (1.11) and Raxacoricofallapatorius and a

trip to Japan in 1336, before Jack was transported from the TARDIS to the *What Not To Wear* studio aboard the Game Station, where he confessed to having considered plastic surgery around the eyes and jaw-line. Following an attempt to rescue Rose from *The Weakest Link*, he was arrested alongside the Doctor and Lynda Moss, and sentenced to imprisonment on the Earth's Lunar Penal Colony. When they eventually escaped and uncovered an army of ships hidden from the Game Station transmitters, Jack recognised them as Dalek ships from the Tenth Dalek Occupation, and willingly deferred to the Doctor's authority, offering to help mount a defence, despite having previously considered himself a coward. Jack rallied the troops aboard the Game Station and served as the Doctor's last line of defence, ultimately facing extermination by the Daleks. He was then resurrected by Rose, who used the power of the Time Vortex to bring him back to life, making him immortal in the process. The Doctor instinctively reacted against Jack's situation, and abandoned him on board the Game Station. (1.12, 1.13)

Stranded in the year 200,100, Jack used his Vortex Manipulator to travel to Earth in 1869, but was forced to live through the entire 20th century when the Manipulator burnt out, waiting for a version of the Doctor that coincided with his own timeline. Jack took this opportunity to visit Rose when she was growing up on the Powell Estate in the 1990s, though without making contact with her, and, knowing that the Doctor would have to return one day to refuel, based himself in Cardiff, on top of the Rift that ran through the city. Jack joined Torchwood Cardiff and, following the Battle of Canary Wharf, rebuilt it in the Doctor's honour to defend the Earth. He had retrieved the Doctor's severed hand after the Sycorax attack, and kept it in order to detect the Time Lord's presence. He then travelled to the end of the universe by clinging to the TARDIS exterior as it dematerialised from Cardiff in 2008, (3.11) before helping the Doctor and Martha defeat the Master upon their return to Earth. Though the Doctor offered to let him continue travelling in the TARDIS once more, Jack returned to his team at Torchwood, but not before the Doctor had disabled his Vortex Manipulator's travel capabilities for a second time. (3.12, 3.13)

Although the Doctor instantly knew of his immortality, Jack himself didn't realise until 1892, when a man shot him through the heart on Ellis Island. He later fell off a cliff, got trampled by horses, lived through two world wars, was poisoned, starved and even got struck by a stray javelin. On his reunion with the Doctor, Jack survived further perils: travelling through the Time Vortex unprotected, electrocution, stet radiation, a laser screwdriver bolt, and a year as the Master's prisoner, where he was repeatedly shot by militia and faced the Toclafane single-handed in order to reach the Paradox Machine.

Charming and flirtatious with everyone he met, regardless of sex or species, the first thing Jack told Rose was that he considered himself to be single and liked to work out. He once, having been sentenced to death, woke up with both his executioners. The various items he carried to assist him in his duties included a sonic blaster, an emergency teleport, psychic paper, a mobile phone, a Compact Laser Deluxe, and a Webley revolver. At one time, he had a fondness for hyper-vodkas containing vermouth, and champagne, explaining to Rose Tyler that he never liked to discuss business with a clear head.

Unable to die, but still able to age, he was concerned by what his future had in store and, before returning to Torchwood, Jack sought advice from the Doctor. Claiming vanity, Jack revealed that he'd been a poster boy where he grew up in the Boeshane Peninsula, and was the first of his people ever to be signed up for the Time Agency. As a result, he told them, he had been nicknamed the Face of Boe, leaving the Doctor and Martha wondering whether Jack would live to become their other old friend, millions of years in the future.

(Played by JOHN BARROWMAN)

Hawtrey's Syndrome: One of the diseases successfully cured by the Sisters of Plenitude in their Hospital on New Earth. (2.1T)

Hazeldine, San: In physics, San Chen, not San Hazeldine, discovered the 15-10 Barric Fields. Rodrick didn't know this when asked by the Anne Droid in *The Weakest Link* aboard the Game Station. (1.12)

Hazelhurst, Ronnie: Composer of the the theme music for British TV sitcom *Are You Being Served?* The opening line of the theme was quoted by the Doctor as he exited the elevator at the top of the Empire State Building. (3.5)

Hazlehead: The Royal Jewellers, Hellier and Carew, were based in this Aberdeenshire town. Queen Victoria was taking the Koh-I-Noor diamond there for its annual re-cutting when she stopped for the night at the Torchwood Estate. (2.2)

HC Clements: Security firm where Donna Noble was temping as a secretary when she met the company's head of Human Resources, Lance Bennett. Donna believed they had fallen in love and she asked Lance to marry her. HC Clements had actually been a subsidiary of the Torchwood Institute for 23 years, supplying Torchwood with various security systems and specialised locks. An underground tunnel linked the basement of HC Clements with a Torchwood facility beneath the Thames Barrier. (3.X)

Head Chef: Food dealer on Floor 139 of Satellite Five, selling, amongst other delicacies, Kronkburgers. (1.7) (Played by COLIN PROCKTER)

Heat Magazine: Celebrity gossip magazine which the Tylers' had a copy of in their living room. The Doctor read it, pointing out that one of the celebrities therein was gay, another an alien. (1.1)

Heathrow: The Doctor told Adam Mitchell to head there on a 3pm flight from the USA when beginning his journey home to Manchester, before agreeing to give him a trip in the TARDIS.

'Heaven and Hell': Show-stopping number at the heart of the New York Revue at the Laurenzi theatre in Manhattan during November 1930. It was sung by Tallulah after the original singer, Heidi Chicane, broke her ankle. (3.4)

HENRIK'S: Chain of London department stores, part of the JC Howell group. One branch, in which Rose Tyler worked, was damaged when the Doctor blew up a Nestene relay device on its roof and was later demolished. (1.1) Elton Pope had been shopping at a branch when he got caught up in the Auton attack. (2.10) Another branch in West London was passed by the Doctor and Donna Noble when he tried to get her to her wedding in Chiswick. (3.X)

Hell: A name often used to describe the Void. (2.12)

Hellier and Carew: Royal Jewellers, based in the Aberdeenshire town of Hazlehead. Queen Victoria was taking the Koh-I-Noor diamond there for its annual re-cutting when she stopped for the night at the Torchwood Estate. (2.2)

Henry V: Play by William Shakespeare. The Doctor used the phrase 'Once more unto the breach' to the writer, which Shakespeare recognised as one of his own. (3.2)

Henry VIII: 15th-century English King. The Doctor offered Martha Jones the chance to meet him, but she declined. (3.13)

'Here Comes The Sun': After being asked a trivia question about The Beatles while heading towards a sun aboard the SS *Pentallian*, the Doctor quoted this George Harrison composition from the group's *Abbey Road* album. (3.7)

Herefordshire: Rural English county that borders east Wales. One of its villages was Farringham, which, in 1913, was the scene of a battle between the Family of Blood and the Doctor. (3.8, 3.9)

Hermethica: Home world of the Wire, leader of a criminal gang there who could transform themselves into pure plasmic energy. (2.7)

Hermits United: The Doctor joked to Professor Yana that he, Martha Jones and Captain Jack were all members of Hermits United to explain why they knew nothing about the Utopia project. (3.11)

Hesperus Galaxy: Initial location of the *Infinite*, provided by the datachip possessed by Gurney. (TIQ)

Hicks, Dale: Boy who vanished while playing football on a front lawn with Tom on 29 July 2012. His was tthe last of the children's disappearances caused by the lonely Isolus and Chloe Webber, who drew him because they needed a friend to play with. He later returned to Tom's front garden after the Isolus left Earth. (2.11) (Played by JAXON HEMBRY)

Hicks, Mr [1]: The distraught parent who added a poster of his son Dale to the posters on a lamp post asking for information about the missing children from Dame Kelly Holmes Close. (2.11) (Played by IAN HILDITCH)

Hicks, Mr [2]: Villager at the dance in Farringham when the Family of Blood attacked, killing Mr Chambers and demanding the Doctor hand himself over to them. John Smith told Hicks to warn the villagers that they should evacuate immediately. (3.9)

High Content Metal: The specific steel John Lumic invented on 'Pete's World' to build his Cyberforms from. (2.5, 2.6)

Himalayas: Mountain range in Tibet, where Harry Saxon had Captain Jack Harkness's Torchwood teammates, including Toshiko Sato, sent on a worthless mission, to stop Jack from contacting them. (3.12)

'Hit Me With Your Rhythm Stick': 1979 number one single for Ian Dury and the Blockheads. The Doctor was playing it to Rose Tyler in the TARDIS when he suggested they go to one of Dury's concerts. (2.2)

Hitchingson, Tom: A news reporter trying his best to report from Westminster Bridge on the Big Ben incident. (1.4) (Played by JACK TARLTON)

Hitler, Adolf: Austrian-born leader of the Nazi Party, Chancellor and then Führer of Germany in the years leading up to and during the Second World War. Wartime posters in London proclaimed that Hitler would give no warning before German air raids during the Blitz. (1.9)

Hockley Terrace: In the fiction created for John Smith's background, John believed this street was adjacent to Broadmarsh Street, where he thought he remembered growing up, in Nottingham. (3.9)

Hoffman, Scott: Multi-instrumentalist musician with the Scissor Sisters, and co-writer of the song 'I Can't Decide', which the Master played and sang one morning aboard the *Valiant* as he pushed the artificially aged Doctor around in a wheelchair. (3.13)

Hoix: Race of aggressive exo-skeletal aliens with an aversion to certain warm liquids. Elton Pope encountered the Doctor and Rose Tyler trying to contain one in Woolwich, London. (2.10) (Played by PAUL KASEY)

'Hollow Men, The': Both the Doctor and Richard Lazarus quoted this poem by TS Eliot to make their points about the benefits and negatives of the GMD that Lazarus had built. (3.6)

Holmes, Dame Kelly: British middle-distance athlete and winner of two gold medals at the 28th Olympic Games. The street in East London where children had been disappearing from had been renamed after her for the 30th Olympiad in 2012. (2.11)

Honesty: Coming in varying strengths, this was one of the Mood Patches available in Pharmacytown in the Undercity of New New York. Cheen was wearing a patch of this, even though she was pregnant. (3.3)

Hoob: In the Pan Traffic culture the month of Hoob is followed by Pandoff, not Clavadoe. Fitch didn't know this when asked by the Anne Droid in *The Weakest Link* aboard the Game Station. (1.12)

Hoodie: The Doctor spotted him taping out the rhythm of the Master's hypnotic signal, being beamed down from the Archangel satellites, in a street in London. (3.12) (Played by RYAN PROBERT)

Hoover, Herbert Clark: The 31st President of the USA, holder of that position at the time of America's Wall Street Crash. All over the States, shantytowns were erected for the homeless and penniless to live in. These were called Hoovervilles, and the one in Manhattan's Central Park, run by Solomon, was attacked by the Cult of Skaro. (3.4, 3.5)

was very proud of his new mobile phone but he was 'eaten' by a Reaper, one of the creatures that broke into the world after Rose Tyler's actions in saving Pete's life created a breach in time. Sonny was returned to life after Pete died again, with no memory of the incidents. (1.8) (Played by FRANK ROZELAAR-GREEN)

Hoskins, Stuart: It was on the way to Stuart's wedding to Sarah Clark that Pete Tyler was killed in a hit-and-run accident. However, when Rose Tyler saved her father's life, time was disturbed, enabling the antibody-like wraiths, the Reapers, to spill into the world of 1987, wiping people out of time and feeding off the resultant chronal energy. Stuart and Sarah had met outside the Beatbox Club. Stuart's father Sonny was a victim of the Reapers but, after Pete Tyler sacrificed his life, Sonny was returned and the wedding took place, with no one recollecting what had occurred other than the unfortunate death of Pete outside the church. (1.8) (Played by CHRISTOPHER LLEWELLYN)

Hooverville: All over the United States of America, shantytowns were erected for the homeless and penniless to live in during the Great Depression. These were called Hoovervilles, named after the then President, Herbert Hoover. The one in Manhattan's Central Park was run by a former soldier, Solomon. Most of the people in Hooverville respected Solomon, but sometimes he had to break up fights between some of the inhabitants, such as the time one man (played by PETER BROOKE) had stolen a loaf of bread belonging to another (played by EARL PERKINS). The bread-owner was the first person to see the Daleks' Pig Slaves when they attacked Hooverville at night, shortly before the Daleks themselves arrived. (3.4, 3.5)

Hop Pyleen: Brothers from Rex Vox Jax who invented Hyposlip Travel Systems. They were guests aboard Platform One to see the Earthdeath spectacle. (1.2)

Hopper, Idris: Margaret Blaine's secretary. He tried, unsuccessfully, to stop the Doctor entering her office as she fled through an open window. (1.11) (Played by ALED PEDRICK)

'Horatius': A poem by Macaulay, quoted by Mr Jefferson in tribute to Scooti Manista after she had been murdered by the possessed Toby Zed. (2.8)

Horsehead Nebula: The Doctor offered to show this to Rose, pointing out that, due to a galactic storm, there were fires a million miles wide burning there, but he could safely fly the TARDIS into the heart of it. (1.5)

Hoskins, Sonny: Father of the groom, Stuart, at the wedding Pete Tyler was due to attend when he was killed. Sonny

Hospital: Massive complex on an island in the bay of New New York run by the Catkind Sisters of Plenitude. In fact the Sisters were breeding a whole new sub-species of humanity with every known plague, virus and illness genetically contained within them, creating a vast store of natural antibodies which could potentially cure any disease. The Hospital was also the secret lair of Lady Cassandra O'Brien and, in Ward 26, the Face of Boe waited to see the Doctor. (2.1)

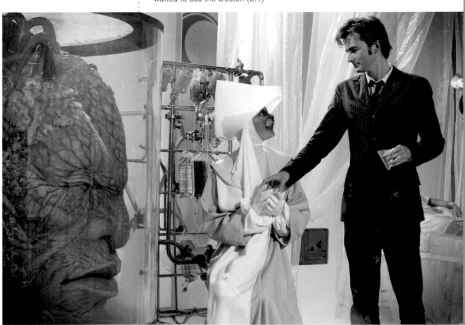

Howling Halls: The Doctor was pursuing a Living Shadow that had escaped from there when he found himself at the Pope household. Mrs Pope had been killed by the Shadow and her four-year-old son Elton saw the Doctor with her body. (2.10)

HP Sauce: An advert for this suggested to Rose Tyler that the TARDIS had brought them to England and not 1956 New York. (2.7)

Hubble Array: Colloquial name for instrumentation aboard the Hubble Space Telescope. Strictly speaking, the arrays aboard the telescope are solar reflectors used to power the device, but Sally Jacobs of UNIT used the phrase as shorthand to report that the Telescope was following the course of the Sycorax ship. (2.X)

Host, the: Young sickly lad, abducted from his village and forcibly infected with the Haemovariform virus, turning him into an eight-foot werewolf. He was released on the Torchwood Estate by the moonlight which the Brethren of St Catherine had arranged for him to be bathed in. When trapped by the Torchwood telescope, and burnt by moonlight via the Koh-I-Noor diamond, the Host briefly asserted control again, begging the Doctor to kill him and destroy the Haemovariform for ever, which the Doctor did. (2.2) (Played by TOM SMITH)

'Hound Dog': Blues song first recorded in 1952 by Big Momma Thornton. Elvis Presley recorded a cover version in 1956, and he later sang it on *The Ed Sullivan Show*, which was watched in eager anticipation by 60 million people in the USA. The Doctor wanted to take Rose Tyler to see this event live in New York. (2.7)

Hour of Woven Words: The time at which the portal linking Earth to the Deep Darkness would open, enabling the Carrionites to dominate Earth, creating a Millennium of Blood. The Woven Words were given to a sleeping Shakespeare by Lilith to be spoken at the end of his play, *Love's Labour's Won*. (3.2)

Housewife: Character in a television advert for a new ghost-inspired cleaning agent, Ectoshine. (2.12) (Played by MADDI CRYER)

Howard: Market-worker that Jackie Tyler had been seeing whilst Rose was off travelling with the Doctor. He left a pair of pyjamas and a dressing gown in Jackie's flat in which she dressed the post-regenerative Doctor. His pockets were filled with fruit, for when Howard got hungry, apparently. (2.X)

Howling, the: The name the Eternals gave to the Void. (2.12)

Hull: Humberside city to which Kathy Nightingale was transported by the Weeping Angel that touched her in Wester Drumlins house. She met her future husband, Ben Wainwright, in a field there. (3.10)

Hull Times: Ben Wainwright showed Kathy Nightingale a copy of this newspaper to prove she was in Hull when she first arrived. (3.10)

Human Point Two: The designation Cybermen gave themselves after they had had the Ultimate Upgrade. (2.5)

Humanish: One of the descriptions used by the humans of five billion years in Rose's future to describe themselves. It implies they are different from the now extinct (bar Lady Cassandra) humans originating from Earth itself. (1.2)

Huon Energy: Ancient energy created by the Time Lords and used for a time in their technology. However, the Time Lords believed they had rid the universe of it billions of years ago, having realised it was lethal. The Racnoss, an enemy from the Dark Times, thrived off the energy, and the Empress, the last of her race, needed an organic key full of it to free her children, trapped at the core of the Earth. When the Torchwood Institute drew the Empress's attention, she recreated Huon Particles artificially in

its labs, subsequently convincing an employee of a Torchwood subsidiary company, Lance Bennett, to force-feed a co-worker, Donna Noble, with potentially fatal doses of Huon particles over six months, thus creating the key she required. Because Donna was getting married, her body became a melting pot of adrenalin and acetylcholine, setting off her endorphins and heating the theoretically inert Huon particles. This caused Donna to be almost magnetically drawn to the only other similar particles in the area, inside the Doctor's TARDIS. (3.X)

Hutchinson: Bullying school captain, who got Timothy Latimer to do his prep for him, including Latin. Latimer was a disappointment to Hutchinson, not the sort of chap he wanted in his House. When Tim had the Doctor's fob watch, he saw a future where he would save Hutchinson's life on a battlefield, and knew therefore that Hutchinson would not die in the battle with the Family of Blood. This vision came true as, a few years later in the trenches of First World War France, Tim indeed saved an injured Hutchinson from a falling German shell. (3.8, 3.9) (Played by TOM PALMER)

Hydra Combination: The door to the Game Station's *Weakest Link* studio was strengthened by this, as was the one to the Observation Deck on Floor 056, although the Daleks still managed to cut through. (1.12, 1.13)

Hydrokinometer: Device aboard the Family of Blood's spaceship that registered the massive energy feedback going through the retrostabilisers and feeding it back through the primary heat converters, because the Doctor had pushed so many buttons. The ship then exploded. (3.9)

Hydroxiding Ribicola: A metal-eating virus the Doctor added to Baltazar's ship, which was made from Pheros living-metal. The race which had developed the virus had long become extinct, but the Doctor possessed a teaspoon, passed through generations of chefs and cooks, made from the virus. When Baltazar broke the spoon, the virus escaped and consumed his ship. (TIQ)

Hyperplex: Specially toughened glass used on 51st-century spaceships that was, all things considered, pretty unbreakable. (2.4)

Hyper-vodka: The result of Captain Jack Harkness instructing his Chula ship's computer to activate Emergency Protocol 417 was the arrival of this drink. Jack recalled that, the last time he had faced execution, he'd had four for breakfast and, instead of dying, ended up in bed with both his executioners. (1.10)

Hyposlip Travel Systems: A form of transportation invented by the brothers Hop Pyleen. (1.2)

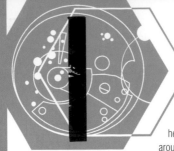

'I Can't Decide': Song by the Scissor Sisters, from their *Ta-Dah* album. The Master played and sang it one morning aboard the *Valiant* as he pushed the artificially aged Doctor around in a wheelchair. (3.13)

'I Could Have Danced All Night': The Doctor returned from the Versailles party with Madame de Pompadour, pretending to be drunk, to fool the Clockwork Robots into letting him pour anti-oil into them. To aid the deception, he sang this song from the musical version of *Pygmalion*, *My Fair Lady*. (2.4)

Iceland: The city of Pola Ventura, not Reykjavik, hosted Murder Spree 20. Rose Tyler didn't know this when asked by the Anne Droid in *The Weakest Link* aboard the Game Station. (1.12)

IE24: News channel on 'Pete's World'. An IE24 newscaster (played by DUNCAN DUFF) tried to warn the population about the Cybermen. (2.5, 2.6)

Il Divo: Multinational pop-opera singing group, of which Jackie Tyler was a fan. When she was flirting with Elton Pope, she played their song 'Regresa A Mi'. (2.10)

'In the Mood': The Doctor and Rose, watched by Captain Jack Harkness, danced to this swing number composed by Glenn Miller in the TARDIS control room. (1.10)

Infinite Temporal Flux: Time is not linear and, as the Doctor explained to Martha Jones, the future can be changed. Although in Martha's world, the Carrionites did not destroy Earth, that didn't mean it couldn't happen in 1599; if it did, the future Martha was from would just fade away, as would she, as time corrected itself to cope with the temporal change. (3.2)

Infinite, the: A mysterious ship from the Dark Times of the universe. Lost for millennia, the ship once contained an ancient entity that could offer someone their Heart's Desire. When the Doctor, Martha Jones and Baltazar located it, the Great Old One who inhabited it had long since died, and only an echo of its power remained, enough to show Martha her Heart's Desire (the Doctor) and Baltazar his (gold and treasures). But these images were illusory, and the Doctor used his sonic screwdriver to deliver a final sonic pulse which weakened the ship and broke it apart for ever. (TIQ)

Intensive Care: Massive area concealed in the Hospital on New Earth where the Sisters of Plenitude had grown human clones, riddled with every disease, virus and contagion known to them. They planned to use the clones as stock for cures, but Lady Cassandra O'Brien let the patients out and they rampaged through the Hospital until the Doctor cured them with their own antibodies mixed into a massive cocktail of drugs. (2.1)

Interface devices: Spherical glowing globes surgically attached to the Ood by their human masters, which enabled the two races to communicate. Once boosted to a telepathy level of Basic 100 by the Beast, the Ood were able to use the interface devices to release a lethal bolt of pure psychic energy against the humans on Sanctuary Base 6. (2.8, 2.9)

International Electromatics: One of the Cybus Industries dummy companies on 'Pete's World' — and the name on the side of the pantechnicon which Mr Crane used to collect people and bring them for Cyber-conversion at the Battersea Power Station factories. (2.5)

International Olympic Committee: News 24 commentator Huw Edwards believed the IOC would have to hold an enquiry into how 80,000 people had disappeared then reappeared at the Olympic Stadium in Stratford, East London in 2012. (2.11)

Ionic power: The power the Isolus used, via Chloe Webber, to transport the children (and cats) away from Dame Kelly Holmes Close and transmute them into living drawings, drawn by Chloe. (2.11)

Ipswich: City in Suffolk, UK. Rose Tyler caustically commented that maybe she could go there instead of being trapped inside a Viewing Gallery on Platform One. (1.2)

Isle of Dogs: Where Blon Fel Fotch Pasameer-Day Slitheen ended up after teleporting out of 10 Downing Street, finding herself in a rubbish skip. (1.5, 1.11)

Isle of Wight: Watching the creation of Earth as it formed around a Racnoss Webstar over four billion years ago, Donna Noble joked to the Doctor that one particular piece of rock was the Isle of Wight, the small island off the British south coast. (3.X)

Isolus: Empathic beings of intense emotion, who drifted through space after leaving the Deep Realms. The Mother Isolus jettisoned roughly four billion offspring, which rode the solar tides in their ovoid podships for thousands of years, their empathic link keeping them connected no matter how far apart they were physically. They could not survive for long if they were alone. They used ionic energy to create make-believe worlds and survived on the love they felt for one another. One Isolus child fell to Earth after its podship encountered a solar flare and, separated from its craft, it sought refuge in the lonely Chloe Webber and used her drawing abilities to create images of the local children. The Isolus then used ionic energy to transport the children away from reality and into an ionic holding pen, where it played with them. This manifested itself in the real world as animated images of the children and animals that Chloe drew. When Rose Tyler located the podship, she returned it to a heat source, the Olympic Torch that was passing by Dame Kelly Holmes Close. Transported warmly in that, the Isolus was then able to return to its collective once the Doctor added the Torch to the Olympic Bowl, creating a massive influx of heat and energy. (2.11)

Isop Galaxy: The oldest inhabitant of this galaxy was the Face of Boe. Rose Tyler knew this when asked by the Anne Droid in *The Weakest Link* aboard the Game Station. (1.12)

'It Had to Be You': Song being sung in the drinking den that the Doctor entered shortly before an air raid, until when he had been unaware of when the TARDIS had landed. (1.9)

ITV: Collective name for a consortium of British independent television channels. The Doctor suggested that the galaxy would implode if their programming was viewed on Christmas Night. He may have been telling a fib. (AotG)

Jabe Ceth Ceth Jafe:
Charming and flirtatious
lead representative from the
Forest of Cheem, who visited
Platform One to witness
Earthdeath. Her ancestors
were from a tropical rainforest
on Earth. She could project
a liana from her wrists. She
presented the Doctor with a
sapling of her grandfather and
later, after learning of his true heritage, devoted herself to helping him save
the space station. Jabe died when the sunfilters surrounding the Ventilation
Chamber collapsed, burning her wooden body in seconds. (1.2) (Played by
YASMIN BANNERMAN)

Jackson [1]: A footman in the service of the MacLeish family in
Torchwood House. He was killed by the Werewolf. (2.2)

Jackson [2]: Schoolboy at Farringham School for Boys in 1913, who hid
alcohol in the cricket pavilion. (3.8)

Jackson, Michael: American pop star infamous for having cosmetic
surgery. Rose Tyler likened Lady Cassandra to him. (1.2)

Jackson, Mr: Villager at the dance in Farringham when the Family of
Blood attacked, killing Mr Chambers and demanding the Doctor hand
himself over to them. (3.9)

Jacob: One of the Lever Room operators responsible for bombarding the
Wall with particle energy via the giant Levers during a Ghost Shift. He was
killed by Cyberleader One, who arrived to take over Torchwood Tower. (2.12)

Jacobs, Sally: An operative in UNIT's Mission Control base beneath the
Tower of London. As her blood group was A+, she was hypnotised by the
Sycorax. (2.X) (Played by ANITA BRIEM)

Jaggit Brocade: A conglomeration of planets, of which Crespallion was
a member. The Brocade was affiliated to the Scarlet Junction as Convex
56. (1.2)

Jagrafess: See *Mighty Jagrafess of the Holy Hadrojassic Maxarodenfoe*

Jailer: Unpleasant man who guided the
Doctor's party around Bedlam as they
sought out Peter Streete, the architect of
the Globe Theatre. (3.2) (Played by
STEPHEN MARCUS)

James, Group Captain Tennant: One
of the arrivals at 10 Downing Street after
the Big Ben incident. An RAF officer, he was
actually a disguised Slitheen, the original
James having been killed previously. (1.5)

Jamie: A young boy who had been wearing his gas mask during an
air raid in the Blitz. He was killed (massive head trauma on the left side,

KYOKO MORITA, ERIKO KURASAWA, MARI YOSHIDA)

Jason: Neighbour of Jackie Tyler's who had A+ blood and was thus affected by the Sycorax's blood control. After the threat had passed, he and his partner Sandra watched as the Sycorax ash fell over the Powell Estate, mistakenly believing it to be snow. (2.X) (Played by PAUL ANDERSON)

partial collapse of his chest cavity on the right and a gash on the back of his right hand) but was reanimated by the Chula nanogenes that had leaked out of a crashed medical transport ship. His only thought was to be reunited with his mother, and he wandered the streets of London, a gas mask of flesh and bone grown from his face, asking everyone 'Are you my mummy?' Because the nanogenes were unaware of what a human looked like, they began transforming all humans they came into contact with into gas mask zombies. In the end the nanogenes were able to use DNA from both him and his mother, Nancy, and restore him to normal. (1.9, 1.10) (Played by ALBERT VALENTINE, voiced by NOAH JOHNSON)

Jamieson, George: Lord Provost of Aberdeen in 1879. Queen Victoria believed, thanks to the Doctor's psychic paper, that he had assigned the Doctor as her protector for her journey to Balmoral Castle. (2.2)

Japan: The Doctor, Rose Tyler and Captain Jack Harkness visited Kyoto when it was still the capital city of Japan in 1336, the year that the civil wars of the Yoshino period began. The Doctor explained that they only just escaped. (1.12) During the year that the Master and the Toclafane ruled Earth, the islands of Japan were destroyed and Martha Jones was the only survivor. (3.13)

Japanese Girls: Three vox pops students who loved the ghosts and wanted to be ghosts because they were really spooky. (2.12) (Played by

Jast, Dalek: Former Force Leader of the Outer Rim Defensive Dalek Battalion, later one of the Cult of Skaro, who brought the Genesis Ark to Earth in a Void ship after the Time War ended. (2.12, 2.13) After fleeing the Battle of Canary Wharf via an emergency temporal shift, along with the rest of the Cult, Jast ended up in Manhattan in 1930. Jast accompanied Dalek Caan for their attack on Hooverville. The Cult used gamma radiation to activate their new Dalek-Human army but, when the army turned on their creators, Jast was destroyed on the stage of the Laurenzi theatre. (3.4, 3.5) (Operated by ANTHONY SPARGO (2.12, 2.13) and DAVID HANKINSON (3.4, 3.5), voiced by NICHOLAS BRIGGS)

Jate: Guard working in the Radiation Room in the Silo base on Malcassairo. When the Futurekind Wiry Woman sabotaged the power systems, all the safety devices went down and Jate died, vaporised by the stet radiation. (3.11) (Played by OLIVER HOPKINS)

Jate, Emperor: The Emperor who defined the measurement of length from his nose to his fingertip as a paab, not a goffle. Rodrick didn't know this when asked by the Anne Droid in *The Weakest Link* aboard the Game Station. (1.12)

Jathaa Sun-Glider: An alien ship that flew across the Shetland Islands ten years before the Battle of Canary Wharf. Torchwood shot it down, accusing it of crossing into Britain's airspace, and then stripped it for resources, including its weaponry, which was subsequently used to destroy the Sycorax ship as it left Earth's atmosphere. (2.X, 2.12)

Jatt, Sister: One of the Sisters of Plenitude, she monitored the experiments on the humans in the secret Intensive Care Unit beneath the Hospital on New Earth. Trying to escape from the infectious patients, Jatt became their first victim when a patient's hand brushed against her face, spreading its numerous viruses into her immunity-free body, killing her instantly. (2.1) (Played by ADJOA ANDOH)

Javit: Catkind car driver in the Fast Lane on the New New York Motorway who tried to warn Milo and Cheen that the Fast Lane was dangerous. (Played by DAISY LEWIS) She had two vestal virgin girls with her (played by HOLLY DYMOCK, HALEY JONES), and all three died when the Macra clawed their way into their car. (3.3)

JC Howell: Parent company for the Henrik's chain of stores. (1.1, 2.10, 3.X)

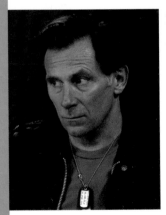

Jefferson, John Maynard: The Torchwood Archive's Head of Security aboard Sanctuary Base 6. A tough, no-nonsense officer, he was greatly impressed by Zachary Cross Flane's leadership after their original captain, Walker, died. He was once married, but something traumatic occurred and, according to the Beast, his wife never forgave him for it. Jefferson led Danny Bartock, Toby Zed and Rose Tyler through the ventilation ducts of Sanctuary Base 6 to escape the pursuing Ood, who were possessed by the Beast. Each duct needed to be flooded with oxygen before they could enter and, as one area was delayed, he volunteered to keep the Ood away while his compatriots escaped. Realising he would not be able to reach his friends in time, Jefferson asked Cross Flane to remove all the air from the area he was in, giving him a quicker death than he'd have had if the Ood had caught him. After his death, Cross Flane entered a commendation into his personal file. (2.8, 2.9) (Played by DANNY WEBB)

Jeffrey: A Welsh civil servant, and father to Cathy Salt's unborn child. (1.11)

Jehovah: Judaeo-Christian deity cited by both Javit and Thomas Brannigan on the New New York Motorway. (3.3)

Jenkins: Schoolboy at Farringham School for Boys in 1913, who had been sent to see the school's Matron with a cold, although he was actually missing his mother. (3.8)

Jenkins, Matilda: Private Jenkins's mother. He struggled to remember her name as he began his transformation into a gas mask zombie. (1.10)

Jenkins, Private: Married soldier who was ill at the Chula ship crash site. Algy left him to guard Nancy, but Jenkins had been infected by Chula nanogenes and transformed into a gas mask zombie. He was kept quiet by Nancy singing 'Rock-a-Bye-Baby'. (1.10) (Played by MARTIN HODGSON)

Jenny: A maid at Farringham School for Boys, she befriended Martha Jones, who was pretending to be in domestic service. Together they suffered the taunts of the boys and early 20th-century society's attitudes and mores. Jenny was a happy-go-lucky girl, always smiling, until she encountered a group of Scarecrows, who kidnapped her and took her to the Family of Blood's invisible spaceship, where she died screaming as Mother of Mine took on her form. (3.8) (Played by REBEKAH STATON)

Jericho Street Junior School: Where Rose Tyler went to school, and joined their Under-7s gymnastics team. (1.1)

Jethro: One of the inhabitants of Hooverville in 1930s Manhattan. Solomon told him to stay with the rest of the people there when they were attacked by the Pig Slaves. (3.5)

Johannesburg: Largest city in South Africa. Hutchinson, House Captain at Farringham School for Boys, heard that his father was going there. Timothy Latimer's uncle had been there on a six-month posting and loved it. (3.8)

John, Elton: British singer and pianist (real name Reginald Dwight) who wrote the music for the song 'The Circle of Life', which the Doctor quoted to the Sycorax Leader. (2.X) Elton Pope's parents named him after the singer. (2.10)

John, Uncle: Eddie Connolly's brother-in-law, who was present at the Connolly's house when Rita threw Eddie out. (2.7) (Played by RICHARD RANDELL)

Jolco and Jolco: Firm of solicitors on Balhoon, who sent the Moxx to represent them at the Earthdeath ceremony on Platform One. (1.2)

Jolie, Angelina: According to Lance Bennett, Donna Noble talked excitedly about this American actor and her on/off relationship with actor Brad Pitt. (3.X)

Jonathan: Young London boy who, like his father and sister, had A+ blood and was thus affected by the Sycorax's blood control. (2.X) (Played by JOSH HUGHES)

Jones, Catherine Zeta: Tish Jones compared the age difference between herself and Professor Lazarus to that between the Welsh actress and her husband Michael Douglas. (3.6)

Jim [1]: Prospective boyfriend for Jackie Tyler, that Rose presumably disapproved of – Jackie promised she'd ditch him if Rose stayed at home and stopped travelling with the Doctor. (1.5)

Jim [2]: One of the young boys Nancy was looking after on the streets of Blitzed London. He had been evacuated to a family in the country, but fled back home to London. Although he couldn't read or write, Jim was determined to send a letter to his missing dad using an old typewriter. After he stopped typing, the 'Empty Child' began psychically using the typewriter. (1.9, 1.10) (Played by JOSEPH TREMAIN)

Jimbo: Nickname given to one of Lady Cassandra's robotic spiders aboard Platform One by the Doctor. (1.2)

'Jingle Bells': The popular name for the song really called 'One Horse Open Sleigh', composed by James Pierpont. It was played by the lethal Christmas Tree placed in the Tylers' flat by the Roboform Santas. (2.X) They played it again while waiting to attack at Donna Noble's wedding reception. (3.X)

Joe: One of the employees at Clancy's Garage, working alongside Mickey Smith. (2.X) (Played by PHILL KIRK)

Jones, Clive: Martha Jones's father, who had abandoned his wife Francine to set up home with a younger woman, Annalise – a source of considerable bitterness among the Jones family. After a row between his girlfriend and estranged wife at his son Leo's 21st birthday party, Clive had an argument with Annalise. Whether they remained a couple after this is unknown. Clive was later captured by Harry Saxon's minions and taken to his old house. There, along with Francine, he tried to persuade Martha to return home, so that she and the Doctor could be captured. Clive warned Martha, though he knew it would mean his own imprisonment. He was also unaffected by the subliminal hypnotic sound being beamed down from the

Archangel satellite network, and realised that Saxon was not exactly what he seemed. After being taken aboard the *Valiant*, he spent a year as a cleaner on the lower decks. As such, when the Paradox Machine was activated, he was one of the few people on Earth for whom the previous 12 months wasn't erased. Martha quit travelling with the Doctor to look after Clive and Francine, who were understandably in shock, although the year's events had brought them closer again. (3.1, 3.12, 3.13) (Played by TREVOR LAIRD)

Jones, Danny: Member of pop group McFly, who endorsed Harry Saxon's campaign to become Prime Minister. (3.12)

Jones, Francine: Businesswoman and mother of Martha Jones. Separated, acrimoniously, from her husband Clive, Francine detested Clive's new girlfriend Annalise, who she saw as an ignorant gold-digger. Francine attended the demonstration of the GMD at LazLabs as a guest of her other daughter, Tish, who was head of PR there. She took her son, Leo, as her escort for the night, and he was injured when the Lazarus Creature attacked. Already suspicious of the Doctor and Martha's friendship, she was distraught when both Martha and Tish remained with the Doctor and pursued Lazarus. A Mysterious Man, who had approached her during the demonstration, returned to warn her about the Doctor – although she was most likely fed a number of lies, as the Mysterious Man was a minion in the employ of future Prime Minister Harry Saxon (aka the Master). Having failed to contact Martha – who had left with the Doctor in the TARDIS – Francine agreed to help Saxon's people if it would rid her daughter of the Doctor's influence, and she allowed a number of her phone calls from Martha to be recorded by a Sinister Woman in an effort to trace the time travellers. Eventually Saxon's people found Clive and brought him home, hoping that a fake reunion between her parents might persuade Martha to break cover. But Clive warned his daughter and, to Francine's horror, the Sinister Woman revealed her true colours and had both of them arrested, along with Tish. Taken aboard the *Valiant*, Francine spent a year as a maid serving the Master, after he had unleashed the Toclafane on Earth, and she had to watch as he slaughtered millions. When the Doctor eventually defeated the Master, the distraught Francine was prepared to shoot him dead, but the Doctor quickly talked her out of it. Because she had been aboard the ship when the Paradox Machine was activated she was one of the few people on Earth for whom the previous 12 months wasn't erased. Martha quit travelling with the Doctor to look after her parents, who were understandably in shock. (3.1, 3.6, 3.7, 3.12, 3.13) (Played by ADJOA ANDOH)

Harriet Jones P.M.

JONES, HARRIET: MP for Flydale North, she arrived at 10 Downing Street for a meeting about Cottage Hospitals (her mother was sick in Flydale Infirmary), but was ignored and ended up hiding in the Cabinet Room. There she discovered that the Family Slitheen had replaced the most senior people in Downing Street. She eventually helped the Doctor and Rose to defeat the Slitheen. (1.4, 1.5) In the wake of these events, she went on to become Prime Minister of Britain, although an Act of Parliament banned her from writing an autobiography. Once in office, she successfully implemented her New Cottage Hospital Scheme. She and the Doctor met again after she had made first contact with the alien Sycorax. However, her time as Prime Minister was cut short when she angered the Doctor by destroying the fleeing Sycorax spaceship. He used just six words, spoken to her aide, to bring down her Government. (2.X) On 'Pete's World', she became President of Great Britain, ushering in a Golden Age that actually saw severe climate change as hothouse gases, exacerbated by the breaches that led through the Void, weakened the planet. The Doctor warned Pete Tyler to be wary of her. (2.13) (Played by PENELOPE WILTON)

Jones, Isham: Co-writer of 'It Had To Be You', the song being performed in the drinking den that the Doctor entered shortly before an air raid. (1.9)

Jones, Leo: 21-year-old brother of Martha Jones. Because of the circumstances surrounding his parents' bitter separation, he was despairing of his proposed birthday party, suggesting to Martha that it be cancelled. It went ahead but, after an argument between his mum, Francine, and his dad's new girlfriend, Annalise, he was forced to head off after Clive to try and smooth the waters. The next night, he accompanied Francine to the LazLabs' party, because his eldest sister, Tish, was working for Professor Lazarus, and he met the Doctor there, who Martha was travelling with. Having been injured during the attack by the Lazarus Creature, he stayed with his distraught mother while Martha and Tish helped the Doctor defeat Lazarus. When Harry Saxon (aka the Master) began to round up the Jones family to get at Martha, Leo and his girlfriend Shonara and their daughter Keisha were having a day in Brighton with a mate, Boxer. Just before the Master broke

through into their phone conversation, Martha warned Leo to stay there, as far away from the authorities as possible, which he did. This meant that, unlike the rest of his family, he wasn't caught up in the Paradox Machine's effects on Earth and had no memory of living through the Year of Hell. He was present at his parents' London home when Martha elected to stop travelling with the Doctor. (3.1, 3.6, 3.12, 3.13) (Played by REGGIE YATES)

Jones, Letitia ('Tish'): Martha Jones's elder sister (by a year). Tish had a job as Head of PR at LazLabs, working for Richard Lazarus. When Lazarus hit on her, she rejected him but, once he had been rejuvenated into his younger self, realised that a little flirting could be a good career move. As a result, she was with him to witness his transformation into the deadly Lazarus Creature, and ended up helping the Doctor and Martha destroy it at Southwark Cathedral. Soon afterwards, Tish took a new PR job, ostensibly overseeing public relations for the new Prime Minister's wife, Lucy Saxon. It transpired that both this job and her post at LazLabs had been set up by Harry Saxon (aka the Master) as part of his plan to bring the Jones family under his control in his pursuit of Martha and, ultimately, the Doctor. Captured by Saxon's minions and herded aboard the *Valiant*, when the Master unleashed the Toclafane onto Earth, Tish was a witness. She spent a year as a maid aboard the *Valiant* alongside her parents, serving food to the incarcerated Captain Jack Harkness. As such, when the Paradox Machine was activated she was one of the few people on Earth for whom the previous 12 months wasn't erased. Martha quit travelling with the Doctor to look after Tish and their parents, who were understandably in shock. (3.1, 3.6, 3.12, 3.13) (Played by GUGU MBATHA-RAW)

Martha Jones

I spent a lot of time with you, thinking I was second best. But d'you know what? I am good!

Daughter of Clive and Francine Jones, sister to Letitia and Leo, aunt to Keisha, and cousin of the late Adeola Oshodi, Martha Jones was a medical student at the Royal Hope Hospital when she first met the Doctor. Under the tutelage of Mr Stoker, she worked alongside Julia Swales and Oliver Morgenstern, and was able to employ CPR to resuscitate the Doctor when a Plasmavore drained his body of blood. (3.1) She was also able to recognise and treat concussion, (3.6) demonstrated the bones of the human hand to Joan Redfern, (3.9) and had worked the late shift in Accident and Emergency. (3.2)

Following her transportation to the Moon and subsequent return to Earth, Martha accepted the Doctor's offer of a single thank-you trip in the TARDIS, despite concerns about her rent and exams. (3.1) Upon materialising in 1599, she was initially cautious about changing history, but quickly learned to embrace the Doctor's time-

travelling lifestyle, using her knowledge of Harry Potter to help Shakespeare defeat the Carrionites. (3.2) The Doctor then took Martha to New New York in the far future, (3.3) before travelling back to old New York in the 1930s, a city she had always wanted to visit. She was identified as possessing superior intelligence by the Daleks, and was taken for their Final Experiment, before being rescued by the Doctor and Laszlo. (3.4)

Following the Daleks' defeat, (3.5) the Doctor took Martha home to 2008, just 12 hours after their departure the previous evening. They attended the reception for Professor Lazarus's rejuvenation demonstration, where Martha introduced the Doctor to her family as one of her work colleagues, and Martha's mother, Francine, became increasingly suspicious of her daughter's behaviour. (3.6) The Doctor then invited Martha to join him as a proper companion, giving her a key to the TARDIS,

and providing her mobile phone with Universal Roaming. (3.7) Some time afterwards, the Doctor made himself human, leaving Martha responsible for the safety of his alter ego, John Smith, in 1913. Smith found Martha employment alongside him at Farringham School for Boys, where she worked as a maid for several weeks, and befriended fellow staff member Jenny. (3.8) She then protected Smith from the Family of Blood's attack in the village hall, and ultimately helped persuade both him and Joan Redfern that the Doctor should be brought back into existence. (3.9)

The Doctor and Martha also watched the Moon landing no fewer than four times, (3.10) and embarked on a quest to find the legendary vessel the *Infinite*. (TIQ) When they were transported

to 1969 by the Weeping Angels, Martha had to find employment as a shop assistant in order to support the Doctor. (3.10) On a trip to the planet Malcassairo at the end of the universe, she met first Captain Jack Harkness and then Professor Yana, who was revealed to be the Master in human form. Eventually they returned to Earth only four days after first meeting the Doctor. Martha's flat was destroyed by the Master, who then took the Jones family into custody in an attempt to lure the Doctor's party into a trap. Having never engaged in any criminal activity, Martha became an unlikely fugitive as part of the Master's plans. She teleported aboard the *Valiant* with the Doctor and Jack, where they were taken prisoner. Escaping with Jack's Vortex Manipulator, Martha was then left on Earth to defeat the Master alone. (3.12)

Unable to return to Britain for an entire year, Martha travelled the world, carrying out the Doctor's instructions. She sailed the Atlantic single-handed and walked across America, travelling from the ruins of New York, to the Fusion Mills of China, and across the Radiation Pits of Europe. She was said to be the only person to have escaped Japan alive, and legends claimed that she had travelled the world in search of a weapon capable of killing the Master. In reality, she had been telling her tale of the Doctor to the world, and used her knowledge of Docherty's son to ensure she was on board the *Valiant* for the Doctor's victory.

Following the Master's defeat, Martha Jones decided to remain on Earth to look after her family, and to seek out Thomas Milligan, who had sacrificed his life for Martha in the year that never was. She also reminded herself of the advice she had given to her friend Vicky, and took the opportunity to escape her unrequited love for the Doctor, her self-confessed Heart's Desire. (TIQ) Parting on good terms, Martha then left her phone with the Doctor, determined that she would see him again one day soon… (3.13)

(Played by FREEMA AGYEMAN)

Joplin, Janis: American singer, originally part of the blues group Big Brother and the Holding Company before finding fame as a solo artist. She gave the Doctor his overcoat. (3.3)

Jordan Road: A street near the Powell Estate in South East London. Pete Tyler was killed there in a hit-and-run accident. (1.8) The TARDIS landed there when the Doctor sent Rose Tyler back to Earth before the Daleks invaded the Game Station. (1.13)

'Journal of Impossible Things, A': Believing that the Doctor and his exploits were just fantasies he was dreaming up, John Smith kept a notebook full of his stories and drawings of all the fabulous places he had seen. He loaned the book to Joan Redfern (and drew a picture of her in it), not realising it was all completely real. When trying to determine if Martha Jones was telling the truth about John's true origins, Joan read to the very end of the book, and its stories convinced her that the consequences of the Family of Blood's victory would be terrible for everyone. After the Doctor was returned, Joan asked him to leave her alone, but kept the journal as a record of John Smith, the man she loved with all her heart. (3.8, 3.9)

Judd, Harry: Member of pop group McFly, who endorsed Harry Saxon's campaign to become Prime Minister. (3.12)

Junction 19: The area of ventilation ducts on Platform One where the Crespallion plumber Raffalo was killed by Cassandra's robot spiders. (1.2)

Junctions: Parts of the New New York Motorway. Junction 5 had been closed for three years, according to an irate White Man. Legend had it that a woman had stood at Junction 47 breathing in the fumes for 20 minutes and her head swelled up to 50 feet. According to Sally Calypso, a multiple stackpile (i.e. crash) had occurred at Junction 509. (3.3)

Jupiter Rising: A holovid series. Rose Tyler was asked a question about it by the Anne Droid in *The Weakest Link* aboard the Game Station. (1.12)

Justicia: A prison planet visited by the Doctor and Rose Tyler. It was the first alien world that Rose went to. (1.11)

JX82: System of origin of the asteroid that was home to the Sycorax. (2.X)

JUDOON: Rhinocerotini species of large-lunged galactic law enforcers, intelligent but over-methodical, frequently missing important details in their determination to do a job quickly and efficiently. The Doctor encountered a Judoon platoon on the Moon, searching out a Plasmavore that had murdered the Child Princess of Padrivole Regency Nine. Because they had no jurisdiction on Earth or for hunting humans, they had used plasma-coil technology to move the Royal Hope Hospital to the Moon. (3.1)

JUDOON CAPTAIN: Commander of the Judoon on Earth's Moon, sent to execute the Plasmavore hiding on Earth. He led his troopers through the Royal Hope Hospital, ensuring that everyone was scanned, logged as human (and given compensation forms for their trouble if necessary). Upon locating the Plasmavore, Judoon justice was swiftly meted out and the Judoon Captain led his troops off the Moon, safely returning the Hospital to Earth, presumably to avoid litigation later. (3.1) (Played by PAUL KASEY, voiced by NICHOLAS BRIGGS)

K 37 Gem 5: Official designation for the black hole in space, connected by a gravity funnel to the planet Krop Tor, impossibly in orbit around it. When the funnel finally collapsed, Krop Tor was drawn back towards the black hole. The survivors aboard Sanctuary Base 6 tried to use an escape shuttle to flee the black hole but were drawn towards it after the Beast, in its human host Toby Zed, was sucked into the event horizon. Using the TARDIS, the Doctor pulled the shuttle to safety, but Krop Tor was eventually destroyed within the black hole's event horizon. (2.8, 2.9)

Kaled God of War: The inhabitants of Skaro had the concept of evil represented by a horned beast in their culture. (2.9)

Kaliko, Captain: In command of the *Black Gold*, a futuristic pirate ship on Bouken, a desert planet overrun by the oil rigs owned by OilCorp. OilCorp were sucking the planet dry of its natural resources in an oil-starved 40th century then selling it at inflated prices. OilCorp's biggest opponents were pirates like Kaliko, who would attack the rigs and steal the oil, selling it at low prices to poorer planets. Kaliko was betrayed by her Skeleton Crew but, after an attack by the OilCorp rigs, she was able to flee her damaged

ship in an escape pod. This though was shot down. She crashlanded on the desert floor, and was then murdered by the despot Baltazar. The Doctor and Martha found her body, retrieving the first datachip they required for their quest to find the *Infinite*. (TIQ) (Voiced by LIZA TARBUCK)

Kate: A friend to Cheen, who had told her of the rumours that something lived below the Fast Lane of the New New York Motorway. Milo put the noises they were hearing down to faulty ventilation ducts, but Kate was proven correct when they were attacked by the Macra. (3.3)

Katherine: Friend of Jeanne-Antoinette Poisson in France. During 1744, they had a conversation about the King's paramour Madame de Chateauroux, who was close to dying, and wondered whether Reinette could catch his eye at the Yew Tree Ball. (2.4) (Played by ANGEL COULBY)

Keisha: The daughter of Leo Jones and his girlfriend Shonara. She was safely with Leo and Shonara in Brighton when the Master began rounding up the rest of the Jones family. (3.1, 3.12) (Played by BAKARI SMART)

Kel: Council worker who had been digging up the road around the time that kids began disappearing from Dame Kelly Holmes Close. Initially accused by some of the neighbours of abducting them in his van, he helped Rose Tyler find the Isolus ship, which had been tarmacked over in

K-9: Specially built version of the Doctor's one-time companion, K-9 Mk III was a gift for Sarah Jane Smith, which she received at Christmas in 1981. K-9 was a mobile computer created in the image of a dog, with circuitry and intelligence far beyond Earth technology of the time. K-9 Mk I had remained on Gallifrey with the Doctor's former companion, Leela, whilst the second K-9 stayed with another companion, Romana, in a pocket universe called E-Space. Sarah Jane was very fond of her friend, with his unique and strong personality, but she had been unable to get spares for him, so, by the time they were reunited with the Doctor at Deffry Vale High School in 2007, he was in serious need of repair. K-9 then sacrificed himself to destroy the Krillitanes that had taken over the school, and Sarah Jane was left sad and alone. However, the Doctor had built her a brand new model, K-9 Mk IV, with all the latest non-degrading parts and an omniflexible hyperlink facility, and the two headed back to her London home ready for new adventures together. (2.3) (Voiced by JOHN LEESON)

the road at a point where cars passing over it lost all their power for a few yards. (2.11) (Played by ABDUL SALIS)

Kelvin, Pilot: A human fighter pilot originally from Myarr who was dedicated to destroying the Mantasphids. However, when the Doctor averted the war, Kelvin ended up brokering the peace deal between the insects and humanity. (TIQ) (Voiced by STEVEN MEO)

Kempe, William: Actor, of the Lord Chamberlain's Men. He played Costard in both *Love's Labour's Lost* and *Love's Labour's Won*. (3.2) (Played by DAVID WESTHEAD)

Kendrick, Dr: On 'Pete's World', Kendrick was a scientist employed by Cybus Industries to oversee the Ultimate Upgrade project. After the first Cyberman was 'born', John Lumic had

Kendrick killed by his own creation to stop him reporting Lumic to the Ethical Committee in Geneva for contravening the Bio-Convention. (2.5) (Played by PAUL ANTONY-BARBER)

Kennedy, John Fitzgerald: The 35th President of the United States of America, he was assassinated in November 1963, an event witnessed by the Doctor. (1.1) Rose Tyler said the word 'assassination' automatically made her think of Kennedy. (2.2)

Kennedy, Victor: Needing to disguise himself as a human, the Abzorbaloff created this eccentric human guise, insisting that he had a virulent skin disease so that no one would be inadvertently absorbed into him before he wanted them to be. He carried an ornate cane which was actually a limitation-field device that stopped the Abzorbaloff stretching his physical form too far. (2.10) (Played by PETER KAY; DEAN HARRIS (2.10T))

Kenny: Schoolboy, not very popular with the other kids at Deffry Vale High School. For medical reasons, he was not allowed to eat chips and so was unaffected by the Krillitane Oil and was not forced to work on the Krillitane plan to solve the Skasas Paradigm. He helped the Doctor and his friends escape the Krillitanes when he realised that, bat-like in their natural form, they wouldn't like loud noises, so he set off the school fire alarms. Later, with the school blown up, he was hailed as a hero by Melissa and the other kids for his involvement in the day's events. (2.3) (Played by JOE PICKLEY)

Keycoder: Device used by Ulysses Mergrass to activate the weaponry he sold to the Mantasphid Queen. After she betrayed him, he fled, taking the keycoder with him, leaving the weapons useless. (TIQ)

Khan, Gus: Co-writer of 'It Had To Be You', the song being performed in the drinking den that the Doctor entered shortly before an air raid. (1.9)

King of Despair: Legendary demon name, one of many attributed to the Beast throughout the galaxies. (2.8, 2.9)

King, Stephen Edwin: American novelist most popularly associated with the horror genre, although he has written outside that sphere many times. Elton Pope misquoted a passage from his novel *The Green Mile* when summing up his new outlook on life after meeting the Doctor. (2.10)

Kings Lynn Players: Assembly whose music was heard on the episode of *What's My Line* playing on a television in Mr Magpie's shop when the Wire first appeared to him. (2.7)

Kirsty: Friend of Trish Webber's who phoned her for a chat. Trish told her Chloe was ill but that a Doctor had come to help. (2.11)

Klein, Alex: UNIT operative assigned to Prime Minister Harriet Jones during the Guinevere One expedition to Mars, he was with her when she was teleported aboard the Sycorax ship. Her premiership crumbled when the Doctor whispered to Alex, 'Don't you think she looks tired' – six words that began a chain reaction leading to her downfall. (2.X) (Played by ADAM GARCIA)

Klingons: According to the local newspapers that drew Mickey Smith's attention to the UFOs above Deffry Vale High School, the invaders were not Klingons from the TV show *Star Trek*. (2.3T)

Koh-I-Noor: Indian jewel, presented to the British monarchy by Prime Minister Disraeli when Queen Victoria was declared Empress of India. It was said to bring good luck to females and bad luck to males. 'Koh-I-Noor' means 'Mountain of Light'. The diamond was regularly resized by Prince Albert until it was ready to be added to the telescope he and Sir George MacLeish had built at Torchwood House to destroy the Haemovariform that had lived in the area for more than 300 years. (2.2)

'Kookaburra': Traditional song by Australian composer Marion Sinclair, popular with societies such as the Girl Guides. The song was sung by Chloe and Trish Webber to bond over, thus keep the drawing of Chloe's abusive dead father from coming to life and hurting her. (2.11)

Krakatoa: Volcanic Indonesian island, which suffered a terribly destructive eruption in August 1883. The Doctor was present but survived by swimming towards the neighbouring island of Sumatra. (1.1)

Krillitanes: A race of aliens who could reconstitute themselves, over generations, by taking on features, both physical and mental, of the races they conquered. After many centuries, the Krillitanes now resembled bat-

like creatures (their characteristics stolen from the inhabitants of a planet called Bessan) but could morph into above-average strength humans at will. A side effect of this evolution was that their own Krillitane Oil was toxic to them, acting as an acid poison if it touched them. However, they needed the Oil, safely stored in sealed drums, to enhance the intelligence of the human children at Deffry Vale High School where they based themselves. With their knowledge and imaginations expanded, the children ought to have been able to solve the Skasas Paradigm, providing the Chosen Few, as these Krillitanes called themselves, with the ability to

harness the basic energies that made up the universe and become gods. Aware of the Great Time War, the Krillitane leader, Brother Lassar, offered to share this knowledge with the Doctor, perhaps enabling him to go back and stop the destruction of the Time Lords. The Krillitanes were eventually destroyed when K-9 heated up and then exploded the drums of Krillitane Oil stored in the school kitchens. (2.3)

Kronkburger: Item of food for sale on Satellite Five. It came ungarnished, or with cheese or pajato. (1.7)

Krop Tor: Ancient Veltino name for the planet beneath which the Beast was imprisoned, which translated as 'the bitter pill'. The planet generated a natural gravity field which, boosted by a gravity funnel, connected it to the

nearby black hole K 37 Gem 5. This enabled the black hole and Krop Tor to remain in synchronous orbit around one another, a hitherto impossible situation. A team were sent from the Torchwood Archive on Earth to explore Krop Tor, because an energy spike had been recorded ten miles beneath its surface, but the mission went awry as their ship encountered the funnel and, although the crew successfully landed on Krop Tor, a number of their personnel died, including their captain, Walker. When the TARDIS brought the Doctor and Rose Tyler to the humans' base, they were just completing their drilling procedure. The Doctor and Science Officer Ida Scott went down in spacesuits to discover the source of the energy readings – which was a huge trapdoor in the surface. Krop Tor's connection to the gravity funnel weakened drastically as they did this and, while the humans aboard the base had to cope with this and the mentally controlled Ood, the trapdoor opened. Leaving Ida by the entrance, the Doctor lowered himself into the depths of the planet and encountered the Beast, whose consciousness was currently split between the Ood and archaeologist Toby Zed. As Krop Tor's orbit finally decayed, the Doctor escaped with Ida aboard the TARDIS, leaving the planet and the Beast to be destroyed within the event horizon of K 37 Gem 5. (2.8, 2.9)

Kurhan: Cold planet which the Doctor suggested he and Martha Jones could visit to go ice skating on its mineral lakes. (3.7)

Kyoto: The Doctor, Rose Tyler and Captain Jack Harkness visited Kyoto in 1336, the year that the civil wars of the Yoshino period began, when it was still the capital city of Japan. The Doctor explained that they had only just escaped. (1.12)

La Viva: Coffee house which the Doctor, Rose Tyler, Mickey Smith and Sarah Jane Smith took K-9 to. Later, they were startled by a Krillitane outside. (2.3)

Lab 003: Torchwood laboratory beneath the Thames Barrier where the Doctor explained to Donna Noble what Huon particles were. (3.X)

Labour camps: Established across Earth by the Master, overseen by the Toclafane, to ensure the building of his war rockets went to schedule. (3.13)

Lad: Occupant of the slave house in Bexley, South London. He listened to Martha's story and was later on the streets saying the Doctor's name, along with the rest of mankind. (3.13) (Played by TOM GOLDING)

Lady Announcer: BBC continuity announcer who announced the credits for *What's My Line* and then declared the end of transmission, while Magpie worked in his shop. The Wire adopted her image to communicate with Magpie and, later, Rose, the Doctor and Tommy. (2.7) (Played by MAUREEN LIPMAN)

Lamb and Flag, the: Sarah Clark's local pub – a number of her fellow regulars were expected at her wedding, but they did not show up. (1.8)

Las Vegas: American city in Nevada, famous for its luxurious hotels and casinos. It also played host to a famous concert by Elvis Presley, and the Doctor was taking Rose Tyler to see Elvis – she wanted his 'Vegas' period, he opted for seeing him perform on *The Ed Sullivan Show* during the late 1950s – but they actually ended up in Muswell Hill in 1953 instead. (2.7)

Laser screwdriver: The Master's own, lethal version of the Doctor's sonic screwdriver, with isomorphic controls, ensuring only he could operate it. It could kill with a laser beam (as it did Thomas Milligan and Captain Jack Harkness) or, when adapted with technology from Professor Lazarus's Genetic Manipulation Device, be used to temporally alter DNA. The Master used it to increase the Doctor's age, firstly by 100 years and then, after suspending his regenerative abilities, he physically aged his body to its full 900 years, leaving him a stunted, shrivelled humanoid. (3.12, 3.13)

Laser spanner: Tool that the Doctor claimed he used to have until it was nicked by suffragette Emily Pankhurst. (3.1)

Lassar, Brother: Leader of the Krillitanes based at Deffry Vale High School. He sought to use the children there, having expanded their minds with Krillitane Oil, to solve the Skasas Paradigm, providing the Krillitanes with the ability to harness the basic energies that make up the universe and become gods. Aware of the Time War, Brother Lassar offered to share this

knowledge with the Doctor, perhaps enabling him to go back and stop the destruction of the Time Lords. Brother Lassar was eventually destroyed when K-9 heated up and then exploded the drums of Krillitane Oil stored in the school kitchens. (2.3)

Laszlo: Young, good-looking stagehand at the Laurenzi theatre, who had a relationship with Tallulah the singer. He was kidnapped by one of the Daleks' Pig Slaves and was being turned into one himself when he escaped halfway through the transformation, leaving him neither one thing nor the other. He met up with Tallulah again in the sewers and realised she wasn't going to abandon him. He helped the Doctor escape from the Daleks, although he knew he was dying. When the Daleks were defeated, the Doctor used their Transgenic Laboratory to find a way to halt the decay and save Laszlo's life. Laszlo opted to live in Hooverville, hoping to continue his romance with Tallulah. (3.4, 3.5) (Played by RYAN CARNES)

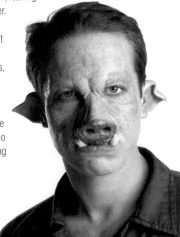

Latimer, Timothy:

Schoolboy at Farringham School for Boys, easily bullied and pushed round by the bigger boys, forced to do their prep, useless at war games and deliberately flunking his lessons so as not to look too bright and become a bigger target for thugs like Baines and Hutchinson. He was mildly psychic, born with a low-level telepathic field, which drew him to the fob watch that schoolteacher John Smith kept on his mantelpiece. The watch contained the essence of the Doctor and, when Tim tried to open it, bits of the Doctor would leak out and give Tim either glimpses of the future, or warnings, with the aim of keeping the fob watch out of the hands of the Family of Blood. One specific warning concerned Tim's own fate, a few years into the future, when he and his schoolboy nemesis, Hutchinson, would be caught in a bombing raid somewhere in the trenches of the First World War – the watch warning him to step to the right and out of a bomb's path. Realising that John Smith needed the fob watch back, he took it to the Cartwrights' cottage where Smith, Martha Jones and Joan Redfern were hiding. Later, having survived the war, Tim lived to a very old age and, decades later at a Remembrance Day ceremony, he saw the Doctor and Martha, unchanged by the ravages of time. (3.8, 3.9) (Played by THOMAS SANGSTER, HUW REES)

Launch Day: The day when the Master planned to launch his two thousand war rockets at the rest of the universe, via a rift in Braccatolian space, and so begin the New Time Lord Empire. (3.13)

Laurenzi, the: New York theatre where the New York Revue was playing. Tallulah was a solo singer there; Myrna and Lois were dancers for the 'Heaven and Hell' routine. Tallulah was also having a relationship with one of the stagehands, Laszlo. Beneath the theatre were the New York sewers, where the Daleks' Pig Slaves roamed, stealing people for use in the Daleks' Final Experiment. The Doctor used the auditorium of the theatre for a final showdown with the Cult of Skaro and their Dalek-Human army, in which three members of the Cult and all of the Dalek Humans died. (3.4, 3.5)

LazLabs: Aka Lazarus Laboratories, the company run by Professor Richard Lazarus, who unveiled his Genetic Manipulation Device at a gala reception in the foyer of the LazLabs building to the press and potential investors. (3.6)

Lee, Brenda: American singer, often referred to as Little Miss Dynamite. Her song 'Rockin' Around The Christmas Tree' was playing in the house where the Graske replaced the parents with changelings. (AotG)

Leeds: British city in Yorkshire, which had elected one of the ghosts (in reality, a Cyberman still semi-existing within the Void) as their MP. (2.12)

Legion of the Beast: The eyes and ears of the Beast, in this case, the entire stock of Ood aboard Sanctuary Base 6, led by the possessed human archaeologist Toby Zed. (2.8, 2.9)

LAZARUS, PROFESSOR RICHARD: Creator of the Genetic Manipulation Device, with which he claimed he could change what it meant to be human. He entered the machine aged 76 and came out nearly 40 years younger, his DNA hvaing been rewritten. However, in undoing his DNA, he brought to the surface a series of molecules that were otherwise dormant in humanity and these quickly became dominant in him, transforming him into a savage arthropod, needing to draw the life energy out of other humans to survive. Believing he had the changes under control, Lazarus continued to maintain that what he was doing was essential to the future of mankind but, with each change, more people had to die. Eventually he sought refuge in Southwark Cathedral, just as he had done as a boy during the Second World War. There the Doctor magnified the sonic resonance of the cathedral's organ, disorienting Lazarus, who fell from the bell tower, dying for good at his true 76 years of age. (3.6) (Played by MARK GATISS)

Lerner, Abi: Medical officer aboard the SS *Pentallian*, she was trying to diagnose what had happened to Korwin McDonnell when he allowed some of the sun that had possessed him to leak out of his eyes, reducing her to an ashen shadow on the wall. (3.7) (Played by VINETTE ROBINSON)

Lerner, Alan Jay: Co-writer of the song 'I Could Have Danced All Night', as sung by the Doctor upon returning from a party in 18th-century France when he was pretending to be drunk. (2.4)

Lever Room: Vast area dominating the top of Torchwood Tower with two huge levers operated by Jacob and Andrew, and a massive blank Wall at one end, through which the Torchwood Institute hoped ghosts would materialise whenever particle energy was fired at it. However, unbeknownst to Torchwood, the ghosts were Cybermen, which had already infiltrated the Tower. These Cybermen used reanimated Torchwood operatives to push the Lever Room to its fullest capacity, enabling tens of thousands of Cybermen to fully materialise on Earth and take over the planet. Following an attack by the Daleks, which had also emerged from the Void via Torchwood, the Doctor reversed the power of the Lever Room, keeping the levers erect long enough for all of the Cybermen and Daleks to be sucked back into the Void from which they had come. Rose Tyler very nearly joined them after losing her grip on one of the levers and was only saved by the 'Pete's World' version of her father, who rescued her and transported her to his home, sealing Rose off from the Doctor, presumably for ever. (2.12, 2.13)

Lewis, Sgt/DI Robert: Fictional character created by Colin Dexter for his range of Inspector Morse novels, later successfully translated into a major television series. Lewis later got his own TV show. The Doctor called Rose Tyler 'Lewis' when he pretended they were both police officers investigating the disappearances of the children in Dame Kelly Holmes Close. (2.11)

Life and Adventures of Martin Chuzzlewit, The: A book cited by the Doctor as one of Charles Dickens' canon that he'd read. The Doctor told Dickens that he didn't like the section set in America. (1.3)

Lilith: Carrionite daughter to Mother Bloodtide and Mother Doomfinger, and leader of the three aliens trying to create their Millennium of Blood – a resurgence of the Carrionite Empire. Lilith was an expert in spellcasting via word-shaping, naming and the use of dolls laced with human hair. When William Shakespeare turned their spellcasting back on them, Lilith and her mothers were trapped inside their crystal ball for eternity. (3.2) (Played by CHRISTINA COLE)

Limehouse Green Station: Railway station close to Albion Hospital and the area of the crashed Chula medical ship that the military were guarding. (1.9, 1.10)

LINDA: Acronymic name created by Elton Pope for the band of Doctor-hunters who met up beneath the old Library on London's Macateer Street. The London Investigation 'N' Detective Agency used to meet and spend more time having fun with their singalongs than searching out aliens – until Victor Kennedy arrived and took charge, giving each member a job. Kennedy was in fact the Abzorbaloff and one by one he absorbed the group until only Elton was left to face him, aided by the Doctor and Rose Tyler. (2.10)

Linda [1]: Housemate alongside Strood, Crosbie and Lynda in the *Big Brother* house some time prior to the Doctor's arrival there. She was forcibly evicted for damaging a camera. Presumably, she ended up on the Dalek mothership and was turned into a Dalek. (1.12)

Linda [2]: One of the Master's minions, working in 10 Downing Street. (3.12)

'Lion Sleeps Tonight, The': Originally a South African song written by Solomon Linda in 1939 as 'Mbube' (Zulu for 'lion'). Various lyrics were added over the years by western musicians. The most popular version was recorded in 1961 by The Tokens, and it was this song which Mr Crane played loudly to cover the screams as Morris and the other homeless people were given the Ultimate Upgrade on 'Pete's World'. It was not The Tokens' version, however, but the 1981 Tight Fit cover version – track 19 on Crane's CD. (2.5

Lion King, The: Disney movie (their first full-length animation not based on a pre-existing work) which featured a song, 'The Circle of Life', that the Doctor quoted to the Sycorax Leader. (2.X)

Lissak, Erina: One of the crew aboard the SS *Pentallian*, she came from a rich family background and chose to go to work on the cargo ship to 'slum it' and make a point to her mother. She signed up after meeting Riley Vashtee in a coffee house, on Torajii Alpha, which her mother owned. (3.7P) She was killed by the sun-possessed Korwin McDonnell. (3.7) (Played by REBECCA OLDFIELD)

Lissak, Stefan: Erina Lissak's elder brother back on Torajii Alpha, favoured by their mother. (3.7P)

Little Girl: Small child who, along with her parents (played by DARIUS WALKER, DURINE HOWELL), was caught up in the Racnoss attack on London, and stood in the path of an energy weapon from the Webstar. She was pulled to safety by her father. (3.X) (Played by ZAFIRAH BOATENG)

Little Lord Fauntleroy: Aspirational 19th-century novel by Frances Hodgson Burnett about an American boy who goes to live in England and becomes part of the aristocracy. Henry Van Statten referred to Adam Mitchell as 'Little Lord Fauntleroy' in a derogatory sense. (1.6)

Little Nell: Heroine from the novel *The Old Curiosity Shop* by Charles Dickens. The Doctor asked Dickens to read the section in which she dies to him. Unsurprisingly, Dickens didn't. (1.3)

Llewellyn, Daniel: Project Manager at the British Rocket Group, charged with overseeing the Guinevere One Space Probe on its mission to Mars. When the Sycorax transported him aboard their ship, he volunteered to make contact with them as the probe had been his responsibility. The Sycorax Leader murdered him with his whip. (2.X) (Played by DANIEL EVANS)

Lloyd George, David: The Doctor tells Rose that he used to go drinking with this Liberal Prime Minister of the early 20th century. (1.4)

Lloyd, Arthur: London householder who reluctantly joined his wife and son in their air-raid shelter when the sirens started during his dinner, in late January 1941. When the raid was over, the Lloyds discovered Nancy attempting to leave their house, after she had allowed the stray children she was protecting to eat the family's evening meal. Nancy then blackmailed him into giving her other things she needed, including a torch and some wire-cutters, by threatening to expose that it was Arthur, not his wife, having an affair with Mr Haverstock, the butcher. (1.9, 1.10) (Played by DAMIAN SAMUELS)

Lloyd, Mrs: London housewife who hurried to get her husband and son into their air-raid shelter when the sirens started during their evening meal, in late January 1941. Many of the locals assumed she was having an affair with the local butcher, which explained how she always had lots of meat to feed her family. (1.9, 1.10) (Played by CHERYL FERGISON)

Lloyd, Timothy: Son of the owners of the house which Nancy broke into, bringing with her the stray former evacuees to eat the Lloyds' food. Nancy was also spooked by the child wearing a gas mask who was wandering the streets, seeking his lost mummy. When Timothy returned to his house, wearing his, Nancy was understandably alarmed. (1.9, 1.10) (Played by LUKE PERRY)

Loch Ness Monster: Sarah Jane Smith told Rose Tyler that, during her time travelling with the Doctor, they had encountered the Loch Ness Monster – in reality, a creature called the Skarasen. (2.3)

Locke, Governor: The real Governor of Volag-Noc. Locke was a robot, and he was sadly lacking in compassion. When the Doctor met him, he'd been rewired under the orders of the new Governor, former inmate Gurney. When the Doctor freed Locke, the robot Governor decided to murder all the inmates of Volag-Noc. This was not part of his deal with the Doctor, who disabled him, returning later and reprogramming him to run a better prison. (TIQ) (Voiced by DAN MORGAN)

Lockley: Schoolboy at Farringham School for Boys in 1913 who was placed in charge of the gathering before the Family of Blood attacked (3.9)

Loewe, Frederick: Co-writer of the song 'I Could Have Danced All Night', as sung by the Doctor upon returning from a party in 18th-century France when he was pretending to be drunk. (2.4)

Lois: Dancer at the Laurenzi theatre in 1930s New York, taking part in the New York Revue. When Martha Jones needed to get across the stage to find Laszlo, she accidentally trod on Lois's costume's tail, causing Lois to tumble. (3.4) (Played by ALEXIS CALEY)

London Credit Bank: Financial institution whose cashpoint machine the Doctor soniced to get it to spew thousands of pounds into the street to distract the Santa Roboforms, giving him the chance to pursue the taxi which had kidnapped Donna Noble. (3.X)

LONDON: Capital city of the United Kingdom. Rose Tyler, Mickey Smith, (1.1) Martha Jones (3.1) and Donna Noble (3.X) and their respective families all lived there. The Doctor met Captain Jack Harkness there. (1.9) Autons, the Nestene Consciousness, (1.1) the Family Slitheen, (1.4, 1.5) Reapers, (1.8) the Chula nanogenes and the resultant gas mask zombies, (1.9, 1.10) Roboform mercenaries disguised as Santas, (2.X, 3.X) Krillitanes, (2.3) the Wire, (2.7) a Hoix, the Abzorbaloff, (2.10) an Isolus, (2.11) Cybermen, Daleks, (2.12, 2.13) the Racnoss, (3.X) Slabs, a Plasmavore, (3.1) Carrionites, (3.2) the Lazarus Creature, (3.6) the Weeping Angels, (3.10) and the Master using the remnants of the human race disguised as the Toclafane (3.12, 3.13) have all been spotted in London at various times. The 'Pete's World' London was overrun by Cybus Industries' Cybermen. (2.5, 2.6) Amongst the London landmarks involved in alien activity have been the London Eye, (1.1) Big Ben, (1.4, 1.5, 2.X) 10 Downing Street, (1.4, 1.5, 3.12) 30 St Mary Axe, (2.X) Alexandra Palace, (2.7) the 2012 Olympic Stadium, (2.11) Canary Wharf, (2.12, 2.13) the Thames Barrier, (3.X) the Globe Theatre, (3.2) and Southwark Cathedral. (3.6) On 'Pete's World', Battersea Power Station was where Cybus Industries set up their Cyber-conversion factories. (2.5, 2.6) Martha Jones claimed she had returned to London to collect from a disused UNIT base the final phial of liquid needed to arm the gun she was supposedly preparing to kill the Master with. (3.13)

London Eye: Also known as the Millennium Wheel and situated on London's South Bank, near Westminster Bridge. The Nestene Consciousness had set up a base below it, and used the shape of the wheel to transmit its activation signal to the dormant Autons throughout London. (1.1)

Lonely Assassins: See *Weeping Angels*

Lonely God, the: Legendary name for the traveller to whom, it was believed, the Face of Boe would impart a great secret. This traveller was in fact the Doctor. (2.1, 3.3)

Lord Provost: Queen Victoria believed, thanks to the psychic paper, that the Lord Provost George Jamieson had assigned the Doctor as her protector for her journey to Balmoral Castle. (2.2)

Los Angeles Crevasse: Area on Earth where Lady Cassandra grew up. (1.2)

Lost Dimension, the: A term used by the Doctor to describe the Void, through which the TARDIS passed to arrive on 'Pete's World'. (2.5)

Louis XV, King: Ruler of France and Navarre, and lover of Reinette in her later life, he was dubious about the Doctor until he was saved by him from the Clockwork Men. When the Doctor arrived back in France in 1764, it was in time to see Reinette's hearse leaving Versailles for the last time, and the King gave the Doctor a letter from his mistress. (2.4) (Played by BEN TURNER)

'Love Don't Roam': Song played at Donna Noble and Lance Bennett's reception to celebrate their non-wedding, which made the Doctor think of Rose Tyler. It was sung by Neil Hannon. (3.X)

Love's Labour's Lost: A play by William Shakespeare. The Doctor and Martha Jones attended a performance at the Globe Theatre, after which William Shakespeare announced the sequel, *Love's Labour's Won*. (3.2)

Love's Labour's Won: Possibly a play by William Shakespeare, thought lost by Martha Jones's time. In fact, Shakespeare had nearly finished it, but the Carrionites influenced the final scene, coercing him to write words that would open up a portal between the Globe Theatre and the Deep Darkness, freeing the other Carrionites trapped there. When Shakespeare used the Carrionites' methods against them and defeated them, all copies of the manuscript were sucked into the Deep Darkness along with the Carrionites. The Doctor convinced Shakespeare not to start the play again. (3.2)

Lovely Bones, The: Novel by Alice Seabold, which the Doctor speed-read in Rose Tyler's flat. (1.1)

Lucifer [1]: The dish Gaffabeque originated on the planet Lucifer, not Mars. Rose Tyler didn't know this when asked by the Anne Droid in *The Weakest Link* aboard the Game Station. (1.12)

Lucifer [2]: Legendary demon name, one of many attributed to the Beast throughout the galaxies. (2.8, 2.9)

Lucky: Title of a book by Jackie Collins, not Jackie Stewart. Rodrick didn't know this when asked by the Anne Droid in *The Weakest Link* aboard the Game Station. (1.12)

Lucy: One of the catering staff employed by Pete Tyler on 'Pete's World' to serve at the party for his wife Jackie's birthday. Whilst serving salmon pinwheels, she told the Doctor who the President of Great Britain was. If she wasn't killed when the Cybermen attacked the party, she was most likely taken to Battersea Power Station and her brain placed into a Cyberform. (2.5)

Luke: Schoolboy at Deffry Vale High School, selected by Mr Wagner to help solve the Skasas Paradigm. (2.3) (Played by BENJAMIN SMITH)

Lumic, John: On 'Pete's World', Lumic was the owner of Cybus Industries. Suffering from a terminal degenerative illness, Lumic had developed the Ultimate Upgrade process. This was a process by which human brains would be transplanted into a Cyberform (or Cyberman) – a body made of Lumic's High Content Metal steel. He tried to sell this concept to the President of Great Britain, not just as a commercial venture but also hoping that, with more research, it might solve his own health problems. When the President refused to support his proposals, Lumic sent the Cybermen that were already operational to kill the President at Pete Tyler's house during Jackie Tyler's birthday party. He then sent his Cybermen out onto the streets, ready to forcibly upgrade the population. After he had been fatally injured by Mr Crane, the Cybermen disregarded his orders and placed his mind inside that of a Cyberform – he became their Cyber Controller. If anything of Lumic was still there after that, it was lost when the Cyber Controller was destroyed. (2.5, 2.6) (Played by ROGER LLOYD PACK)

Lunar Penal Colony: Where the Game Station Security Guard told the Doctor, Captain Jack Harkness and Lynda Moss they would be sent to, without trial. (1.12)

Lupine-Wavelength-Haemovariform: According to the Doctor, this was the correct name for the werewolf that prowled Torchwood House. (2.2)

Lute: Taller of Jabe's two associates from the Forest of Cheem aboard Platform One. He was distressed to hear of Jabe's death from the Doctor. (1.2) (Played by ALAN RUSCOE)

Lynam, Des: Former presenter of the Channel 4 quiz show *Countdown*. After the Toclafane invasion, *Countdown* was cancelled, much to the chagrin of Professor Docherty. (3.13)

Lyndstep Crescent: Road close to the Powell Estate where the Doctor walked with Rose Tyler after the Auton arm had attacked them both in her mum's flat. (1.1)

Lynley: Master of the Revels in 1599, whose job it was to read and approve plays and decide if they were fit to go before the public. He threatened to ban *Love's Labour's Won* from being performed as he'd not had the chance to read it, so Lilith the Carrionite used her spellcasting to drown him in a dry street, then give him a heart attack. (3.2) (Played by CHRIS LARKIN)

Lynn, Auntie: Guest at the wedding of her nephew Stuart Hoskins and Sarah Clark. She hadn't arrived, nor had her husband Steven. (1.8)

Lynne, Jeff: British producer, composer and singer for the Idle Race, The Move, the Travelling Wilburys plus solo artists such as Tom Petty, Roy Orbison and George Harrison. However, he was most famously associated with the Electric Light Orchestra, of which Elton Pope was a huge fan. (2.10)

M4: London to South Wales motorway the Roboform taxi driver took Donna Noble on instead of turning off for Chiswick. (3.X)

Ma: Passenger in a car on the New New York Motorway. Tired of the endless delays, her husband overrode the onboard computer that registered how many adults were aboard and lied to the computer at the Transit Authority. Saying that there were three adults in his car gave them access to the Fast Lane, where they were attacked and killed by the Macra. (3.3) (Played by JUDY NORMAN)

Macaulay, Thomas Babbington: Author of the poem 'Horatius', quoted by Mr Jefferson as a tribute to Scooti Manista after she had been murdered by the possessed Toby Zed. (2.8)

Macateer Street, Unit 4b: Location of the basement room beneath a deserted library where LINDA had their fun-filled meetings until Victor Kennedy arrived and forced them to work harder at hunting down the Doctor and Rose Tyler. (2.10)

Mackeson: One of the soldiers under Captain Reynolds protecting Queen Victoria in 1879. (2.2)

MacLeish, Lady Isobel: Wife of Sir Robert and lady of Torchwood House, she bravely tried to keep spirits up among her staff when they were imprisoned by the Brethren of St Catherine and faced the Haemovariform. She led her maids and cook to the kitchens where they filled pans and buckets with mistletoe to distract the werewolf. After her husband's sacrifice, Lady Isobel opted not to remain at Torchwood House, and it passed to the Crown. (2.2) (Played by MICHELLE DUNCAN)

MacLeish, Sir George: Father to Sir Robert, and friend of Prince Albert. A polymath, equally au fait with science and legends and folklore as was the Queen's consort, he designed and built a huge telescope which, when linked to the Koh-I-Noor diamond, would create a beam of light powerful enough to destroy the Haemovariform. (2.2)

MacLeish, Sir Robert: Having inherited his home from his father, Sir Robert never understood the work his father and Prince Albert, the Queen's consort, had undertaken in the Observatory of Torchwood House. When the Brethren came, he was unable to stop them taking the house over and setting a trap for the Queen – his wife, Lady Isobel, and the entire household were held captive. After the Haemovariform escaped, Sir Robert realised the only way to salvage his family name and reputation was to sacrifice himself to protect the Queen – and so he held the werewolf

off for a few vital seconds outside the Observatory before becoming its final victim. (2.2) (Played by DEREK RIDDELL)

MacNannovich, Cal 'Spark Plug': He and an unnamed companion were guests aboard Platform One to see the Earthdeath spectacle. (1.2)

Macra, the: Massive crustaceans living beneath the lanes of the enclosed New New York Motorway, feeding off the exhaust fumes which most likely escaped from the New New York Zoo at some point. The Macra had once run an empire of enslavement and terror centuries before, but over the aeons had devolved into mindless brutes, acting only on instinct. As a result, cars reaching the lowest level, the Fast Lane, tended to be swatted down by the Macra, who regarded them as pests to be knocked aside. When the Doctor opened the covered Motorway and freed the cars trapped inside, the Macra were left down there, presumably to be rehoused in the Zoo at some point as the exhaust fumes they thrived on would soon dissipate. (3.3)

Macrae Cantrell, Suki: An eager young journalist, hoping that her work would get her noticed. Born in the Independent Republic of Morocco

Maddock Way Surgery. The TARDIS landed there a year after taking Rose away (1.4) and later crashlanded there after the Doctor's regeneration. (2.X)

Maeve: Elderly resident of Dame Kelly Homes Close who suspected that the disappearances of the neighbourhood kids weren't natural and had her suspicions about Chloe Webber. She thanked Rose when the kids were returned safely. (2.11) (Played by EDNA DORE)

Mafeking: South African town that was the scene of a 217-day siege in 1899–1900, during the closing months of the Second Boer War, which was decisive in the British victory in that conflict. The definitive account of the siege was written by Aitchinson Price, according to history teacher John Smith. (3.8)

Magna-clamp: Alien magnetic technology that made anything heavy virtually weightless and therefore easy to move. Jackie Tyler thought that would be handy for carrying the shopping. The Doctor used them to hold himself and Rose Tyler to the wall when opening the Lever Room entrance to the Void, as the Daleks and Cybermen were sucked back in. Rose Tyler lost her grip on hers while trying to operate a Lever and was only saved by the 'Pete's World' version of her father, who rescued her and transported her to his home, sealing Rose off from the Doctor, presumably for ever. (2.12, 2.13)

in 199'89, her hobbies included reading and archaeology and she took a job on Satellite Five to cover her sister's university fees then applied for a promotion to Floor 500. This was successful but, when Suki got there, she discovered what was really in control of Earth – the Jagrafess. The Editor, the Jagrafess's human associate, revealed that he knew the truth about Suki; that she was not the humble journalist she pretended, but was in fact self-declared anarchist Eva Saint Julienne, the last known member of the Freedom Fifteen, a group determined to prove that Satellite Five was being manipulated by outside sources. The Jagrafess killed Suki/Eva and reanimated her corpse via her chip implant to work for him. However, when the Jagrafess was destroyed, a tiny spark of Suki/Eva still existed and she stopped the Editor from escaping the carnage, resulting in both their destructions. (1.7) (Played by ANNA MAXWELL-MARTIN)

Madame de Pompadour, SS: Spaceship in the 51st century, run by Clockwork repair robots, which were using time-window technology to travel back to 18th-century France to find the real Madame de Pompadour and, in their skewed logic, remove her brain to enable them to fly the ship properly – at a point when she was 37, the same age as the ship. The crew had already been sacrificed, their body parts integrated unsuccessfully into the ship's workings. When the Clockwork Robots were all deactivated, their mission failed, the lifeless SS *Madame de Pompadour* continued floating aimlessly through space. (2.4)

Maddock Way: Road running through the middle of the Powell Estate in South East London, with shops along it such as Maddock Cleaners and the

Magpie, Mr:

Small businessman, running his own shop selling electrical goods such as radios and televisions in Muswell Hill during the early 1950s. The alien criminal known as the Wire inhabited one of his television sets, spreading its influence across many others in his store, which he then sold across the area. He worked for the Wire out of fear – the creature promised not to steal his face if he followed her orders. Under the Wire's guidance, he built a primitive portable television which he took to the Alexandra Palace television mast, through which the Wire would be able to spread itself further afield. When Magpie finally decided to fight back, the Wire vaporised him. (2.7) (Played by RON COOK)

Magpie's Electricals: Retail business based on Mafeking Road, in Muswell Hill in North London, and owned by Mr Magpie in the 1950s, specialising in the then-new television sets and aerials. Thanks to the upcoming Coronation and his own very low prices, Magpie was able to see an upswing in sales. (2.7) The business was still running nearly 60 years after the death of Mr Magpie, reportedly initially taken over by his son, as the loudspeakers used by the DJ at Donna Noble's wedding reception (3.X) and Martha Jones's television set (3.12) were both supplied by Magpie's Electricals. One of its delivery men set up the television set for the Connolly family. (2.7T) (Played by KEVIN HUDSON)

Malcassairo: Planet on the very edge of the universe, where the human refugees of the year 100,000,000,000,000 had gathered. The Malmooth who originally dominated the planet were all but gone and, after the rocket took off, the effectively dead world of Malcassairo was left in the hands of the bestial Futurekind. (3.11)

The Master

And I looked down upon my new dominion, as Master of all. And I thought it good.

Plagued by the never-ending sound of drumming in his head, the Master was one of the Doctor's childhood friends, driven insane after looking into the Untempered Schism on Gallifrey when he was just eight years old. Like the Doctor, the Master was responsible for choosing his own name, and stole a TARDIS in order to flee Gallifreyan society and explore the universe. Unlike the Doctor, however, the Master craved domination, and sought alliances with a number of alien races during his early attempts to conquer the Earth – including the Nestene Consciousness, Axons, Daleks and Sea Devils. It was also during this time that he and the Doctor came to the attention of organisations such as UNIT and Torchwood. Despite running out of regenerations and eventually dying, the Master's consciousness was revived by the Time Lords during the course of the Time War, when he was resurrected to serve as the perfect warrior.

The Master was present when the Dalek Emperor took control of the Cruciform, but fled to the end of the universe in order to escape, making himself human in the process. After 17 years hiding as Professor Yana on Malcassairo, it was a chance encounter with the Doctor, Martha Jones and Captain Jack Harkness that caused the Master to regain his identity, encouraged by echoes of his past incarnations contained within the Professor's fob watch. He promptly seized the opportunity to steal both the Doctor's severed hand and the TARDIS, and return to Earth – but not before suffering a fatal gunshot from the Professor's companion, Chantho, and undergoing a regeneration. (3.11)

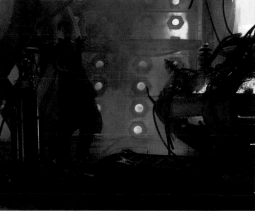

before publicly announcing his relationship with the Toclafane to the world. It was during first contact with the Toclafane on board the *Valiant* that the Master revealed his true identity and ordered the assassination of US President Winters at the hands of the Toclafane. Assuming authority over the entire Earth, the Master then used the Paradox Machine to allow the Toclafane to invade from the end of the universe, and ordered the decimation of the planet's populace, keeping an aged Doctor, Jack and the Jones family prisoner aboard the *Valiant* in order to watch his victory. (3.12)

Abandoning the Doctor in the far future, the Master travelled to Earth in 2007, shortly after the downfall of Harriet Jones PM. He then met Lucy Saxon, and took her to the end of the universe to see Utopia, where the human race had devolved and were converted into the Toclafane. Returning to Earth, the Master married Lucy and assumed the role of Harry Saxon, creating an entire history for his alter ego. As Saxon, the Master claimed to have attended and graduated from Cambridge University, gone into business, succeeded in his athletics career, and even written a novel, *Kiss Me, Kill Me*.

Over the course of a year, the Master constructed an army of 200,000 war rockets in shipyards around the world, and was planning to open a rift in Braccatolian space as part of his bid to launch a new Time Lord Empire, and adopt a new Gallifrey alongside it. Egotistical and overindulgent, the Master had his likeness carved into the face of Mount Rushmore and recreated across the globe in the form of colossal statues. He also collected wives from across the continents in addition to Lucy, and would insist upon receiving a massage every day at three o'clock. It was through such predictability – the Doctor knew he couldn't resist a countdown – that the Doctor was able to rejuvenate himself and defeat the Master, restoring time to a point before the Toclafane ever invaded.

During this time, the Master cannibalised the TARDIS and converted it into a Paradox Machine, as well as starting work for the Ministry of Defence, where he was responsible for launching the Archangel mobile phone network, shooting down the Racnoss Webstar on Christmas Eve, and funding Richard Lazarus's rejuvenation experiments. He also assisted in designing the *Valiant* aircraft carrier for UNIT. He would later incorporate Lazarus's findings into the functions of his own laser screwdriver, enabling it to age individuals beyond their natural life spans, whilst also dispensing deadly laser bolts at his attackers.

As a fellow Time Lord, the Doctor took responsibility for the Master's actions, and intended to spend the rest of his lives caring for him within the safety of the TARDIS. When the Master was shot dead by his abused wife, he refused to regenerate in spite of the Doctor's wishes, willingly allowing himself to die in order to secure one final victory over his opponent. His body was then set upon a funeral pyre and burned by a devastated Doctor, though his ring was later removed from the embers by a mysterious female hand... (3.13)

The Master was elected Prime Minister of Great Britain in 2008, assisted by the mesmeric influence of the Archangel network, which tricked the Earth into believing his deceits, whilst also concealing his presence from the Doctor. His supporters at this time included Sharon Osbourne, pop group McFly and Ann Widdecombe MP. As Saxon, the Master also ensured that Tish Jones was able to secure jobs with both LazLabs and himself, whilst simultaneously using his operatives to spread disinformation about the Doctor to Francine Jones. In the role of Prime Minister, his first unofficial duty was to oversee the execution of the Cabinet in his office,

(Played by ROGER DELGADO, ANTHONY AINLEY, DEREK JACOBI, JOHN SIMM, WILLIAM HUGHES)

M

Male Crewmember: Realising that the SS *Madame de Pompadour* was about to be caught up in an ion storm, he and his fellow crewmember sent a mayday back to Earth. When the ion storm struck, he was left unconscious but safe, until a Clockwork Robot arrived on the bridge. (2.4T) (Played by DAVID MARTIN)

Malmooth: Blue-skinned insectoid race which once dominated Malcassairo but had almost died out. Only Chantho survived, helping Professor Yana for 17 years as he tried to launch a rocket that would take the human refugees to Utopia. (3.11)

Man: Passer-by in the street in 1883 at Christmas, when a young street urchin was kidnapped by the Graske. (AotG) (Played by ROGER NOTT)

Manchester: Metropolis in North West England. Home of the Mitchell family, including Adam, who briefly travelled with the Doctor and Rose Tyler. (1.7)

Manchester Suite [1]: Where Platform One held the reception for alien dignitaries to observe Earthdeath. Its sunfilters were momentarily lowered, causing the deaths of some visitors, including the Moxx of Balhoon. (1.2)

Manchester Suite [2]: Where the reception for the non-wedding of Donna Noble and Lance Bennett was held. The reception guests were attacked by Roboform mercenaries searching for Donna. (3.X)

Manhattan: Island district of New York, often separated into three regions, Lower, Midtown and Upper. The Cult of Skaro ended up there after fleeing the Battle of Canary Wharf and began plotting to create a New Skaro from a Transgenic Laboratory they had converted in the sewers beneath the Empire State Building. (3.4, 3.5)

Manista, Scootori: 20-year-old Torchwood trainee Maintenance Officer on Sanctuary Base 6. She discovered the possessed Toby Zed standing unharmed on the exposed surface of Krop Tor but, when she tried to report

116   DOCTOR WHO: THE ENCYCLOPEDIA

this, he psionically locked the doors, trapping her in one area, which he then opened to the elements, sending Scooti to her death in the vacuum of space. (2.8) (Played by MYANNA BURING)

Manservant: Sent by Madame Poisson to retrieve her daughter from her room, he was shocked to discover the Doctor there. (2.4) (Played by GARETH WYN GRIFFITHS)

Mantasphid Queen: A manipulative insect. She controlled the hive mind of the Mantasphids, an incredibly intelligent insectoid race, who colonised fertile planets full of dung. The Queen set up home on Myarr, then exiled the human colonists already there and thus found herself leading her people into a war with the Earth Empire of the 40th century. Ultimately she faced defeat and total annihilation at the hands of the humans until the Doctor stepped in and pretended to Earth Control that it was he, Doctor Vile, who had forced the Mantasphids to attack the humans on his behalf. The Doctor then fled Myarr, leaving the Mantasphids and humans to broker a peace deal. (TIQ) (Voiced by LIZZIE HOPLEY)

Mantasphids: An incredibly intelligent alien insectoid race. They colonised fertile planets full of dung, including Myarr, then exiled the human colonists already there and thus found themselves at war with the Earth Empire of the 40th century. (TIQ)

Marbella: Popular beach resort in Spain's Costa del Sol. The Doctor told Rose Tyler that they could easily head there in 1989, and leave the Daleks to destroy humanity in 200,100. (1.13)

Marcie: Front Desk Officer at the police station where Billy Shipton was a detective inspector. (3.10)

Marconi's Disease: An illness that took years to recover from but by using a cell-washing cascade, the Sisters of Plenitude on New Earth had developed a cure that took two days. (2.1)

Maria: Shakespearian character from *Love's Labour's Lost* and later *Love's Labour's Won*. (3.2)

Maria Leszczynska, Queen: Wife of King Louis XV of France and friend to Madame de Pompadour, despite her being the King's lover. She was present when Clockwork Robots from the 51st century attacked a party at the Palace of Versailles and the Doctor saved Madame de Pompadour's life. She died in 1768. (2.4) (Played by GAYLE ANN FELTON)

Mark, John: Olympic Torch-bearer at the 1948 Olympic Games in North London whom the Doctor admired. (2.11)

Market Tavern: Pub where the Jones family celebrated Leo Jones's 21st birthday, until a row erupted between Francine Jones and Clive's new girlfriend, Annalise. (3.1)

Marley, Jacob: Ghostly character in Dickens' *A Christmas Carol*, which the author read to an enrapt Welsh audience on Christmas Eve 1869. (1.3)

Marr, Andrew: BBC reporter outside 10 Downing Street after the Big Ben incident, who wondered where the Prime Minister was. (1.4)

Mars: Jackie Tyler and her friends drunkenly toasted the supposed 'Martians' that crashed a spaceship into Big Ben and then the Thames. (1.4) Adam Mitchell pretended to be a student visiting Satellite Five from the University of Mars. (1.7) The Guinevere One space probe was headed to Mars when the Sycorax ship intercepted it. Major Blake of UNIT knew the Sycorax weren't natives of Mars because Martians looked completely different. (2.X) When unexpectedly travelling in the TARDIS, Jackie told the Doctor that, if he took her to Mars, she'd kill him. (2.12) Donna Noble assumed the Doctor was from Mars when she first met him. (3.X)

Martian Boondocks: Area on Mars known to be associated with the University there. (1.7)

Martian Drones: In social security, the payment given to Martian Drones was Default. Colleen knew this when asked by the Anne Droid in *The Weakest Link* aboard the Game Station. (1.12)

Marx Brothers: Fraternal American film comedy troupe of the 1920s, 1930s and 1940s, whose movie *Duck Soup* gave the Doctor the fictitious name of Freedonia, the country he told William Shakespeare that Martha Jones hailed from. (3.2)

Master of the Revels: Official 'censor' of the Elizabethan era, based in Clerkenwell. The holder of the job had the power to halt any entertainment if, in their opinion, it failed to meet the criteria of good taste. The Master of the Revels when William Shakespeare was writing *Love's Labour's Won* was Mr Lynley, who was murdered by one of the Carrionites. (3.2)

Matt: Driver of the car that killed Pete Tyler in Jordan Road in 1987. Rather than checking on his victim, Matt panicked and drove away, never reporting the crime or being caught. When Rose Tyler's actions saved Pete's life, a breach in the fabric of time opened up and Matt and his car were projected a few miles down the road to St Christopher's Church. Matt was caught in an endless cycle of driving and panicking around the church until Pete Tyler realised what had happened. He ran out in front of the car and was killed. This time Matt did the right thing, and stayed put, while Pete died in the arms of a mysterious blonde no one ever traced. In fact, this was Rose Tyler. (1.8) (Played by CRISPIN LAYFIELD)

Mauve: The universally recognised colour for danger, according to the Doctor as the TARDIS pursues a Chula warship through the Time Vortex. (1.9)

Max: Nickname for the Mighty Jagrafess of the Holy Hadrojassic Maxarodenfoe, given to it by its human associate, the Editor. (1.7)

McAllister, Ewan: One of the arrivals at 10 Downing Street after the Big Ben incident. The Deputy Secretary for the Scottish Parliament, he was actually a disguised Slitheen, the original McAllister having been killed previously. (1.5)

McCrimmon, Dr James: Pseudonym the Doctor adopted for the benefit of Queen Victoria. Jamie McCrimmon had been a travelling companion of the Doctor during his second incarnation. (2.2)

McDonnell, Kath: Acerbic and quick-witted captain of the SS *Pentallian*, and ultimately responsible for the decision to use a fusion scoop to get matter from the living sun that then threatened her crew, because it was too expensive to scan for life first. As the sun-possessed version of her

husband, Korwin, began murdering her crew, she tried to understand what had happened, but it was only when the Doctor made contact with the living sun and became sun-possessed himself that she finally realised what had to be done. She led Korwin into an airlock and opened it into space, allowing herself and her husband to be sucked into the sun, where they died together. (3.6) (Played by MICHELLE COLLINS)

McDonnell, Korwin: Husband of Kath, the captain of the SS *Pentallian* which he was aboard. They had been married for 11 years and chose the ship together. He was the first victim of the living sun, angry that the *Pentallian* had scooped out part of its body – so it consumed Korwin and used him as a walking weapon aboard the ship, wrecking engineering and

so setting the ship on a course into the sun, thus regaining what it had lost. Korwin also began killing the crew one by one, although he infected Dev Ashton rather than killing him, needing a partner. However, the sun-possessed Korwin was notably weaker for doing this and Orin Scannell believed he had killed Korwin by freezing him with the ice vents. However, Korwin soon defrosted himself and began his relentless march through the ship, so Kath led him into an airlock, and opened it into space, allowing herself and her husband to be sucked into the sun, where they died together. (3.6) (Played by MATTHEW CHAMBERS)

McFly: British pop group, who endorsed Harry Saxon's campaign to become Prime Minister. (3.12)

McFly, Marty: The Doctor used the 1985 movie *Back to the Future* and its time-travelling lead character Marty McFly to explain to Martha Jones the complexities of the Infinite Temporal Flux. (3.2)

McKillan, Jane: One of the children drawn by Chloe Webber, who thus disappeared from Dame Kelly Holmes Close to become a friend for the Isolus. She later returned to the street after the Isolus left Earth. (2.11) (Played by GABRIELLE EVANS)

McKillan, Mrs: Mother of missing child Jane, who wept with joy when her daughter was returned to her after the Isolus left Earth. (2.11) (Played by KAREN HULSE)

McMillan: Torchwood Archive representative who sent Captain Walker and his crew to Krop Tor to examine the energy source detected ten miles beneath its surface. (2.8T) (Played by RI RICHARDS)

Medical: The area on Floor 016 of Satellite Five where Adam Mitchell went to receive an implant to give him access to the technology of the Spike Rooms. (1.7)

Medusa Cascade: The Doctor once single-handedly sealed a rift there. The Master reminded the Doctor of this when taunting him over his current defeat. (3.13)

Melanie: See *Safka-Schekeryk, Melanie Anne*

Melissa: Schoolgirl at Deffry Vale High School, she was one of the students mesmerised into helping solve the Skasas Paradigm. (2.3) (Played by LUCINDA DRYZEK)

Mellow: Coming in varying strengths, this was one of the Mood Patches available in Pharmacytown in the Undercity of New New York. (3.3)

Memphis: One of the cities Van Statten suggested dumping the mind-wiped Polkowski in. (1.6)

Ménière's Disease: Infection of the inner ear that causes vertigo. Martha Jones wondered if Florence Finnegan's dizzy spells were a symptom of this. (3.1)

Mergrass, Ulysses: A freelance military adviser and gunrunner, Mergrass had a reputation for finding anything for anyone, and was especially popular with the inmates of Volag-Noc. An amphibious lizard from Anura, he could only survive in non-water-based atmospheres by travelling everywhere with a liquid breathing tank. After selling weapons to the Mantasphids on Myarr but being betrayed by their Queen, Mergrass opted to flee, only to encounter his old enemy Baltazar, who murdered him by shattering his water tank. When the Doctor and Martha Jones found his dehydrated corpse, all they could do was retrieve the second datachip they needed to complete their quest to locate the *Infinite*. (TIQ) (Voiced by PAUL CLAYTON)

Merrick, John: The Doctor joked to Queen Victoria that he'd had the choice of buying either Rose Tyler or the disfigured Merrick, aka the Elephant Man, for sixpence. (2.2)

'Merry Xmas Everybody!': Christmas 1973 number one hit for Slade. It was playing on the radio in Clancy's Garage when Mickey Smith heard the TARDIS landing in the Powell Estate. (2.X) It was also being played a year later at the disco to celebrate the non-wedding of Donna Noble and Lance Bennett. (3.X)

Meta Sigmafolio: The Doctor suggested taking Martha Jones there, to see a burst of starfire over its coast. (3.13)

Metaltron: The name given to the Dalek in Henry Van Statten's underground Vault, because it refused to speak and reveal its identity. (1.6)

MI5: A division of the British Security Service, focusing on counter-intelligence. One of its operatives, Margaret Blaine, was murdered by Blon Fel Fotch Pasameer-Day Slitheen, and her body was used as a disguise. (1.4, 1.5) The fake Blaine later became Lord Mayor of Cardiff. (1.11)

Michael: Child at the reception for Donna Noble and Lance Bennett's non-wedding. Donna checked up on him after the attack by the Roboform Santas. (3.X)

Mick: Soldier based at Albion Hospital who led the search for the augmented pig that the Slitheen had launched into space, ensuring the subsequent crash back to Earth would cause a huge distraction and enable them to take over the British Government. (1.4)

Mighty Jagrafess of the Holy Hadrojassic Maxarodenfoe: Vast gastropodic creature that lived in the freezing ceiling of Floor 500 aboard Satellite Five. His vast metabolism required very low temperatures and he could potentially live for 3,000 years. As Editor-in-Chief, it controlled, via its human associate the Editor, the news and information gathered and disseminated around the Fourth Earth Empire. Its plan was to weaken the Empire, making it xenophobic and closing it off from other empires. In truth, it was installed at the behest of the Bad Wolf Corporation, and was controlled by the Daleks as part of a grand master plan by the Dalek Emperor. It was destroyed when the temperature, normally carefully controlled, was raised considerably, and the Jagrafess exploded. (1.7) Rose Tyler pretended to have authority granted to her by the Mighty Jagrafess to demand the Sycorax leave Earth. (2.X)

Millennium of Blood: The state of chaos the Carrionites wished to create on Earth by bringing the rest of the Carrionites to Elizabethan London. (3.2)

Millennium Square: Colloquial name for the large paved area at the front of the Millennium Arts Centre in Cardiff, stretching down to the Bay. Its main attraction is a water tower sculpture. Unknown to the vast majority of humans is that the area directly beneath the Square's concrete ground is a network of tunnels and rooms that make up Torchwood 3, a secret organisation specialising in investigating alien incursions into Wales, run by Captain Jack Harkness. (1.11, 3.11)

Miller, Alton Glenn: American jazz musician who seemingly died in 1944 while en route to France to entertain the troops. Captain Jack Harkness and Rose Tyler danced before the face of Big Ben atop an invisible Chula ship to Miller's composition 'Moonlight Serenade'. (1.9) The Doctor and Rose, watched by Jack, later danced to his 'In the Mood' tune in the TARDIS control room. (1.10)

Milligan, Thomas: Former paediatrician who had survived the Toclafane purges because he was considered useful as a member of the Peripatetic Medical Squad. In fact, he was part of the British resistance and helped bring Martha Jones back to Britain after a year away, believing she was

assembling a special gun with which to kill the Master. Thomas was killed defending Martha on the streets of London, but after time jumped out of synch and erased the previous year, Martha was delighted to discover that Thomas was alive again and working in a children's hospital. (3.13) (Played by TOM ELLIS)

Milo [1]: Studious boy at Deffry Vale High School, who knew much more information than he should have done, due to eating chips cooked in Krillitane Oil. (2.3) (Played by CLEM TIBBER)

Milo [2]: Young man in New New York who was heading to Brooklyn for a job in the Foundries there, thus creating a new home for himself, Cheen and their unborn son, away from the Undercity. He and Cheen kidnapped Martha Jones so that they could legitimately register as having three adults aboard their car and gain access to the Fast Lane. Once down there, the car was attacked by the Macra and Milo switched off everything in the vehicle to avoid attracting their attention. Realising that they would run out of air, Milo reactivated the car and they took their chances at trying to get away from the creatures. When the Doctor reopened the cover of the Motorway, Milo and Cheen were able to drive up to the Overcity and start a new life up there. (3.3) (Played by TRAVIS OLIVER)

Ministry of Asteroids: The Doctor planned to pretend to be a Doctor John Smith working for this fictitious government department when he arrived in London during the Blitz. (1.9)

Minneapolis: One of the cities Van Statten suggested dumping the mind-wiped Polkowski in. (1.6)

Minogue, Kylie: Australian actress and singer. The Doctor quoted her song 'Never Too Late' to Tommy Connolly as they headed to Alexandra Palace to put a stop to the Wire's Time of Manifestation. (2.7)

Minto Road: Trying to interest Rose Tyler, Mickey Smith asked Jackie Tyler if she'd been to a new pizza parlour on Minto Road, which had previously been a Christmas shop. (1.13)

Mirror: National UK tabloid paper. They were prepared to pay £500 to interview Rose Tyler after the explosion at Henrik's department store. (1.1)

Missouri: American state where some of the citizens of Manhattan's Hooverville were from. (3.4)

Mistletoe: The Brethren of St Catherine had trained the Haemovariform they unleashed to hate mistletoe, and they wore the plant for protection against it. Lady Isobel MacLeish and her staff filled buckets and pans with mistletoe and threw it over the werewolf, disorientating it for long enough to gain a brief respite from its attack. (2.2)

MITCHELL, ADAM: English genius, fresh out of university, and working for Henry Van Statten. He had hacked into the Pentagon's computer systems when he was eight years old. Van Statten employed Adam to go through the flotsam and jetsam of alien tech he collected and discover what it was, how it worked and to suggest ways of utilising it for Geocomtex. Adam was a bit of a dreamer and was fascinated by the universe, wondering what it was like out there. He and Rose Tyler were pursued by the Dalek once it had escaped the Vault in Henry Van Statten's underground base and, although Adam got away, Rose was captured. After the Dalek was destroyed, Rose persuaded the Doctor to take Adam in the TARDIS. (1.6) The TARDIS then took him to visit Satellite Five. Wandering off by himself, Adam had a technological implant grafted into his forehead that gave him access to a knowledge database. Using information from the future, Adam planned to make a fortune back home and, via Rose's Universal Roaming-enabled mobile phone, began leaving messages on his parent's answerphone. When the Doctor discovered this, he furiously escorted Adam home, destroyed the messages and abandoned him, still with the implant grafted into his head. (1.7) (Played by BRUNO LANGLEY)

Mitchell, Geoff: Wife of Sandra, father to Adam. He was out when his wife found that Adam had returned to their home in Manchester, complete with the Type Two info-spike chip in his forehead. (1.7)

Mitchell, Peggy: Fictional owner of the Queen Vic pub in the BBC soap opera *EastEnders*, set in Walford. Jackie Tyler explained to the Doctor that, in recent episodes of the serial, Peggy had heard a noise in the cellar which had turned out to be the ghost of former publican Den Watts. (2.12) (Played by BARBARA WINDSOR)

Mitchell, Sandra: Adam Mitchell's mother who, on his return home to Manchester, discovered to her horror that her son had alien tech permanently grafted into his skull. (1.7) (Played by JUDY HOLT)

Mo, Cousin: Relative of Jackie and Rose Tyler, who had left London and gone to live in the Peak District. (2.X) Before leaving for New Earth with the Doctor, Rose reminds Jackie to call Mo. (2.1)

Mobile phone: Communications device popular on 21st-century Earth. The Doctor adjusted both Rose Tyler's (1.2) and Martha Jones's (3.7) so they had Universal Roaming, which meant that they could make and receive calls to and from anywhere in space and time.

Mobile Phone Man: A guest at the reception for Donna Noble and Lance Bennett's non-wedding. The Doctor borrowed his phone and souped it up with his sonic screwdriver to learn more about HC Clements. (3.X) (Played by BEN McLEAN)

Molecular fringe animation: The science used by Son of Mine to create and activate his army of straw Scarecrows. (3.8, 3.9)

Mongrels: How Lady Cassandra O'Brien referred to humans who were, unlike her, not born on Earth. (1.2)

Moon, the: Natural satellite which orbits the Earth. The Judoon used plasma coils to transport the Royal Hope there, so they could gain access to the fugitive Plasmavore they knew was hiding in the hospital . (3.1)

'Moonlight Serenade': Captain Jack Harkness and Rose Tyler danced before the face of Big Ben atop a Chula ship to this jazz number composed by Glenn Miller. (1.10)

Moore, Mrs: Mature member of the Preachers on 'Pete's World', who was their driver, their techie and very good at building electromagnetic hand grenades. Her real name was Angela Price, but she adopted the 'Mrs Moore' identity from a book she'd read, hoping to protect her husband and children. She used to work for Cybus Industries but realised what they were doing was illegal as well as immoral, going to join the Preachers when the information she knew made her a target. She accompanied the Doctor into the Battersea Power Station Cyber-conversion factory, accessing it via Deepcold Six. There they discovered that the Cyberforms had emotional inhibitors, shortly before Mrs Moore was electrocuted by the grip of a Cyberman. (2.5, 2.6) (Played by HELEN GRIFFIN)

Moore, Sir Patrick: Television astronomer and expert on the heavens. Rose Tyler cheekily suggested to the Doctor that Moore was the biggest expert in alien knowledge. (1.4)

Morgenstern, Oliver: Intern at the Royal Hope Hospital who coped better at being transported to the Moon than most. He was the first person to communicate with the Judoon Captain and, as a result, followed him as the Judoon Troopers went through the Hospital scanning people, Morgenstern advising everyone they'd be safe. Once back on Earth, Morgenstern became the person the media went straight to for comments about the ordeal. (3.1) (Played by BEN RIGHTON)

Morocco: North African country where Donna Noble and Lance Bennett were planning to go to for their honeymoon. (3.X)

Morris [1]: A homeless man on 'Pete's World' lured into the back of Mr Crane's pantechnicon on the promise of limitless food. He was later turned into a Cyberman. (2.5) (Played by ADAM SHAW)

Morris [2]: Schoolboy at Farringham School for Boys in 1913, who was told to maintain a position over the stableyard before the Family of Blood attacked. (3.9)

Morrison, Jim: Lead singer of The Doors, mentioned by the Doctor when he realised that the Graske's hatchery had, he reckoned, more doors than Jim Morrison. (AotG)

Mortlock, Madame: A medium who worked in the Butetown district of Cardiff in the 1860s. (1.3)

Moss, Lynda: Contestant on *Big Brother* aboard the Game Station in 200,100, being broadcast on Channel 44,000. Like all the contestants in all the *Big Brother* houses and other games on the Station, Lynda was selected to be on the show, rather than having to apply. When the Doctor decided to break out, Lynda followed him, eager to discover the truth behind the Game Station – and saw him as a possible way out of her drab life by travelling in the TARDIS. When the Daleks were revealed to be behind everything, Lynda enthusiastically worked with the Doctor to stop them. She was reporting back from an observation deck on Floor 056, when a Dalek appeared outside, floating in space and blasted the Exoglass away, killing her instantly. (1.12, 1.13) (played by JO JOYNER)

Most Haunted: Television show about ghost hunters. With the world populated by friendly ghosts, its presenter Derek Acorah lamented that he was out of a job. (2.12)

Mother of Mine: Mother of the Family of Blood, who verbally greeted schoolboy Jeremy Baines when he stumbled across their invisible spaceship in Cooper's Field, Farringham. Baines was killed, his body inhabited by Son of Mine, and one by one the Family found themselves bodies. Mother of Mine was the last to do so, taking on the form of Jenny, a maid at the school. Posing as Jenny, she encountered Martha, sensing she had something to do with the Time Lord the Family sought. She later joined her Family at the village dance, enjoying the carnage they created there and shortly afterwards at the school itself. Having regained his Time Lord form and blown up the Family's spaceship, the Doctor threw Mother of Mine into the event horizon of a collapsing galaxy where she would remain for eternity. (3.8, 3.9) (Played by REBEKAH STATON)

Motorway: Vast series of tunnels and road lanes, including the legendary Fast Lane, beneath New New York's Undercity. The drivers believed they were actually getting somewhere, albeit only a couple of feet a day, but in fact they had been kept down there by the Face of Boe until such a time as the Overcity was contamination-free. It had been for quite a while, but Boe lacked the energy to reopen the covered tunnels and set the drivers free. (3.3)

Motorway Foot Patrol: When the Doctor jumped from the base of Brannigan's car and into the White Man's vehicle on the New New York Motorway, he told Whitey that he was from the Motorway Foot Patrol, doing a survey. He used this excuse a couple more times as he jumped into various other cars. (3.3)

Mount Rushmore National Memorial: Vast sculpture in the rock face of Mount Rushmore, in South Dakota, with four former US Presidents carved into it. The Master had his face added. (3.13)

Mount Snowden: A spaceship found buried at the foot of this North Wales mountain contained a couple of Magna-clamps, which the Torchwood Institute appropriated. (2.12)

Mount Stuart Square: London road in which was located the police station where Sally Sparrow met DI Billy Shipton. (3.10)

Moxx of Balhoon, the: From the firm of solicitors Jolco and Jolco, he was sent to observe Earthdeath from Platform One. He died after Lady Cassandra O'Brien had the sunfilters around the Manchester Suite lowered. (1.2) (Played by JIMMY VEE, voiced by SILAS CARSON)

'Mr Blue Sky': Number six hit for the Electric Light Orchestra in 1978, a song often danced to by Elton Pope in the privacy of his own room, as he was a huge fan of the band.

MRI: Magnetic Resonance Imaging, a process used at the Royal Hope Hospital for non-invasive observation of patients. The Plasmavore intended to use the MRI there as a weapon – to increase its magnetic output to 50,000 tesla, which would fry the brains of everything within 250,000 miles. The Plasmavore, protected by a screen, would be safe and, with the humans and Judoon dead, could make its escape. After the Judoon executed the Plasmavore, they left the MRI still building up its power – the results of the mono-magnetic pulse of no interest to them as they would be long gone and out of range. The Doctor was able to disconnect the scanner and save everyone. (3.1)

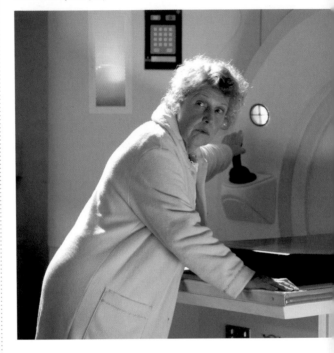

Muffin the Mule: Children's puppet show, which ran between 1952 and 1955, presented by Annette Mills. An episode of this was among the first things watched by the Connollys on their new television set. (2.7)

Multi-grade anti-oil: The Doctor pourcd this into one of the Clockwork Robots, pretending it was red wine, to save Rose Tyler and Mickey Smith from being dissected by them. (2.4)

Mum [1]: London woman whose family had A+ blood and thus were affected by the Sycorax's blood control. (2.X) (Played by CATHY MURPHY)

Mum [2]: A London woman kidnapped by the Graske at Christmas, and replaced with a changeling. She was eventually returned home with no memory of her experiences. (AotG) (Played by LISA PALFREY)

Mummies: Sarah Jane Smith told Rose Tyler that, during her time travelling with the Doctor, they had fought Egyptian Mummies – in reality these were powerful Servo Robots, created by the Osirans. (2.3)

Munchkin-Lady: A bizarre alien who, the Doctor and Rose Tyler recalled, had breathed fire from her mouth. (2.5)

Muppet Movie, The: Listing things of importance that happened in 1979, the Doctor told Rose Tyler that this film was released. (2.2)

Murder Spree 20: The city of Pola Ventura hosted Murder Spree 20, not Reykjavik. Rose Tyler didn't know this when asked by the Anne Droid in *The Weakest Link* aboard the Game Station. (1.12)

Muswell Hill: North London area, in the shadow of Alexandra Palace and home to streets such as Florizel Street and Damascus Street in 1953. (2.7)

Mutt and Jeff: American comic-strip characters created by Bud Fisher in the 1920s. Mutt was the tall rich one, Jeff, his shorter insane companion. The Doctor likened Rose Tyler and Adam Mitchell to them when aboard the space station Satellite Five. (1.7). He later used the same name to describe Rose and himself working as a team in the Torchwood Institute Lever Room as they prepared to destroy the invading Cybermen and Daleks. (2.13)

My Fair Lady: The Doctor sang 'I Could Have Danced All Night' from this musical upon returning from a party in 18th-century France. (2.4)

My Invasion Blog: Ursula Blake's online diary about the Doctor's involvement with alien incursions on Earth, which drew her and Elton Pope together, and thus led to the formation of LINDA. (2.10)

Myarr: Arable planet colonised by humans generations before the Mantasphids invaded and threw them out. This was the final straw in an ongoing war between the Earth Empire and the Mantasphids, and Earth Control opted to obliterate the planet and sacrifice it, thus eliminating the Mantasphids once and for all. The Doctor intervened and saved Myarr, leaving the humans and Mantasphids to find peace. (TIQ)

Myrna: Dancer at the Laurenzi theatre in 1930s New York, taking part in the New York Revue. When Martha Jones needed to get across the stage to find Laszlo, she used Myrna to shield her from the audience. (3.4) (Played by FLIK SWAN)

Mysterious Man: An employee of Harry Saxon who approached Francine Jones at the cocktail reception at LazLabs to plant seeds of doubt in her mind about the Doctor's ability to keep her daughter Martha safe from harm. (3.6) (Played by BERTIE CARVEL)

Mystery of Edwin Drood and the Blue Elementals, The: Charles Dickens decided to finish his serialised novel as soon as he returned to London after his adventure with the Doctor in which they defeated the Gelth, who resembled the blue elementals he elected to use in the new title. The story was never finished, as Dickens died six months later. (1.3)

Naming, the: A Carrionite spell in which powerful words end with an object or person being named, which in turn causes the target injury or even death. The Doctor, when he works out that Mother Doomfinger is a Carrionite, names her and transports her back where she came from. Martha tries the same trick on Lilith, but a Naming doesn't work when it is repeated. Instead Lilith knocks out Martha by Naming *her*, and tries to stop the Doctor's heart by Naming Rose Tyler. (3.2)

Nancy: Teenage girl who took it upon herself to look after various children who had been evacuated from London during the Blitz but had returned as strays. She told the Doctor this was because her younger brother Jamie had died during an air raid. She also explained about the strange 'empty' child walking the streets, wearing a gas mask and asking everyone 'Are you my mummy?' She suggested the Doctor should talk to a doctor at Albion Hospital, the nearest hospital to Limehouse Green Station where an unexploded bomb had fallen shortly before the child began walking the streets. Nancy later went to the site of the bombing and revealed to the Doctor that the child was Jamie – not her brother but her son. The Chula nanogenes that had brought the dead Jamie back to life then conjoined Nancy and her son's DNA, returning Jamie to normal. (1.9, 1.10) (Played by FLORENCE HOATH)

Nanodentistry: One of the areas within the Hospital on New Earth run by the Sisters of Plenitude. (2.1)

Nanogenes: Smart subatomic robots that inhabited all Chula ships and could restore living tissue to its pristine form, provided they had been programmed with what that pristine form was. The nanogenes aboard Captain Jack's ship were familiar with humans, due to his presence – the

ones aboard the medical ship he had forced to crash in war-torn London were not. They reanimated a dead boy and assumed that was how all humans should be, so rewrote the DNA of all those they encountered to resemble that child. They were reprogrammed when they encountered mother and son together, recognising the mother's superior DNA, and they repaired all the damage they had done, actually improving the health of many they had infected. (1.9, 1.10)

Nano-termites: Installed in Adam Mitchell's throat as part of the Vomit-o-Matic when he had the Type Two chip inserted into his head. As soon as the doors in his forehead whirred open and he saw his own brain, Adam threw up, but the Nurse told him that the nano-termites had frozen the waste created by his gag reflex. (1.7)

Naples: The Doctor hoped to take Rose Tyler there for the first Christmas of the newly unified Kingdom of Italy. They ended up in the Cardiff of 1869. But still at Christmas. (1.3)

National Trust: Preservation authority who owned Earth five billion years in Rose Tyler's future. (1.2)

NATO: The North Atlantic Treaty Organisation – a military alliance which went to red alert when the Sycorax ship approached Earth. (2.X)

Naturists: A nude couple driving on the New New York Motorway, encountered by the Doctor as he jumped from car to car. (3.3) (Played by CHRIS ILSTON, ZOE JEFFRIES)

Navarre, King of: Character from Shakespeare's *Love's Labour's Lost* and later *Love's Labour's Won*, played by Richard Burbage. (3.2)

Nav-Com: The Chula navigational system on Jack's stolen ship.

Neighbour [1]: A resident of number 3 in the same street as the Finch family, he put out a wheelie bin near Mickey Smith's car while Rose Tyler was visiting Clive Finch. The bin was used by the Nestene Consciousness to kidnap Mickey and replace him with an Auton facsimile. (1.1) (Played by ALUN JENKINS)

Neighbour [2]: An anxious mother who suggested that council worker Kel was responsible for kidnapping the missing children of Dame Kelly Holmes Close. (2.11) (Played by ERICA EIRIAN)

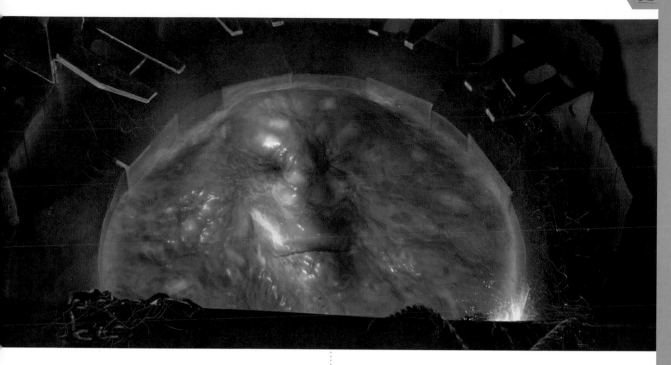

Neo-Classic Congregational and Neo-Judaism: Two of the many religions practised in the 42nd century. (2.9)

Nerys: One of the guests at Donna's wedding. Donna assumed that Nerys had arranged her transportation from the church to the TARDIS. When Donna finally got to her reception, she was not amused to find Nerys moving in on Lance Bennett, her fiancé. (3.X) (Played by KRYSTAL ARCHER)

Nestene Consciousness: Disembodied energy form that could manipulate any form of plastic and use it was a weapon. It fled the Time War after the destruction of its home planet, and may have been a signatory to the Shadow Proclamation. It had attempted to invade Earth more than once but, after it took on a liquid-plastic form, the Ninth Doctor used antiplastic to destroy it, presumably for ever. (1.1) (Voiced by NICHOLAS BRIGGS)

'Never Can Say Goodbye': Cover version of the Jackson 5 hit, performed by The Communards and being played nearby when the TARDIS materialised in 1987 prior to Pete Tyler's death in a hit-and-run accident. (1.8)

'Never Gonna Give You Up': Number one hit for Rick Astley in 1987. It was playing on Pete Tyler's car radio as he took Rose to St Christopher's Church for the wedding of Stuart Hoskins and Sarah Clark. (1.8)

'Never Too Late': 1989 hit for Kylie Minogue, quoted by the Doctor to Tommy Connolly as they headed to Alexandra Palace to put a stop to the Wire's Time of Manifestation. (2.7)

New American Alliance: The Emperor Dalek's forces bombed this Earth continent in 200,100. (1.13)

New Amsterdam: Original name for New York. (3.4)

New Atlantic: Ocean off the coast of New New York where, according to Sally Calypso, the sun was blazing high in the sky, creating a perfect setting for the Daily Contemplation. (3.3)

New Earth: A planet the same shape, size and orbit as the original Earth, but 50,000 light years away, in the Galaxy M87, and settled on by humans nostalgic for their home world, which had been destroyed by the expansion of the Sun. The Doctor took Rose Tyler to visit it, where they encountered Lady Cassandra O'Brien trying to blackmail the Sisters of Plenitude. (2.1) The Doctor returned there with Martha Jones at a time, 30 years later, when the planet had been quarantined for 24 years after the Mood Patch Bliss had mutated and wiped out most of the planet's inhabitants. (3.3)

New Fifth Avenue: Street intersection on the New New York Motorway where, according to Sally Calypso, a spate of car-jackings had occurred. (3.3)

New Gallifrey: Once the Master had created his New Time Lord Empire, he hoped to found a new home planet for himself. (3.13)

New Germany: European country on 'Pete's World', which Pete Tyler suggested to John Lumic as an alternative place to establish the Ultimate Upgrade project. (2.5)

New Humans [1]: One of the names used by the humans of five billion years in Rose's future to describe themselves. It implied they were different from the now-extinct (bar Lady Cassandra) humans originating from Earth itself. (1.2)

New Humans [2]: In a massive Intensive Care Unit beneath the Hospital on New Earth, the Sisters of Plenitude had grown new humans, riddled with every known disease, virus and contagion. Their plan was to use the

NEW NEW YORK: The 15th place to bear the name New York, this city was located on New Earth in Galaxy M87, and everyone on New Earth lived in the city and its environs, surrounded on one side by the New Atlantic and on the other by the New Pacific. New New York was ruled over by a Senate and was an ultra-sophisticated high-rise cityscape, dominated by two main species, Humans and Catkind. The areas of New New York, usually named after those of the 21st-century New York on Earth (such as Brooklyn, Battery Park and Manhattan), were linked by a series of covered motorway tunnels. Over the years, the city had become divided into two distinct areas, the Overcity and the Undercity. While the rich and powerful, such as the Senate and the Duke of Manhattan, lived above, the lower levels became home to the poor, the dispossessed and the dealers of Mood Patches in Pharmacytown. The Doctor and Rose Tyler's visit to New New York in 5,000,000,023 centred on a small headland where a vast Hospital had been built, run by the Sisters of Plenitude, an order of Catkind nuns. (2.1) Thirty years later, he took Martha Jones to the Undercity and learned that a new mood, Bliss, had mutated and wiped out the Overcity, leaving the people on the Motorway the only survivors apart from Novice Hame and the Face of Boe, who were striving to maintain the city's energy levels. The Macra, who inhabited the lowest levels of the Motorway, were rumoured to have escaped from the New New York Zoo. (3.3)

humans as stock for cures, but Lady Cassandra O'Brien let the patients out of their cells, and they rampaged through the Hospital until the Doctor was able to cure them with their own antibodies in a massive cocktail of drugs. Once they were cured, the Doctor described them as a new species. (2.1)

New New Jersey Expressway: Part of the New New York Motorway where, according to Sally Calypso, 15 extra lanes had been opened to assist traffic flow. (3.3)

New Roman Empire: The Empire that ruled Earth in the year 12,005. (1.2)

New Skaro: The Cult of Skaro intended to use their Dalek-Human army to turn Earth into New Skaro. (3.5)

New South America: Devastated area of 'Pete's World' with a huge homeless problem. (2.5) According to the mysterious Gemini, 265,000 people had disappeared from New South America since 2004. (2.5T)

New Times Square: The Businessman driving his car on the New New York Motorway compared the arrivals of first the Doctor and then Novice Hame in his car with the hustle and bustle of New Times Square. (3.3)

New Venus Archipelago 27: Place where 200 people died in sandstorms, according to Bad WolfTV. (1.7)

New York: Colloquial name for New York City, the largest city in America, and the main city of New York State. Base of the United Nations, who were debating what to do in light of the massive weapons of destruction the faux British government (in reality, the Family Slitheen) had convinced them existed in space, requiring a nuclear strike to destroy them. (1.5) Location of the studios for *The Ed Sullivan Show*, where the Doctor planned to take Rose Tyler to see Elvis Presley perform 'Hound Dog' live in 1956. (2.7) Captain Jack Harkness tried to enter New York during the year Ellis Island became the immigration entry point – Jack was shot while there, and discovered then that he couldn't die. (3.11) Martha Jones walked across the Earth, including New York, telling her story about the Doctor, preparing people for the right moment to chant his name. (3.13)

New Time Lord Empire, the: The Master intended to set this up by going to war with everyone else in the universe, aided by the Toclafane. To this end he was using labour camps across the Earth to build 2,000 massive war rockets, each with a black hole converter inside. Time Lord technology had been based on the harnessing of black holes, and the Master reasoned that this would be the perfect foundation for his New Empire. (3.13)

New York Record: Daily newspaper, which alerted the Doctor and Martha about the disappearances from Hooverville in 1930s Manhattan. (3.4)

New York Revue: The musical show playing at the Laurenzi theatre in 1930, which featured Tallulah singing 'Heaven or Hell'. (3.4)

Newport: On 'Pete's World', the name of the London Borough which, on Rose Tyler's version of Earth, was called Waterloo. (2.6)

Newsreaders: A male BBC News 24 studio newsreader commented on the Big Ben incident. A female newsreader reported on the arrival of UNIT officers from Geneva. (1.4) The American AMNN news anchor reported on the Big Ben incident, on the Sycorax's message being relayed to Earth, and on President Winters' address to the Toclafane. (1.4, 2.X, 3.12) (Played by LACHELE CARL) Another News 24 anchor reported on the Guinevere One space probe. (2.X) (Played by JASON MOHAMMAD) Another reported on the Sycorax's contact with Earth. (2.X) (Played by SAGAR AYRA) A French presenter told his public that the President of France had decided that ghosts would not receive the Légion d'honneur. (2.12) (Played by ANTHONY DEBAECK) An Indian newsreader warned visitors to the Taj Mahal that the ghosts should be treated as sacred guests. (2.12) (Played by HAJAZ AKRAM) In Japan, a newsreader explained that the ghosts were the latest craze to sweep Japan. (2.12) (Played by TAKAKO AKASHI) A young newsreader tried to warn her viewers and her family about the Dalek and Cyberman invasion, but was cut off mid-broadcast by one of the alien invaders. (2.13T) (Played by ADRIENNE O'SULLIVAN) A News 24 anchor warned the public about the Doctor, Martha Jones and Captain Jack Harkness after the Master arranged for them to be declared public enemies. She later commented on the Toclafane arrival. (3.12) (Played by OLIVIA HILL) A Chinese newsreader warned the People's Republic that watching British newscasts about the Toclafane was illegal. (3.12) (Played by DANIEL MING)

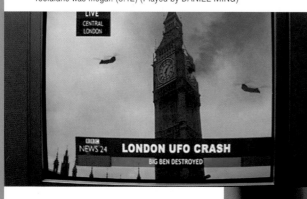

Nightingale, Katherine Costello: Best friend of Sally Sparrow. When Sally came to her flat late one night, spooked about the message she had found addressed to her at Wester Drumlins, Kathy agreed to accompany her back to the house the next day for another look. They were then disturbed by the arrival of a man claiming to be Kathy's grandson, just as Kathy was touched by a Weeping Angel and sent back in time, to December 1920. She found herself in Hull and eventually settled there, with a young farmer called Ben Wainwright. They married (although Kathy lied about her age, claiming to be only 18) and had three children, one of whom was named Sally in Sally Sparrow's honour. After Ben died, Kathy had grandchildren, one of whom was Malcolm Wainwright, and she wrote a letter explaining what had happened and asked him to deliver it to Sally at the exact moment she had

disappeared from Wester Drumlins in 2007. She died in 1987, not long after writing the letter. (3.10) (Played by LUCY GASKILL)

Nightingale, Lawrence: Brother to Kathy, who had been wandering around his sister's flat naked the first time he met Sally Sparrow. After Kathy disappeared and Sally received a letter from her from 1987, she tracked Larry down to Banto's DVD shop where he worked, and tried to explain that Kathy had had to go away. She was intrigued by the DVDs that Larry had – he was a bit of a geek about 17 particular DVDs all of which had Easter eggs on them, each with clips of a man called the Doctor apparently having one half of a conversation. When Sally

next contacted Larry and told him the 17 discs matched all the DVDs she owned, he agreed to meet her at Wester Drumlins with copies of them. Together they learned about the Weeping Angels, and were promptly attacked by one. While Sally looked for a way out of the house, Larry tried not to blink, but he eventually gave in and followed Sally to the cellar where they found and entered the TARDIS. After they'd inserted one of the DVDs into the console, the TARDIS dematerialised around them and went back to 1969 to locate the Doctor and Martha Jones. Larry was relieved to realise that it had been a lure for the Weeping Angels, which had been holding the TARDIS as it vanished – with the police box gone, they had been left staring at one another, freezing them for eternity. During the next 12 months, Larry and Sally bought Banto's store and set up their own shop selling old books and rare DVDs, naming it Sparrow and Nightingale, and the two briefly met the Doctor in the street. Sally handed the Time Lord all her files on their encounter, realising she was now starting off the chain of events. (3.10) (Played by FINLAY ROBERTSON)

Donna Noble

Can't you reverse, or warp, or beam, or something?

The daughter of Sylvia and Geoff Noble, and fiancée to Lance Bennett, Donna was halfway up the aisle of St Mary's Church when she found herself accidentally transported aboard the TARDIS, a side effect of the Empress of the Racnoss's plans. Convinced that she had been deliberately abducted by the Doctor on behalf of her nemesis Nerys, Donna vowed to return to Chiswick in time for her wedding, but was abducted by a Roboform mercenary masquerading as a taxi driver. She was rescued by the Doctor in a high-speed motorway chase, but missed the ceremony itself.

Donna first recalled meeting Lance when she was temping as a secretary for HC Clements, six months before their eventual wedding day, when he offered to make her a simple cup of coffee. In reality, he was dosing her with Huon Energy in liquid form on behalf of the Empress of the Racnoss, who was using her body to catalyse the Huon particles, enabling her to release the remaining Racnoss from the centre of the Earth. The Doctor later deduced that it was when these particles inside Donna

had magnetised with those inside the TARDIS that she was initially drawn on board, and was then able to reverse the process, summoning the TARDIS to materialise around them. The Doctor confirmed that all the Huon Energy, deadly to humans, had been drained from Donna by the Empress before she returned home.

Prior to HC Clements, Donna lived alone with her dog in London, where she worked as a temp, and had a tendency to show off

– even her mother noted that, on her first day at school, she had been sent home for biting. She liked Pringles, lifestyle fads and celebrity gossip, and disliked Christmas to the extent that she deliberately scheduled her wedding for Christmas Eve, with a honeymoon to follow in Morocco. The Doctor also observed Donna's tendency to miss big events playing out around her, having been hung over during the Sycorax invasion at Christmas and scuba-diving in Spain when the Cybermen manifested across the globe.

Although her time with the Doctor helped put everything into much greater perspective, Donna turned down the opportunity to travel with him following their encounter with the Racnoss, choosing instead to give up temping and go travelling instead. She did, however, hope that their paths might cross again, one day… (3.X)

(Played by CATHERINE TATE)

Nina: Orphaned schoolgirl eaten by Hector Finch at Deffry Vale High School. (2.3) (Played by HEATHER CAMERON)

NNYPD: The New New York Police Department arrested the Sisters of Plenitude on New Earth after their scheme had been thwarted. (2.1) By the time the Doctor and Martha Jones investigated the Motorway on New New York in 5,000,000,053, the NNYPD had ceased to exist and instead drivers were fooled into thinking they were still there via a series of recorded messages going out automatically. (3.3)

Noble, Geoffrey: Somewhat hen-pecked (by his wife Sylvia) father-of-the-bride (Donna). He took charge of seeing to the injured in the wake of the Roboform Santas bombing the wedding reception, and was overjoyed when Donna returned home after her adventures with the Doctor, having feared his daughter was dead. (3.X) (Played by HOWARD ATTFIELD)

Noble, Sylvia: Donna's mother, quick to criticise and used to getting her own way, but ultimately overjoyed when Donna returned home after her adventures with the Doctor, having feared her daughter was dead. (3.X) (Played by JACQUELINE KING)

Norway: Having been trapped on 'Pete's World' for some months, Rose Tyler heard the Doctor calling to her in a dream. She, Mickey, Jackie and Pete followed the voice, driving from Britain all the way to Norway, where the Doctor, as a hologram, and Rose were reunited for two minutes on the beach at Dårlig Ulv Stranden, able to say a final, heartfelt goodbye. (2.13)

Nottingham: Midlands city where, in the fiction the Doctor created for John Smith's background, John believed he came from. He told Joan it lay on the River Leen and other basic details, but couldn't give her more personal recollections of it. (3.8, 3.9)

Novice: Rank of young Time Lords as they entered the Academy on Gallifrey for the first time. (3.12)

Nuclear Plant Seven: Research area where Professor Docherty worked for the Master, although the Resistance counted her as a major player in their ranks. (3.13)

Nurse [1]: She looked after Adam Mitchell on Floor 016 of Satellite Five and oversaw the implantation of the Type 2 chip into his forehead. (1.7) (Played by TAMSIN GREIG)

Nurse [2]: A Krillitane who had taken human form and worked at Deffry Vale High School. She was killed when K-9 heated up the drums of Krillitane Oil in the school kitchen and blew the Nurse, the school and himself to pieces. (2.3) (Played by SUZANNE CASENOVE)

O'Connor, Des: Presenter of Channel 4 quiz show *Countdown*. After the Toclafane invasion, *Countdown* was cancelled, much to the chagrin of Professor Docherty. (3.13)

Oakham Farm: Farm owned by Mr Clark, who was murdered by the Family of Blood. (3.8, 3.9)

Observatory: Room atop Torchwood House containing a telescope designed and built by Sir George MacLeish and Prince Albert. (2.2)

Oddie, Bill: British comedian and ornithologist, famous for his bird-conservation television programmes. When the TARDIS arrived on Pheros, Martha Jones saw the bird eyrie and suggested they were in Bill Oddie heaven. (TIQ)

OilCorp: Galactic corporation that was sucking planets such as Bouken dry of their natural resources in an oil-starved 40th century, then selling the oil at inflated prices. OilCorp's biggest opponents were a number of pirates who would attack the rigs and steal the oil, selling it at low prices to poorer planets. OilCorp created sentient robotic rigs that could defend themselves against the pirates, and on Bouken they placed a spy, Swabb, aboard the ship the *Black Gold*, commanded by Captain Kaliko. (TIQ)

Oklahoma: The Trine-E android aboard the Game Station described Captain Jack Harkness's outfit as having an 'Oklahoma farm boy look' during the *What Not to Wear* programme. This was a reference to the 46th

American state, famed for its farming and oil production. (1.12) Some of the residents of Manhattan's Hooverville were from this state. (3.4)

Old Curiosity Shop, The: A novel by Charles Dickens that includes a celebrated scene in which the heroine, Little Nell, dies. The Doctor asked Dickens to read that specific section for him, but he didn't. (1.3)

Old Earth: Referred to in questions by the Anne Droid aboard the Game Station, during the *Weakest Link* quiz. (1.12)

'Old Rugged Cross, The': Every day at the same time, the drivers of the cars on the New New York Motorway took a few moments to sing together, as one voice, a hymn to celebrate their lives. When the Doctor was with the Brannigan family, and Martha Jones with Milo and Cheen, the hymn sung was this 20th-century Christian anthem – perhaps suggesting that the New New Yorkers were primarily Christians (Thomas Brannigan and Javit both mentioned Jehovah, and the occupants of the cars later sang another Christian anthem, 'Abide With Me'). (3.3)

Olive Woman: One of the posh guests at the LazLabs reception party, who thought that choking on an olive was a greater threat than anything that the GMD experiment could have created, until she became the second victim of the Lazarus creature. (3.6) (Played by LUCY O'CONNELL)

Oliver Twist: A book cited by the Doctor as one of the Charles Dickens canon that he'd read. (1.3)

Om-Com: The communications system on Chula ships. It allowed both Captain Jack Harkness (when he was on his ship) and the 'empty' child (because he was infused with Chula nanotechnology) to communicate through anything with a speaker grille. (1.10)

Oncoming Storm, the: The name the Daleks gave to the Doctor in their own legends. (1.13) Rose Tyler sarcastically reminded him of this when he turned up in the 51st century, apparently drunk after celebrating in the 18th. (2.4)

Ood: Hive-minded race of aliens, who believed they were bred to serve, and thus were treated as slaves by humanity in the 42nd century. They were considered so unimportant that human computers were not even programmed to recognise Ood as proper life forms. They communicated on a low-level telepathic field with one another, and with their human masters via cybernetically attached communication spheres called interface devices. Sanctuary Base 6 had a complement of 50 Ood and, although they were docile, when the Beast of Krop Tor awoke, he raised their telepathic

field to Basic 100. Normally this would kill any sentient being, but it allowed the Beast to use the Ood as mobile eyes and ears in the Base, as well as enabling the Ood to deliver a lethal pulse of psychic energy via the interface devices. When the Beast was stopped, the Ood were left free of its mental control but abandoned on Sanctuary Base 6 as it was drawn into the singularity of a black hole, where they all undoubtedly perished. The human survivors of Sanctuary Base 6 awarded them all posthumous commendations. (2.8, 2.9) (Voiced by SILAS CARSON)

Operation Market Stall: Part of Detective Inspector Bishop's scheme to solve the mystery of the faceless people populating Muswell Hill in 1953. When he and his associate Crabtree drove a newly captured victim back to the cage where he was keeping them, two undercover policemen would cover the entrance to his base with a fake set of market stalls, creating a dead end littered with trucks and signage, including a removals firm, B Clancy and Son, and two business estate agents: W Carter & Co and Gardiner Lawson of 27 Paddock Street. (2.7)

Osbourne, Sharon: Television personality who endorsed Harry Saxon's campaign to become Prime Minister. (3.12)

Oshodi, Adeola: Torchwood operative based in the Lever Room in the Torchwood Tower. She and her colleague Gareth went to the upper floors for an illicit snog, only to find that the area under construction was a new conversion site for the Cybermen. Adeola was killed, then reanimated via a Cybus Industries ear pod that was connected directly into her cerebral cortex. When the Doctor discovered this, he jammed the signal to the ear pod and the already dead Adeola died once again. (2.12) Her cousin, Martha Jones, later became the Doctor's companion, and commented that Adeola had vanished during the Battle of Canary Wharf. The Doctor opted not to confirm Adeola's death or his part in it. (3.1) (Played by FREEMA AGYEMAN)

Ostrich: Cassandra brought gifts aboard Platform One, including the last ostrich egg from Earth. She mistakenly believed the ostrich had a wingspan of 50 feet and breathed fire from its nostrils. (1.2)

Outer Worlds: Erina Lissak wanted to go backpacking across these as all her mates had done, but her mother forbade it. Instead, Erina signed up for a tour of duty aboard the cargo ship SS *Pentallian*. (3.7P)

Overcity: The upper echelons of New New York. Ruled by the Senate, everyone there was killed by a virus when a mutated Mood Patch called Bliss infected the very air of New New York. (3.3)

O'BRIEN DOT DELTA SEVENTEEN, LADY CASSANDRA: The last 'pure' human alive at the time of Earthdeath, although she was nothing more than a thin area of skin hung tautly across a wire frame, with only her eyes and mouth left functioning. Her vain, selfish and arrogant brain was kept safely in a jar beneath her skin, and she was regularly moisturised by her two surgeons. She resented all the various hybrid humans and mutations that existed across the cosmos that, ironically, kept the human race alive. She claimed she'd been married a number of times, that her father was from Texas, her mother from the Arctic Desert and they were the last humans buried on Earth, that she had endured over 700 operations to preserve her, and that she was born male. Using her robot spiders and the Adherents of the Repeated Meme, Cassandra's plan was to stage a hostage situation, with herself as one of the victims, then collect all the ransom and insurance monies herself. When the Doctor exposed her plan, she teleported away, leaving Platform One to be destroyed, and intended to take over each of the deceased dignitaries' holdings. However, the Doctor brought her back to the space station without her surgeons to moisturise her, so her skin, now dry, snapped. (1.2) Cassandra didn't die however and, 23 years later, the Doctor and Rose encountered her on New Earth. Now with her face rebuilt using skin from her posterior, she was able to use a psychograft to place her mind in Rose. Assisted by a force-grown clone, which she called Chip, Cassandra was caught up with the Sisters of Plenitude's attempts to breed drone humans with every disease in their systems, thus creating perfect anti-serums. After leaving Rose, she took over the Doctor's body and even one of the drone patients before finally accepting her time was up. The dying Chip volunteered his own body for Cassandra's final resting place and, before she died for good, the Doctor took Cassandra to witness her real self many years earlier. 'Chip' died in the younger Cassandra's arms, after telling her how beautiful she was. (2.1) (Played by ZOË WANAMAKER, BILLIE PIPER, DAVID TENNANT, JOANNA CROZIER, SEAN GALLAGHER)

Pa: Driver of a car on the New New York Motorway. Tired of the endless delays, he overrode the onboard computer that registered how many adults were aboard and lied to the computer at the Transit Authority. Saying that there were three adults in his car gave him access to the Fast Lane, where he and his wife were attacked and killed by the Macra. (3.3) (Played by GRAHAM PADDEN)

Paab: The measurement of length defined by Emperor Jate as being from his nose to his fingertip was a paab, not a goffle. Rodrick didn't know this when asked by the Anne Droid in *The Weakest Link* aboard the Game Station. (1.12)

Pacifica: The Emperor Dalek's forces bombed this Earth continent in 200,100. (1.13)

Pacoo, Mr and Mrs: They were guests aboard Platform One to see the Earthdeath spectacle. (1.2)

Padrivole Regency Nine: The society which had employed the Judoon to trace the Plasmavore which had murdered its child princess. (3.1)

Pale Woman: A young, depressed woman who came to Pharmacytown to buy a Forget Mood Patch after her parents had left the Undercity to travel on the Motorway. (3.3) (Played by LUCY DAVENPORT)

Pallidome Pancrosis: A lethal disease that killed its victims in ten minutes. The Sisters of Plenitude on New Earth found a cure. (2.1)

Pallushi: A mighty civilisation which spanned a billion years and was destroyed for ever when its solar system, the Scarlet System, was destroyed by the black hole, K 37 Gem 5. (2.8)

Pan Traffic Culture: In their calendar, the month of Hoob is followed by Pandoff, not Clavadoe. Fitch didn't know this when asked by the Anne Droid in *The Weakest Link* aboard the Game Station. (1.12)

Pandoff: In the Pan Traffic culture, the month of Hoob is followed by Pandoff, not Clavadoe. Fitch didn't know this when asked by the Anne Droid in *The Weakest Link* aboard the Game Station. (1.12)

Pankhurst, Emmeline: One of the founders of the British Suffragette movement in the early 20th century. She stole the Doctor's laser spanner. Allegedly. (3.1)

Papua New Guinea: Their Olympic Team surprised everyone in the Shot-Put in the Games of 2012, according to the Doctor. (2.11)

Paradox Machine: Device built by the Master and fitted to the TARDIS whilst aboard the *Valiant*, after he travelled, with Lucy Saxon, to Utopia in the year 100,000,000,000,000. With the TARDIS's unlimited power, the Paradox Machine created a rent in time and space, enabling the Toclafane to travel to 21st-century Earth from Utopia, to wipe out their own ancestors. When Captain Jack Harkness destroyed the Paradox Machine, the rent closed, sealing the Toclafane in the future and, because time needed to heal, it shunted the *Valiant* back to the exact moment it had begun operation. This erased the previous year for everyone on Earth apart from those aboard the *Valiant*. (3.12, 3.13)

Paris: Capital of France. Jeanne-Antoinette Poisson was living here as a child when the Doctor first met her. (2.4) Mickey Smith and Jake Simmonds set off in the Preacher's van towards Paris to liberate it from whatever Cybermen still existed there. (2.6)

Parker-Bowles, Camilla: Rose Tyler likened Madame de Pompadour's determination to get on in the 18th-century French Royal court as similar to that of Prince Charles's second wife in the Britain of the 21st century. (2.4)

Parsons, Luke: Technician in UNIT's Mission Control base beneath the Tower of London. As his blood group was A+, he was vulnerable to the Sycorax's blood control. (2.X) (Played by JOHNIE CROSS)

Parsons, Mr: A history teacher at Deffry Vale High School who was a bit dubious about new Headmaster Finch and some of the other members of staff who had also arrived in the previous three months. He was, along with the other human teachers, eaten by the Krillitanes. (2.3) (Played by ROD ARTHUR)

Pash Pash: One of the many religions practised in the 42nd century. (2.9)

Patient: A human suffering from Hawtrey's Syndrome, who was cured by the Sisters of Plenitude in the Hospital on New Earth. She was subsequently threatened by an unknown force, and may have been killed. (2.1T) (Played by SOPHIE HIGGS)

Patients: The New Humans being bred by the Sisters of Plenitude on New Earth. One of them (played by SIMON JUDDERS) awoke in his incubation tank, and Sister Jatt incinerated him. Another (played by JOANNA CROZIER) killed Matron Casp and was briefly inhabited by the consciousness of Lady Cassandra O'Brien. (2.1)

Pavale, Davitch: One of the Programmers on the Game Station, alongside his female counterpart. They answered to the Controller but, when the Doctor exposed the Game Station as a fraud and the Controller was transmatted aboard the Dalek mothership and exterminated, the two Programmers joined forces against their foe. They joined Captain Jack Harkness, who took a shine to Davitch, and he was still flirting outrageously with the Female Programmer when she was exterminated defending Floor 499. Angrily, he returned fire but was likewise cut down by the Daleks. (1.12, 1.13) (Played by JO STONE-FEWINGS)

Peace Treaty 5.4/cup/16: A treaty which forbade the use of teleportation devices such as the TARDIS and the one possessed by Lady Cassandra aboard Platform One. (1.2)

Peace, Mrs: Elderly lady who died and was laid to rest at Sneed and Company. An alien Gelth took over her corpse, reanimating it. Mrs Peace then murdered her grandson and fled to the Taliesin Lodge where Charles Dickens was giving a reading – the last place the real Mrs Peace had been intending to visit prior to her death. When the Gelth left her body to return to its gaseous form, Mrs Peace's body collapsed in the auditorium. (1.3) (Played by JENNIFER HILL)

Pierpont, James: Composer of 'Jingle Bells', famously the first song ever beamed back to Earth by a human being in space. It was played by the lethal Christmas Tree placed in the Tylers' flat by the Roboform mercenaries. (2.X)

Pemberton: Schoolboy at Farringham School for Boys in 1913 who took part in the war-games there, manning the Vickers Gun. He was later charged with loading the spare magazines with real bullets before the Family of Blood attacked. (3.8, 3.9)

Pentallian, SS: Cargo ship touring the Torajii system, it was separated into a series of Areas which, in an emergency, could be individually locked, requiring a two-man team to open the deadlock-sealed doors using machinery and a special password. Run-down and battered, the crew were similarly exhausted and overworked, which led the captain, Kath McDonnell to use an illegal fusion scoop to steal vast amounts of energy from a sun without doing the standard procedure of scanning for life beforehand – scanning taking time, and time costing money. As a result, the living sun took over the bodies of two of her crew, including her husband, and they sabotaged the ship, ensuring it would crash into the sun, thus returning what they had taken. The Doctor was able to discover the truth and convince the surviving crew to jettison the fuel back into the sun, and thus avoid a fiery death. The Doctor and Martha Jones departed, leaving the *Pentallian* and its two surviving crew awaiting rescue by the authorities. (3.7)

Perception filter: The Doctor surrounded the Gallifreyan fob watch into which he downloaded his essence from the chameleon arch with a perception filter. This meant that it could only be seen if the observer really wanted to see it, otherwise it would always seem to be just on the periphery of their vision. This meant that John Smith could never inadvertently pick the fob watch up and open it, thus restoring the Doctor and alerting the Family of Blood to his whereabouts. (3.8, 3.9) Martha Jones realised Professor Yana had never really noticed the fob watch he carried, due to a perception filter. (3.11) The Doctor created a similar field on each of their TARDIS keys, using bits from Martha Jones's mobile phone and Captain Jack Harkness's laptop. When they wore these keys around their necks, people didn't really notice them. The Master was immune to the perception filters, however, and saw all three of them clearly on the deck of the *Valiant*. (3.12) When Martha escaped from the *Valiant* using Jack's Vortex Manipulator, her key's perception filter allowed her to travel the Earth unnoticed by the Toclafane. (3.13)

Perganon: A civilisation lost during the Great Time War. (2.3)

Peripatetic Medical Squad: A mobile group of doctors, given permission by the Master and the Toclafane to go between labour camps, administering their services where necessary. Thomas Milligan worked for one, which was useful cover for his Resistance activities. (3.13)

'Pete's World': The Doctor gave this name to the parallel Earth on which he, Rose Tyler and Mickey Smith fought the Cybermen. The Cybermen and other humans from 'Pete's World', including Pete Tyler himself, then went back and forth between it and the Earth where Rose was born. The two Earths were almost identical, but there were subtle differences: Mickey Smith was Ricky Smith; his grandmother Rita-Anne was still alive; Cuba Gooding Jnr was born in February not January; Cybus Industries dominated the business world from their Zeppelin airships; Pete Tyler was a millionaire, married to Jackie Tyler but without a daughter (instead, their terrier was called Rose). The Britain of 'Pete's World' was a Republic, run by a President, and was suffering not just from severe global warming but also from the breaches created by the Cybermen and Jake Simmonds' troopers travelling back and forth between the two Earths. The Doctor was able to repair these breaches, sealing off both worlds for ever and trapping millions of Daleks and Cybermen in the Void between the two. However, this meant that Jackie, Mickey and Rose had to stay on 'Pete's World' for the rest of their lives, officially listed among the dead after the Battle of Canary Wharf on Rose's home Earth. (2.5, 2.6, 2.12, 2.13)

Peterson: Schoolboy at Farringham School for Boys in 1913, who did something his headmaster found unacceptable before the Family of Blood attacked. (3.9)

Petrifold Regression: A terminal disease of the flesh that turns people to stone. The Duke of Manhattan on New Earth was suffering from it and, although the Doctor believed there wouldn't be a cure for another thousand years, the Sisters of Plenitude cured him. (2.1)

Pharmacists: Stallholders in Pharmacytown, part of the Undercity of New New York. They sold Mood Patches and were told by an angry Doctor to be prepared to be closed down. After freeing the cars from the Motorway, the Doctor returned to Pharmacytown and found they had moved on voluntarily. (3.3) (Played by TOM EDDEN, NATASHA WILLIAMS, GAYLE TELFER STEVENS)

PIG SLAVES: When they first arrived in Manhattan, the Dalek began a series of genetic experiments, at first attempting to create new Dalek embryos. When that failed, Dalek Sec realised the way forward was to merge himself with a human but, to ensure they would be compatible, the Cult began using kidnapped humans and merging them with pigs, porcine flesh being the closest to human, creating a race of Pig Slaves. The resultant physical trauma meant that the Pig Slaves had a limited life span, but it was long enough to use them to kidnap more humans, the less intelligent of which were also turned into Pig Slaves. The more intelligent ones went on to join the other aspect of the Final Experiment: the creation of a hybrid Dalek-Human army. Most of the Pig Slaves were killed in the Empire State Building when Martha Jones used iron poles to conduct electricity from a lightning strike into their ranks. Once the Daleks were defeated, any survivors would have roamed the sewers until they died naturally. (3.4, 3.5)

Pharmacytown: Part of the Undercity of New New York where stallholders sold Mood Patches and were told by an angry Doctor to be prepared to be closed down. After freeing the cars from the Motorway, the Doctor returned to Pharmacytown and found the stallholders had moved on voluntarily. (3.3)

Phelan, Sally: When the Doctor and Mrs Moore went further into Deepcold 6 on 'Pete's World', they stopped a Cyberman using an electromagnetic bomb. When the Doctor tried to examine the fallen Cyberform, he realised its emotional inhibitor was damaged. The human within tried to reassert its personality, revealing itself to be a girl, Sally Phelan, who had been Cyber-converted the night before her wedding to Gareth. Using his sonic screwdriver, the Doctor sorrowfully switched the life support in the Cyberform off, giving Sally final peace. (2.6) (Voiced by NICHOLAS BRIGGS)

Pheros: Planet of living metal, a huge eyrie for the giant metal birds that dominated the planet. Baltazar used the living metals to build himself a vast warship from which he became the scourge of the galaxies, along with his first mate, Caw, one of the Pheros bird creatures. (TIQ)

Phillips, Mr: The bursar at Farringham School for Boys, who was murdered by Son of Mine, inhabiting the body of schoolboy Jeremy Baines. (3.8, 3.9) (Played by MATTHEW WHITE)

Pick-up truck: Jackie Tyler borrowed one from her friend Rodrigo, and Mickey Smith used it to wrench open the TARDIS console, flooding Rose Tyler with the Time Vortex. (1.13)

Picosurgeon: Surgeon who administers the Type Two chip to Adam Mitchell to give him full access to the information spikes on Satellite Five. (1.7)

Pilot Fish: The Doctor likened the mercenary Roboforms, who disguised themselves as Santa Clauses on two consecutive Christmases, to pilot fish. (2.X, 3.X)

Pirates: A regular fear of the drivers on the New New York Motorway was that they could be car-jacked by pirates. (3.3)

Pit, the: The area on Krop Tor sealed by a 30-foot-wide metal trapdoor. The trapdoor opened when the humans from Sanctuary Base 6 drilled through to the cavern it was in, revealing the Pit, within which lived the body of the Beast. (2.8, 2.9)

Pitt, Brad: According to Lance Bennett, Donna Noble talked excitedly about this American actor and his on/off relationship with actor Angelina Jolie. (3.X)

Plasma coils: Artificial energy source, used throughout the galaxy. A platoon of Judoon transported a set to Earth and placed it around the Royal Hope Hospital. Over two days it began creating electrical storms that would power the H2O Scoop that they would use to transport the hospital to the surface of Earth's Moon. (3.1)

Plasmavores: Race of shape-changing aliens who lived off the richest veins of haemoglobin they could find. A Plasmavore was hiding in the Royal Hope Hospital on Earth, disguised as Florence Finnegan. (3.1)

Plasmic energy: The energy that the Wire was composed of, which it also used to drain the life force out of its television-viewing victims. (2.7)

Platform One: Vast space station, overseen by a computerised Control (voiced by SARA STEWART), consisting of Suites, Viewing Galleries, ventilation ducts, private rooms, a massive Ventilation Chamber and other areas. On Platform One, a number of alien dignitaries arrived to observe Earthdeath, as did the Doctor and Rose Tyler. Although nearly destroyed when the protective force field was temporarily shut off by Lady Cassandra O'Brien, Platform One survived. Other Platform space stations included Platform Three, Platform Six and Platform Fifteen. (1.2)

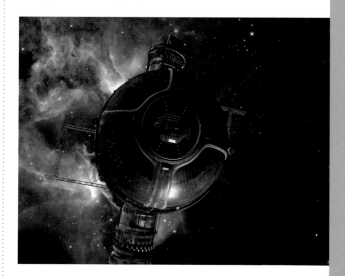

PlayStation: Mickey Smith told Rose Tyler that he had learned to fly a Zeppelin on his PlayStation games console. (2.6)

Pleasure Gardens: An area of the Hospital on New Earth. Access to it required coloured ID cards, and taking cuttings from the Gardens was forbidden. (2.1)

Plymouth: City in Devon, on the south-west coast of the UK with the largest naval docks in Western Europe. The submarine HMS *Taurean* was just ten miles away from Plymouth when Mickey Smith helped the Doctor launch one of its sub-Harpoon missiles at 10 Downing Street. (1.5)

Poisson, Jeanne-Antoinette: As an adult, Reinette, as she had been known when a child, met the Doctor in her bedroom for the first time since her seventh year, having previously assumed he was a dream. They next met face to face in 1745 when he, Rose Tyler and Mickey Smith went through a time window from a ship in the 51st century to stop a Clockwork Robot attacking her in the palace at Versailles, where she had recently moved. Sending Rose and Mickey back, the Doctor strove to find out why they were interested in Reinette and they linked minds – she gaining access to his as much as he to hers. Their friendship seemed to be growing deeper (he stayed for a good party). Her next encounter with the future was via Rose in 1753, by when she had become Madame de Pompadour. Rose told her that the Robots would be back one last time, in 1758, when she would be the same age as the spaceship. Sure enough, at a party in Versailles, the Clockwork Robots were back, and the Doctor crashed through a mirror on the back of Arthur the Horse, breaking the Robots' link to the 51st century and cutting them off from their power source. They collapsed, inert. Reinette was told by the Doctor he could never go back – she however had had the Paris fireplace moved to Versailles, and the mechanism connecting it to the future still worked. The Doctor asked her to accompany him to the stars and she agreed, preparing for his return once he'd found Rose and Mickey. She never saw him again and died in 1764. (2.4) (Played by SOPHIA MYLES)

Poisson, Madame: Mother to Jeanne-Antoinette Poisson, aka Reinette, who was anxiously waiting to take her away from their Paris home for the evening, when the Doctor encountered the adult Reinette for the first time. (2.4)

Pok Baint, Stella: She was famous for her hats, not for shoes. Rose Tyler didn't know this when asked by the Anne Droid in *The Weakest Link* aboard the Game Station. (1.12)

Pola Ventura: The city of Pola Ventura, not Reykjavik, hosted Murder

Spree 20. Rose Tyler didn't know this when asked by the Anne Droid in *The Weakest Link* aboard the Game Station. (1.12)

Police: A young officer took notes from Rose Tyler when she returned home after being missing for a year. (1.4) (Played by CERIS JONES) A police officer observed the A+ hypnotised victims of the Sycorax making their way to the tops of tall buildings. (2.X) (Played by SEAN CARLSEN) A policeman tried to stop Rose Tyler reaching the Olympic Torch so she could power the Isolus spaceship. (2.11) (Played by STEPHEN MARZELLA) Two police officers stopped members of the public, including Tish Jones, getting to the site where the Royal Hope Hospital had stood until the Judoon took it to the Moon. (3.1) (Played by BRIAN MORGAN and SONAL MANTA)

Police Commissioner: Metropolitan officer who asked the public to remain calm as more 'ghosts' appeared. When the ghosts transformed into Cybermen, he urged people to stay in their homes. (2.12) (Played by DAVID WARWICK)

Polkowski: Henry Van Statten's chief aide, who warned his boss against having the US President replaced. As a result, Van Statten had Polkowski fired and mind-wiped, leaving him to live his life as a vagrant. (1.6) (Played by STEVEN BECKINGHAM)

Polycarbide: The alloy used to create the outer casing of a Dalek. It is usually combined with Dalekanium, although Dalek Sec's was made from Metalert. (2.13, 3.4, 3.5)

Pompeii: Captain Jack Harkness likened London during the Blitz to Pompeii as a great place to put things you want destroyed surreptitiously. Pompeii was destroyed when a volcano buried it in lava and ash in AD 79. (1.10)

Pool, Mr: Teacher at Farringham School for Boys who didn't want his afternoon tea, so Cook gave it to Martha Jones. (3.8)

Pope, Elton: As a four-year-old, Elton found his mother dead, and the Doctor standing over her body. The Doctor had been trying to track a Living Shadow which had escaped the Howling Halls. The Shadow had killed Elton's mother, but Elton's memories of

exactly what had happened remained blurred for many years. However, as Elton found himself in the same shopping centre as Jackie Tyler during the Auton invasion, watching the Slitheen ship smash through Big Ben, and had his windows blown out by the passing Sycorax ship, he gained an interest in alien incursions on Earth. He found a blog on the net, My Invasion Blog, set up by Ursula Blake to record such things, which led him to join a like-minded group of gentle people all searching for the Doctor. They called themselves LINDA and, before long, they were all close friends. Elton was especially close to Ursula Blake. After their group was infiltrated by the Abzorbaloff, posing as Victor Kennedy, Elton was forced to make friends with Jackie Tyler (who he actually really liked) and ultimately betray her as he searched for information about her daughter Rose. Rebelling against Kennedy, Elton ended up as the only survivor of LINDA, although Ursula lived on as a face embedded in concrete, so she still stayed with him in his flat. Finally meeting the Doctor gave Elton the closure he needed over his mother's death and he was able to continue with his life. (2.10) (Played by MARC WARREN)

Pope, Mrs: The Doctor was pursuing an elemental shade that had escaped from the Howling Halls when he found himself at the Pope household. Mrs Pope had been killed by the Shadow and her four-year-old son Elton saw the Doctor with her body. (2.10) (Played by LARMORNA CHAPELL)

Posh Mum and Posh Dad: Visitors to Ward 26 in the Hospital on New Earth. They were leaving the ward when the infected New Humans tried to burst through the door, and the mum was killed. (2.1) (Played by HELEN IRVING and DAVE BREMNER)

Post-Op: One of the areas within the Hospital on New Earth run by the Sisters of Plenitude. (2.1)

Powell Estate: Part of the North Peckham Estate in South East London, postcode SE15 7GO, where the Tyler family lived, and where Mickey Smith lived (at number 90 Bucknall House) after the death of his grandmother, Rita-Anne. The Tylers lived at 48 Bucknall House. Other estate residents included Debbie, the Changs, Tina the Cleaner and Sandra and Jason. (1.1, 1.4, 1.5, 1.8, 1.13, 2.X, 2.1, 2.6, 2.10, 2.12, 3.X)

Poynter, Dougie: Member of pop group McFly, who endorsed Harry Saxon's campaign to become Prime Minister. (3.12)

Preacher: Gloomy predictor of Earth's imminent destruction in 1599. When the portal to the Deep Darkness opened, he seemed curiously delighted that his prophecies were about to come true. (3.2) (Played by ROBERT DEMEGER)

Preachers, the: Underground resistance group on 'Pete's World', dedicated to bringing down Cybus Industries, aided by the mysterious Gemini. They took their name from the fact they planned to tell the world 'the gospel truth' about John Lumic's plans. Amongst its members were Mrs Moore (the group's driver and techie), Jake Simmonds (reconnaissance), Ricky Smith

(planning) and Thin Jimmy (leader). After Thin Jimmy's capture, Ricky became leader. When Ricky and Mrs Moore died fighting the Cybermen, Mickey Smith took Ricky's place and headed to the continent with Jake to locate more Cybermen. (2.5, 2.6) Jake Simmonds later led an armed group from 'Pete's World' to the real Earth to fight Cybermen. Whether these were new Preachers or an entirely new group is unknown. (2.13)

Prentice, Grandad: Jackie Tyler's father, who died from a heart attack in the late 1980s, but according to Jackie came back as a friendly ghost. The 'ghost' was in fact a Cyberman, breaking through the Void as a means of travelling to Earth from 'Pete's World'. (2.12)

Presenter: TV personality who alerted the public to the disappearances of the children from Stratford in 2012. (2.11T) (Played by DANIEL ROCHFORD)

President of the People's Republic of Great Britain: On 'Pete's World', Britain was a republic. The President refused to fund the Ultimate Upgrade project, so Lumic had him killed. (2.5) (Played by DON WARRINGTON) He was succeeded by Harriet Jones, under whom the People's Republic took over the Torchwood Institute. (2.13)

President of the United States of America: The President was due to address the American nation live from the White House on the evening of the Big Ben incident. (1.4) The President wanted to bypass Harriet Jones and make contact with the Martians that later turned out to be Sycorax. (2.X) President Winters attempted to take control of the Toclafane situation from Harry Saxon (aka the Master) and make contact with the spheres aboard the *Valiant* but was murdered by the alien invaders. (3.12, 3.13)

Presley, Elvis Aaron: American singer, generally considered the King of Rock 'n' Roll. The Doctor suggested the Sycorax could hypnotise someone to sing like Elvis, but not convince them to die. (2.X) The Doctor and Rose were on their way to see Elvis in Las Vegas but ended up in Muswell Hill. (2.7) The crew of the SS *Pentallian* had set a trivia question on one of their door seals, regarding who had the most UK number one hits before the download era out of Elvis and The Beatles. (Elvis won!) (3.7)

Price Family: On 'Pete's World', Angela Price worked for Cybus Industries until she learned their secrets and fled, joining the Preachers to try and bring the corporation down. To protect her husband and children, she assumed the name Mrs Moore. After her death, the Doctor told Jake Simmonds and Mickey Smith to find Mr Price and tell him how brave his wife had been. (2.6)

Price, Sergeant: Police officer who oversaw security at 10 Downing Street in the wake of the murder of the UNIT personnel, academics and military officers, unaware that the murderers were actually the people he took his orders from – Slitheen family members disguised as humans. When the Doctor managed to have a sub-Harpoon missile launched at the building, it was Price's job to get everyone out but, when he saw the Slitheen in their true forms, he happily left them to their fate. (1.5) (Played by MORGAN HOPKINS)

Prime Minister: The head of the British Government, the Prime Minister disappeared at the start of the Big Ben incident. Margaret Blaine of MI5 told General Asquith that she personally saw the PM into his car, but Margaret was really a disguised Slitheen, and the Prime Minister had actually been murdered and stuffed into a cupboard in 10 Downing Street. (1.4) Once the Slitheen attack had been defeated, Harriet Jones was elected Prime Minister by a landslide. She then had to deal with the Sycorax spaceship over London, until the Doctor intervened. Using Torchwood to destroy the alien craft after it began its retreat, she angered the Doctor, who whispered the phrase 'Don't you think she looks tired' to her aide. Within days, Harriet Jones's leadership was crumbling, (2.X) an event that enabled the Master to create a fake personality, Harry Saxon, and begin his campaign to become Prime Minister and destroy Earth via the mysterious Toclafane. (3.12, 3.13)

Pringles: According to Lance Bennett, Donna Noble got excited over a new flavour of these crisp snacks. (3.X)

Prison Cell 8447: The cell on Volag-Noc that contained the real Governor, Locke. The Doctor was erroneously placed in with Locke, and together the two escaped. (TIQ)

Private Gallery 15: Area aboard Platform One where the TARDIS landed. (1.2)

Private Legislation 16: The rule under which the Doctor was arrested aboard the Game Station. (1.12)

Protein One: One of the foodstuffs eaten by the inhabitants of Sanctuary Base 6. Other Protein supplements included Protein Two and Protein Three. (2.8, 2.9)

Protohumans: One of the names the humans of five billion years in Rose's future used to describe themselves, implying they were different from the then-extinct (bar Lady Cassandra) humans from Earth itself. (1.2)

Psychic Paper: Special paper, apparently blank, housed in a wallet, and used by the Doctor. It projected a low-level telepathic field that caused its viewer to see on it whatever they expected to see (e.g. a security pass or a business card). This enabled the Doctor and his companions to access many places they would otherwise not have been allowed to enter. The

employees from the Torchwood Institute (2.12) and William Shakespeare (3.2) were among those immune to the psychic paper. The Doctor also used it to discover other people's identities by getting them to hold it and then reading whatever they unwittingly project onto it, as he did with Gurney, the fake Governor of the prison on Volag-Noc. (TIQ)

Psychograft: A device activated by Chip to transplant the consciousness of Lady Cassandra O'Brien from her dying brain into Rose Tyler's body on New Earth. The psychograft's energy remained within Cassandra's mind, enabling her to jump from body to body for some while afterwards. (2.1)

Queen's Arcade: Shopping mall in South London where Rose Tyler's mother and Clive Finch's family were attacked by Autons. (1.1)

Queen Street: Location of Banto's DVD store, where Larry Nightingale worked. After defeating the Weeping Angels together, Larry and Sally Sparrow bought Banto out and turned the shop into an antique book and rare DVD store. (3.10)

Queen Victoria, the: Fictional Walford pub featured in the BBC soap opera *EastEnders*. Publican Peggy Mitchell had discovered the ghost of previous tenant Den Watts in the cellar of the pub, in episodes being watched by Jackie Tyler. (2.12)

Quizmania: ITV Play television series of which Annalise, the girlfriend of Clive Jones, presumably watched repeats. According to Clive's estranged wife, the show was too difficult for Annalise to handle. (3.1)

Quoldonity: One of the many religions practised in the 42nd century. (2.9)

Racnoss: Omnivorous, giant, eight-legged, semi-humanoid race from the Dark Times, who devoured entire planets because they were born starving. Believed destroyed by the Fledgling Empires, a Webstar ship carrying Racnoss young, the Secret Heart, was caught in the gravity field of a star, and a world was formed around it – the Earth. Billions of years later, the last of the Racnoss, their Empress, returned to Earth, eager to free her ever-hungry young, using an organic key charged with Huon particles. However, the Doctor blew up the walls of the Torchwood base which flooded the tunnel through which the children were escaping, wiping out all the Racnoss young. The Empress herself was aboard her Webstar when it was destroyed moments later, bringing an end to one of the longest-surviving races in the universe. (3.X)

Radford Parade: Area of Nottingham where, in the fiction the Doctor created for John Smith's background, John believed he grew up. (3.9)

Radiation Pits of Europe: Martha Jones walked across the Earth telling her story about the Doctor, preparing people for the right moment to chant his name. Amongst the places she visited were the Radiation Pits of Europe. (3.13)

Radiation Room: Part of the Silo base on Malcassairo, where stet radiation was being used to power the rocket's drives. Stet radiation was utterly lethal to humans – and when the Futurekind's Wiry Woman turned the power off, Guard Jate was instantly vaporised by it. (3.11)

Radio Enthusiast, The: Magazine about radio and the burgeoning television industry. Tommy Connolly was reading a copy when trying to persuade his father to buy a television set. (2.7)

Raffalo: A Crespallion maintenance worker aboard Platform One who Rose talked to. She was killed when Cassandra's robot spiders dragged her into a ventilation duct. (1.2) (Played by BECCY ARMOURY)

Rage: Coming in varying strengths, this was one of the Mood Patches available in Pharmacytown in the Undercity of New New York. (3.3)

Rago Rago 5 6 Rago: Location of a famous university. Chosen Scholars from Class 55 were guests aboard Platform One to see the Earthdeath spectacle. (1.2)

Raleigh, Sir Walter: Nobleman during the reign of Elizabeth I who reportedly laid his cloak across a puddle to avoid his monarch's feet getting wet. This chivalrous act seeped into history and Queen Victoria likened Sir Robert MacLeish to Raleigh when he offered to climb through a window first, better to help her out afterwards. (2.2)

Ralph: One of the Lord Chamberlain's Men, an actor and stagehand in Shakespeare's company at the Globe Theatre. He was charged with distributing drafts of *Love's Labour's Won* to the rest of the company. (3.2)

Ramsay: One of the soldiers under Captain Reynolds protecting Queen Victoria in 1879. (2.2) (Played by CHARLES DE PAULA)

Ravel, Maurice: French composer whose most famous work, Boléro, was being listened to by Toby Zed while working on the ancient Veltino inscriptions he found on the surface of Krop Tor. It switched off when the Beast contacted his mind. (2.8)

Raxacoricofallapatorius: A world of burgundy seas and four polar regions, part of the Isop Galaxy, Raxacoricofallapatorius was considered a peaceful place. Its chief inhabitants were the calcium-based Raxacoricofallapatorians – but their society had a darker side, epitomised by the exiled Family Slitheen, a gang of ruthless criminals. Criminals were executed by being boiled alive in acetic acid until they became soup. Female Raxacoricofallapatorians had lethal defence mechanisms: a poison dart that could be ejected from their claws, and they could exhale poison gas. (1.4, 1.5, 1.11) Henry Van Statten had the arm of a Raxacoricofallapatorian in his exhibit room in Utah. (1.6) Rose Tyler pretended to have authority granted to her by the Raxacoricofallapatorian Parliament to demand the Sycorax leave Earth. (2.X) The Graske held a Raxacoricofallapatorian, which the Doctor identified as a member of the Family Slitheen, prisoner in his base on Griffoth. (AotG) Raxacoricofallapatorius had a sister planet, Clom, and the Abzorbaloff came from there. (2.10)

Reapers: When Rose Tyler stopped her dad dying in a hit-and-run accident on the day of Sarah Clark and Stuart Hoskins' wedding in 1987, she caused a tear in the fabric of time, allowing the antibody-like wraiths the Reapers to spill into the Earth of 1987, wiping people out of time and feeding off the resultant chronal energy. The survivors hid within St Christopher's Church, a building so old the Reapers had a hard time getting in, with the Doctor's age being an added protection. However, when Rose met her younger self, as a baby, and they touched, the safety net broke as the additional surge of chronal energy from this paradox weakened the Church. The Reapers burst in, and the Doctor became their next victim, although one of them was destroyed when it touched the TARDIS. Pete Tyler, having worked out who Rose really was and why the Reapers were there, sacrificed his life, putting time back on track and expelling the Reapers, and returning to life all those they'd taken. No one there was left with any memory of the events, except the Doctor and Rose. (1.8)

Red Division: A troop of security guards under the command of Bywater, working for Henry Van Statten in his Vault, deep below Utah. (1.6)

Red Falls Five: Place that the Shafe Cane family came from before arriving as refugees on Malcassairo. (3.11)

Red Hatching: According to Martha Jones, she and the Doctor were in a hurry and couldn't speak to Sally Sparrow in 2008 because a migration had begun and the red hatching would be starting within twenty minutes. Exactly what the red hatching was remained a mystery to Sally, but she discovered from the Doctor that it involved four things and a lizard. (3.10)

Red People: A number of the humans who lived on New Earth came in extreme colours, including red and white. In the Hospital on New Earth, a Red Woman was being repainted as a cure for Marconi's Disease by some of the Sisters of Plenitude. (2.1) (Played by CLAIRE SADLER) As the Doctor dropped from car to car on the New New York Motorway, he encountered a Red Man driving one vehicle. (3.3) (Played by ANDREW CAMERON)

Red Velvets: Rodrick knew that Hoshbin Frane was the President of the Red Velvets when asked by the Anne Droid in *The Weakest Link* aboard the Game Station. (1.12)

Redfern, Nurse Joan: Matron at Farringham School for Boys and charged with overseeing their welfare. Over the few weeks that John Smith had been teaching history at the school, Joan had become attracted to him and he to her, and they began a courtship, much to the chagrin of Martha Jones. She knew their relationship was doomed because, before long, she would have to open the fob watch containing the essence of the Doctor, so John Smith would no longer exist. When the Family of Blood attacked first the village and then the school, Joan found herself tested. She deplored the fact that the boys were educated in the art of war, because her husband Oliver had died during the Boer War, and yet she accepted that the school needed to defend itself from the Family and their Scarecrow foot soldiers. She eventually led Smith and Martha to the Cartwrights' cottage, where she and John discussed the fact that he clearly was this Doctor that the Family and Martha had claimed he was. Eventually, John opened the fob watch, and the Doctor was reborn. Joan realised that, no matter how much she had loved John Smith, the Doctor was a wholly different person, and one she did not like at all. The Doctor offered Joan the chance to travel with him, because somewhere inside him whatever had drawn John Smith to her still existed. But Joan was resolute and asked him to leave, keeping his 'Journal of Impossible Things' as a reminder of the second man in her life to have died. (3.8, 3.9) (Played by JESSICA HYNES)

REGENERATION: A Time Lord process whereby the entire cellular make-up of a Time Lord is rearranged, literally replacing his body with a new one, although the mind, perhaps a bit shaken up at first, remains the same. After Rose Tyler had absorbed the Time Vortex and destroyed the Dalek Emperor and his fleet from aboard the Game Station, the Doctor kissed Rose and drew all that devastating power out of her and into his own body. Tragically, although he saved Rose, that amount of power damaged his body fatally, requiring him to regenerate. (1.13) He later told Rose he couldn't change back. (CiN) At about the time the TARDIS was transported aboard the Sycorax ship, the Doctor became fully acclimatised to his new body and took the Sycorax Leader on in combat. The Doctor's right hand, which had a weak dorsal tubercle, was lopped off by the Leader's sword but, as his regenerative cycle was still under 15 hours old, he was instantly able to grow a new one – one better suited for combat. (2.X) The Master was forced to regenerate when Chantho, last survivor of the Malmooth, shot him in the stomach. (3.11) When that incarnation of the Master stole the severed hand of the Doctor, he was able to use DNA from it to programme his laser screwdriver, using technology from Professor Lazarus's GMD, to suspend the Doctor's regenerative capabilities and age him to his full 900-plus years. The Master was once again shot in the stomach, this time by Lucy Saxon, but he refused to trigger a regeneration, choosing to die and leave the Doctor alone in the universe – his final revenge. (3.13)

Redfern, Oliver: Late husband of Joan Redfern, Matron at Farringham School for Boys. He died at Spion Kop, one of the famous battles of the Boer War, in January 1900. (3.8)

Redford: Schoolboy at Farringham School for Boys in 1913, who was told to secure the courtyard before the Family of Blood attacked. (3.9)

Redpath, Mr: Young grandson of Mrs Peace, whose body was lying in Gabriel Sneed's Chapel of Rest. When the Gelth inhabited Mrs Peace's body, she throttled Redpath to death and another Gelth later took over his corpse. (1.3) (Played by HUW RHYS)

Registrar: Council official who married Jackie Prentice to Pete Tyler in a registry office in 1982. (1.8) (Played by ROBERT BARTON)

'Regresa A Mi': Spanish-language version of the song 'Un-Break My Heart', sung by Il Divo and played by Jackie Tyler to Elton Pope in her flat. (2.10)

Reinette: Nickname given to Jeanne-Antoinette Poisson, better known in later life as Madame de Pompadour. As a seven-year-old, Reinette met the Doctor for the first time when he talked to her from the 51st century via the fireplace in her Paris bedroom. He later crossed through to see her, but some months had passed for Reinette. Together they discovered a Clockwork Robot hiding under her bed. (2.4) (Played by JESSICA ATKINS)

Rels: Dalek measurement of time. (2.13, 3.5)

Remembrance Day: Annual service held across Britain each November to remember and honour the dead of the wars of the 20th century. As a very old man, Timothy Latimer was at one when he saw the Doctor and Martha Jones for the first time since he was 14. (3.9)

Resistance: A network of resistance cells existed after the Master and the Toclafane took over the Earth. Amongst their members were Professor Allison Docherty, Thomas Milligan and Martha Jones. (3.13)

Rex Vox Jax: Planetary home of the Hop Pyleen brothers, inventors of Hyposlip Travel Systems. (1.2)

Rexel 4: A planet in the Rexel planetary configuration. (3.2)

Rexel planetary configuration: The home system of the Carrionites. Legend had it that the specific alignment of the configuration was the prison door created by the Eternals to seal the Carrionites within the Deep Darkness. (3.2)

Reykjavik: The city of Pola Ventura hosted Murder Spree 20, not Reykjavik. Rose Tyler didn't know this when asked by the Anne Droid in *The Weakest Link* aboard the Game Station. (1.12)

Reynolds, Captain: Commander of the soldiers charged with guarding Queen Victoria against would-be assassins on her way to Balmoral in 1879. He was killed by the Haemovariform at Torchwood House. (2.2) (Played by JAMIE SIVES)

Rhodri: Official wedding-video recordist for Donna Noble and Lance Bennett. He recorded Donna's disappearance and showed it to the Doctor, which enabled the Doctor to realise she had been fed Huon particles and thus the biodamper she wore wouldn't protect her. Rhodri was considering selling the tape to the TV show *You've Been Framed*. (3.X) (Played by RHODRI MEILIR)

Rice, Tim: British lyricist, responsible for the song 'The Circle of Life', which the Doctor quoted to the Sycorax Leader. (2.X)

Richard, Cliff: British singer (real name Harry Webb) who Jackie Tyler was a fan of. The Doctor was not surprised by this. (2.7)

Ricky: Deliberately trying to wind him up, the Doctor often referred to Mickey Smith as Ricky. (1.4, 1.11) On 'Pete's World', Mickey's counterpart really was called Ricky Smith. (2.5, 2.6)

Rift, the: An unexplained space and time phenomenon that crossed through the centre of Cardiff, its exact start and end points unknown. Various kinds of energy bled through it and, in 1869, it formed a gateway to Earth for would-be invaders called the Gelth. (1.3) The Doctor's TARDIS was re-energised by absorbing Rift energy. When it was connected to a tribophysical waveform macro-kinetic extrapolator, energy beamed up from the TARDIS into the Rift, tearing it open and causing a series of earthquakes across Cardiff. (1.11) The Doctor and Martha Jones later returned to Cardiff to refuel the TARDIS. Captain Jack Harkness had previously begun working at the Torchwood base beneath Cardiff, knowing that the Doctor would return eventually for this purpose. (3.11)

Rigs: Robotic oil rigs patrolled the planet Bouken, harvesting its rare oil reserves. They had a low level of sentience and advanced weaponry. (TIQ)

Ring: The Master wore a ring, with the LazLabs logo on it, which he habitually tapped out the pulse-beat his Archangel Network was hypnotising humanity with. After his death and immolation, a mysterious female hand removed the Master's ring from his funeral pyre. (3.12, 3.13)

Rio de Janeiro: City in Brazil where Great Train Robber Ronald Biggs fled to. (3.1)

Rita Logistics: Haulage company that Elton Pope worked for. (2.10)

Rita-Anne: Mickey Smith's blind grandmother, who took Mickey in after his mother ran away and Jackson Smith, his father, moved to Spain. She was a strict disciplinarian, but loved Mickey a lot. She died about five years before Mickey met the Doctor, by tripping over loose stair-carpet. Mickey felt guilty about this – she had asked him to repair it a few times. On 'Pete's World', Mickey was delighted to see she was still alive, although her grandson was called Ricky and, much to her consternation, hung out with the Preachers. (2.5) (Played by MONA HAMMOND)

Roboforms: Robotic scavenging mercenaries based on Earth, camouflaged as Christmas Santas. They carried weapons disguised as musical instruments and attacked Rose Tyler (and Mickey Smith by default, as he was with her) and later the Doctor because they were drawn to him and the TARDIS and intended to replenish their batteries from his chronon energy. (2.X) A year later, the Doctor encountered them again, this time being used by the Empress of the Racnoss, who had sent them to kidnap Donna Noble. (3.X)

Rocastle, Mr: Headmaster of Farringham School for Boys. A strict disciplinarian, he could nevertheless be quite fair when necessary. As a former soldier in the Boer War, he saw it as his duty to instil in his boys an aptitude for warfare, fearing that it would not be long before they would need those skills. When the Family of Blood attacked first the village and then the school itself, the initially sceptical Rocastle, along with Mr Phillips the school's bursar, went to investigate. Phillips was murdered by the aliens, and Rocastle realised the danger his school and pupils were in. He organised the defence against the Family's Scarecrow soldiers. However, he refused to believe that the body of six-year-old Lucy Cartwright could be host to an alien – a mistake, as she promptly disintegrated him. (3.8, 3.9) (Played by PIP TORRENS)

'Rock-A-Bye Baby': American lullaby, generally accepted as the first written on American soil, but based on the British ballad 'Lillibullero'. Nancy sang it to Private Jenkins to keep him calm after he had become a gas mask zombie. (1.10)

'Rockin' Around The Christmas Tree': A seasonal 1958 hit song for Brenda Lee, this was playing in the house where the Graske replaced the parents with changelings. (AotG)

Rodrick: One of the players of *The Weakest Link* aboard the Game Station. He was ruthless and tactical, getting rid of the stronger links so he would go head to head with Rose Tyler, who he thought was a bit thick, and thus win. He did indeed win, by default, but never received his money. He was amongst the angry contestants and Game Station staff gathered on Floor 000 when the Daleks invaded the station, and he was exterminated. (1.12, 1.13) (Played by PATERSON JOSEPH)

Rodrigo: Male friend of Jackie Tyler's who, she claimed, owed her a favour. She borrowed his pick-up truck, with which Mickey Smith was able to wrench open the TARDIS console. (1.13)

Roedean: Exclusive British girls' school in Sussex. Lucy Saxon went there. (3.12)

Roentgen radiation: A form of radiation transmitted by the X-ray machine installed in the Royal Hope Hospital. The Doctor used a huge amount to flood the room, destroying a Slab and filling his body as well, though Time Lords were immune to its destructive capabilities. He managed to shake the radiation out through his foot, soaking his shoe with it in the process – he threw away the shoe. When he was a child, the Doctor used to play with Roentgen blocks. (3.1)

Rook, Vivien: British journalist, working for the *Sunday Mirror*. Claiming to be doing a story about Lucy Saxon, she made her way through Downing Street to warn Lucy about Harry Saxon. As one of the two per cent of the population not affected by the Master's hypnotic pulse beaming down from the Archangel network (like Lucy Saxon and Clive Jones), she had discovered he was a fake. Realising this, the Master had her killed by the Toclafane, but Vivien had already uploaded a message and all her files to Torchwood, hoping someone would stop Saxon. (3.12) (Played by NICHOLA McAULIFFE)

Room 802: Room in Albion Hospital where Dr Constantine made taped recordings of his sessions with Jamie, the gas-mask-wearing 'empty' child. When the gas mask zombies tried to surround the Doctor, knowing they were all behaving like a four-year-old boy, he told them to go to their rooms. Eventually Jamie made his way to Room 802, believing it to be his room. (1.10)

Rose: In 'Pete's World', Jackie Tyler's pet Yorkshire Terrier was called Rose. This Tyler family had never had a daughter. (2.5) (Played by TINKERBELL)

Rose of the Powell Estate, Dame: The title bestowed upon Rose Tyler by Queen Victoria after the Doctor destroyed the Haemovariform that threatened her life at Torchwood House. Victoria then exiled Rose and the Doctor from the British Empire. (2.2)

Roswell: The New Mexico home of the legendary 'Area 51', where many conspiracy theorists believe alien autopsies have occurred and extraterrestrial spaceships and weaponry are stored by the US Government. Henry Van Statten had a milometer from a Roswell spaceship in his exhibit room deep under the surface of Utah. (1.6)

Rogue Traders: Australian rock group, whose single 'Voodoo Child'

was played by the Master aboard the *Valiant* as the Toclafane began their descent. Lucy Saxon danced along to it, too. (3.12)

Rowling, JK: Author of the Harry Potter novels. The Doctor told Martha Jones he had cried at the end of *Harry Potter and the Deathly Hallows*. Martha used a word from the books, 'Expelliarmus', to help William Shakespeare send the Carrionites back into the Deep Darkness. (3.2)

Royal Hope Hospital: Thameside hospital where Martha Jones was training to become a doctor and which was unwittingly harbouring a fugitive Plasmavore. As a result it was transported wholesale to the Moon, where the alien Judoon, who had no jurisdiction to land on Earth, came searching for the Plasmavore. Once the Plasmavore had been executed, the hospital was returned safely to Earth. (3.1)

Rubicon: North Italian river which, according to legend, Caesar crossed as a deliberate act of war. The Doctor told Rose he could take her to witness this. (2.2)

Russia: The largest country on Earth, turned into the massive Shipyard Number One by the Master and the Toclafane. The shipyard ran from the Black Sea to the Bering Strait. (3.13)

Rutherford, Ernest: Often associated with splitting the atom (he didn't, it was actually John Cockcroft and Ernest Walton), but generally he is seen as the main exponent of that branch of science. Richard Lazarus likened the importance to mankind of his own work with the Genetic Manipulation Device to Rutherford's work. (3.6)

Sabre-toothed gorillas: Alien creatures which the Doctor warned Martha Jones about when they arrived on the planet Myarr. (TIQ)

Sacramento: One of the cities Goddard suggested dumping the mind-wiped Henry Van Statten in. (1.6)

Safka-Schekeryk, Melanie Anne: American singer, whose most famous song, 'Brand New Key', was sung by a couple of the female members of LINDA at one of their meetings. (2.10)

Saint Julienne, Eva: See *Macrae Cantrell, Suki*

Salt, Cathy: Reporter for the *Cardiff Gazette*, who read some of Mr Cleaver's postings about the Blaidd Drwg project's shortcomings. She confronted Margaret Blaine, the Lord Mayor of Cardiff, with her story, not realising Blaine was actually responsible for the design faults. Blaine was preparing to kill her when she learnt that Cathy and her boyfriend Jeffrey were expecting a child. (1.11) (Played by MALI HARRIES)

Salt Lake City: The nearest populated area to Henry Van Statten's underground base. The Doctor predicted that if the Dalek escaped the Vault Salt Lake City's one million inhabitants would be just the first to die. (1.6)

Samson: A horse owned by Gabriel Sneed and used to pull his undertaker's cart. (1.3)

Samuel: Identity assumed by Mickey Smith once back in his home reality, so he could infiltrate the Torchwood Institute as one of Dr Singh's associates. (2.12)

San Andreas Fault: An 800-mile stretch of geological fault line in

California caused by tectonic plates moving northwards and southwards, often resulting in earthquakes. The Doctor likened the Rift threaded through Cardiff to the San Andreas Fault. (3.11)

San Claar: One of the many religions practised in the 42nd century. (2.9)

San Diego: One of the cities Goddard suggested dumping the mind-wiped Henry Van Statten in. (1.6) Martha Jones claimed to have gone there and collected one of the phials of liquid needed to arm the gun she was allegedly preparing to kill the Master. (3.13)

San Kaloon: Place visited by the Doctor, Rose Tyler and Captain Jack Harkness, famous for its glass pyramids. (1.11)

Sanctuary Base: Portable kit-constructed bases that could be assembled on any planet, moon or asteroid, on surfaces or beneath water.

Sanctuary Base 6: Constructed on the surface of Krop Tor where the Doctor encountered the Ood. The crew of Sanctuary Base 6 were explorers on behalf of the Torchwood Archive, their ship having crashed after riding a gravity funnel between the black hole which Krop Tor orbited and the surface. They were carrying out their mission, drilling ten miles below the surface of the planet, to discover the unexplained power source that had registered down there. (2.8, 2.9)

Sandra: Neighbour of Jackie Tyler's whose partner, Jason, had A+ blood and was thus affected by the Sycorax's Blood Control. Once the threat had passed, they watched as ash from the Sycorax ship fell over the Powell Estate, mistakenly believing it to be snow. (2.X) (Played by SIAN McDOWELL)

Santini Khadeni, Cathica: A journalist on Satellite Five, Cathica desperately wanted to be noticed for her work, especially in the Spike Room, and was appalled when Suki Macrae Cantrell was promoted to Floor 500 first. Although initially resistant to the Doctor's coaxing about what was actually wrong with Satellite Five, her journalistic instincts served her well when she made her own way to Floor 500 and discovered the truth about what was really in control of Earth – the Jagrafess. Linking via her implanted chip to an abandoned Spike Room, Cathica disconnected the other Spike Rooms' news feeds and raised the temperature on the Floor 500. This broke the link between the Jagrafess and the zombie humans operating the computers and eventually caused the creature to explode, taking the contents of Floor 500 with it, including the Editor. Cathica remained on Satellite Five, determined to return the Earth Empire's news-gathering to more honest, investigative ways. (1.7) (Played by CHRISTINE ADAMS)

Santori, Goddess: Catkind deity worshipped by the Sisters of Plenitude. Other Catkind worshipped the more traditional Christian God, referrerd to by them as Jehovah. (2.1, 3.3)

Satan: Legendary demon name, one of many attributed to the Beast throughout the galaxies. (2.8, 2.9)

Sato, Toshiko: Undercover Torchwood operative who arranged to be in charge of the investigation into the supposed alien that crashlanded in the Thames. She and the Doctor determined that it was just a normal pig that had been augmented by alien technology. (1.4) (Played by NAOKO MORI)

Saul: A friend of Jenny, the maid at Farringham School for Boys. When confronted by the Scarecrows about to kidnap her, Jenny briefly thought they might be a practical joke by Saul. (3.8)

Saxon, Harry: Character created by the Master to become the Prime Minister of Great Britain. See *The Master*

Saxon, Lucy: Schooled at Roedean and St Andrews, the wife of Harry Saxon, the new Prime Minister of Great Britain, met her husband while working at the publishing house that published his book. She was well aware of his real identity as the Master, and was a willing accomplice in his plans with the Toclafane, having travelled 100,000,000,000,000 years into the future, to Utopia. She betrayed Vivien Rook to him, and danced as the Toclafane invasion began. However, as the year of Toclafane domination went on, Lucy seemed to lose favour with the Master, receiving beatings at his hands that changed her view of him, and she became more withdrawn, the spell broken.

When the Toclafane were stopped and the world was sent back a year so that the majority of Earth had no idea what had transpired, Lucy remembered. As the Master surrendered, she shot him, exactly as Chantho had shot his previous incarnation. What happened to Lucy after the *Valiant* returned to Earth is unknown. (3.12, 3.13) (Played by ALEXANDRA MOEN)

Scannell, Orin: Onc of the crew aboard the SS *Pentallian*, he was horrified to learn that Korwin McDonnell had destroyed the engineering equipment, setting the cargo ship on a course for a nearby sun. He and Captain McDonnell, Korwin's wife, tried to find a way to jump-start the ship using the generators. When that failed, due to the sun-possessed Ashton hacking the ship's systems, he concentrated on helping the Doctor get Martha Jones and Riley Vashtee back from the jettisoned pod that was taking them closer to the sun. When Vashtee was safely back aboard, he and Scannell made it to the auxiliary controls and, on Martha Jones's orders, vented all the fuel that had been scooped from the sun. This shot straight back into the injured sun and they managed to get the ship off its predetermined collision course. When the Doctor and Martha said their goodbyes, Scannell and Vashtee stayed aboard the *Pentallian*, waiting for rescue by the authorities. (3.7) (Played by ANTHONY FLANAGAN)

SATELLITE FIVE: A vast space station, with 500 floors, populated almost entirely by humans. Its main remit was as a broadcaster, delivering news across the Fourth Great and Bountiful Human Empire over the previous 91 years. The workers all aspired to reach Floor 500, where they believed they would be well rewarded. Floor 500 was, however, occupied by the true master of Satellite Five, the Jagrafess, and his minion, the Editor. Unlike the rest of the station, the temperature on Floor 500 was barely above freezing, and the humans manning it were all dead – corpses animated through their implants and manipulated by the power of the Jagrafess, via the Editor. (1.7) When the Jagrafess was destroyed, Satellite Five ceased broadcasting but, instead of freeing humanity from the Jagrafess domination, the Doctor's intervention had actually started another century of social decay for humanity. The Jagrafess was actually just one part of a long-term plan of the Emperor Dalek, who went on to place his own agent, called the Controller, aboard Satellite Five, now renamed the Game Station. Humanity believed the Game Station was 500 floors of makeover and game shows with lethal twists. In fact, no one was dying when they lost – they were being teleported to the Dalek mothership hovering at the edge of the solar system and were being turned into Daleks. The Daleks were not thwarted until Rose Tyler absorbed the powers of the Time Vortex from the heart of the TARDIS and reduced the Daleks to atoms. When Rose and the Doctor left, the Game Station's only remaining living occupant was Captain Jack Harkness, who used his damaged Vortex Manipulator to try and track his friends down. (1.12, 1.13, 3.11)

Scarecrows: Straw-filled foot soldiers created by Son of Mine, using molecular fringe animation. Relentless, untiring, with rudimentary intelligence, even after being cut down by machine-gun fire, they could be reanimated. After the Family of Blood were imprisoned for eternity by the Doctor, the Scarecrows probably fell apart or just become traditional scarecrows, placed in fields and meadows across Britain. (3.8, 3.9)

Scarlet Junction: A conglomeration of planets and systems of which the Jaggit Brocade was an affiliate, designated Convex 56. (1.2)

Scarlet System: A star system the inhabitants of Sanctuary Base 6 observed being destroyed as it was consumed by the black hole K 37 Gem 5. It was home to the Pallushi, who perished at the same time. (2.8)

Schwarzenegger, President: The Trine-E android aboard the Game Station described an outfit it and the Zu-Zana android had given to Captain Jack Harkness as having a 'tweak of President Schwarzenegger' during the *What Not to Wear* programme. (1.12)

Science Foundation: Human cadre of scientists who postulated the concept of Utopia and formulated the Utopia Project thousands of years before Professor Yana got the rocket launched away from Malcassairo and towards Utopia. (3.11)

Scissor Sisters: American glam band, whose album *Ta-Dah* spawned the song 'I Can't Decide', which the Master played and sang along to one morning aboard the *Valiant* as he pushed the artificially aged Doctor around in a wheelchair. (3.13)

Scooby-Doo: Famous American cartoon dog who, with a gang of human helpers, solved mysteries, usually more by accident than design. On 'Pete's

World', Pete Tyler likened the Preachers to the Scooby Doo gang. (2.6) Larry Nightingale told Sally Sparrow that the Wester Drumlins house resembled something out of a Scooby-Doo episode. (3.10)

Scott, Ida: Science Officer on Sanctuary Base 6 who, according to the Beast, only joined the Torchwood Archive to run away from her father. She accompanied the Doctor beneath the surface of Krop Tor, but he left her safely above the trapdoor that led to the Beast's prison. However, when the planet began moving towards the nearby black hole, the atmosphere of Krop Tor was drained away and Ida collapsed unconscious, all the air in her spacesuit's tanks used up. Reunited with the TARDIS, the Doctor had the time to collect Ida, revive her and return her to the survivors of the Base aboard their shuttle craft. (2.8, 2.9) (Played by CLAIRE RUSHBROOK)

Scribble Creature: A ball of literal pencil scribbles animated by the ionic energy of the Isolus channelled through Chloe Webber. Chloe drew it to prevent Rose Tyler from interfering with what was going on in her room at 53 Dame Kelly Holmes Close. The Doctor later rubbed out part of it with a simple pencil eraser. (2.11)

Scrooge, Ebenezer: Main character in Dickens' novel *A Christmas Carol*, which the author read to an enrapt Welsh audience on Christmas Eve 1869. (1.3)

Sea Devils: Colloquial name given to prehistoric reptile men living on Earth beneath the sea who once emerged to reclaim what they saw as their world. The Master aided and abetted them in their attempts but was defeated by the Doctor. The Master reminded the Doctor of this when taunting him over his current defeat. (3.13)

Seabold, Alice: American novelist and writer of *The Lovely Bones*, which the Doctor speed-read in Rose Tyler's flat. (1.1)

Seamus: One of the inhabitants of Hooverville in 1930s Manhattan. Solomon told him to stay with the rest of the people there when they were attacked by the Pig Slaves. (3.5)

Searchwire: Internet search engine used by Rose Tyler to find out information about the Doctor. (1.1)

Seattle: One of the cities Goddard suggested dumping the mind-wiped Henry Van Statten in. (1.6)

Sebastian: One of the Torchwood soldiers present when the Doctor first arrived at the Torchwood Tower, he showed the Doctor an alien particle gun. He later helped defend the Tower against the Cybermen on the top floor of the Tower and was presumably killed at some point during the battle. (2.12, 2.13)

Secret Heart, the: The name of the Webstar ship that carried the Racnoss children away from the war with the Fledgling Empires. The ship later became the centre of Earth as the planet formed around it. (3.X)

Secretary: While researching sightings of the Doctor from his office, Victor Kennedy came across details of LINDA. His secretary came in with tea and was promptly absorbed. If not killed there and then, she was when the Abzorbaloff was destroyed after Elton Pope broke his cane. (2.10T) (Played by OLWEN REES)

Secretary General: Head of the Secretariat of the United Nations. He told people to 'watch the skies' in the wake of the Big Ben incident. (1.4)

Security Guard: He arrested the Doctor aboard the Game Station after the apparent murder of Rose Tyler by the Anne Droid. Quoting Private Legislation 16 of the Game Station Syndicate, he told the Doctor, Captain Jack Harkness and Lynda Moss that they would be transported to the Lunar Penal Colony without trial. The Doctor then knocked him out. (1.12) (Played by SAM CALLIS)

Security Protocol 712: A holographic projection of the Doctor appeared to Sally Sparrow and Larry Nightingale when they entered the TARDIS, alerting them that the DVD Larry was carrying had been recognised by the ship's

systems as carrying programmed flight instructions and could be inserted into the console. Larry did so and the TARDIS began to dematerialise. (3.10)

Segway PT: Motorised one-person transport. The Doctor, Donna Noble and Lance Bennett had fun using these to get from the basement of HC Clements to the Torchwood base beneath the Thames Barrier. (3.X)

Sellards, Jason: Lead singer of the Scissor Sisters, and co-writer of the song 'I Can't Decide', which the Master sang along to one morning aboard the *Valiant* as he pushed the artificially aged Doctor around in a wheelchair. (3.13)

Senate: Government of New New York and, by implication, of the whole of New Earth, its members were wiped out by the mutated Bliss virus – their last act was to put the planet into a 100-year quarantine. The Face of Boe took charge of the survivors, giving his own life energies to keep the Motorways and Undercity powered so that one day, when the Motorway could be opened, the Overcity could be repopulated. (3.3)

Sergeant: An army sergeant based at Albion Hospital who organised the search for the augmented pig that the Slitheens had launched into space. The subsequent crash back to Earth had caused a huge distraction and enabled the Family Slitheen to take over the British Government. (1.4)

Sexton: A churchwarden whose dead body had been reanimated by the Gelth that existed in Gabriel Sneed's Cardiff undertakers. The Sexton's corpse later walked into his own memorial service. (1.3)

Shadmoch: A planet in the Rexel planetary configuration, which had a hollow moon. (3.2)

SEC, DALEK: Former Commander of the Seventh Dalek Incursion Squad, later the leader of the Cult of Skaro, inhabiting a special black Dalek armoured shell, its Dalekanium enhanced with Metalert on the express orders of the Dalek Emperor during the Great Time War. Establishing a mobile strategy chamber within the Void ship after fleeing the apparent destruction of the Daleks, Sec brought with him the Genesis Ark, waiting to emerge on a planet and set free the millions of Daleks held prisoner within, courtesy of Time Lord technology. Needing the genetic imprint of a humanoid time traveller, the Cult waited patiently to emerge onto Earth, breaking further into Earth's reality whenever either the Cybermen or Yvonne Hartman and her Torchwood colleagues created a breach in the Void. When the Doctor found a way to send the Daleks and Cybermen back into the Void, Sec led his Cult into an emergency temporal shift and they escaped. (2.12, 2.13) Arriving on Earth in New York, 1930,

Sec realised the Cult needed to scale back their ambitions as that time zone was too primitive. He studied the millions of humans and gradually understood why the Emperor had given the Cult the capacity to think and reason. Sec masterminded the Final Experiment. Firstly, the Cult kidnapped humans – the smart ones they would use to create a Dalek Human army, the denser ones were transformed into hybrid Pig Slaves. Another part of the experiment was to merge himself with a human, Mr Diagoras, giving him full mobility again. Unfortunately for the Cult, the Dalek Sec Hybrid began displaying human qualities such as compassion and an appreciation of morality. Sec's fellow Daleks turned on him, chaining him to Dalek Thay and dragging him to the Laurenzi theatre to confront the Doctor. Sec understood that the Doctor was possibly the only person who could help the Dalek race evolve to another level and, when Daleks Thay and Jast threatened to kill the Doctor, Sec put himself in the line of fire. Whether his death was the result of deliberate self-sacrifice or an accident remains unknown. Shortly after his death, Sec's Final Experiment failed when the Dalek-Human army turned on their creators and destroyed Thay and then Jast before Caan killed them all and fled that time zone. (3.4, 3.5) (Operated by NICHOLAS PEGG (2.12, 2.13), ANTHONY SPARGO (3.4, 3.5), voiced by NICHOLAS BRIGGS, (2.12, 2.13, 3.4) ERIC LORENS (3.4, 3.5))

Shadow Proclamation: A treaty between various interplanetary races and empires. Quoting Convention 15 enabled someone to seek peaceful contact with a potential enemy, as the Doctor did with the Nestene Consciousness. (1.1) Rose Tyler cited this to the Sycorax Leader in an attempt to make him leave Earth. (2.X) The Doctor cited it to communicate with the Isolus child that had possessed Chloe Webber's body in 2012. (2.11)

Shafe Cane, Beltone: Brother of Padra Fet and son to Kistane, a human on Malcassairo who, once reunited, took off in the rocket ship to Utopia. Whether they themselves or their descendants were turned into the Toclafane by the Master is unknown. (3.11) (Played by MAT IRELAN)

Shafe Cane, Kistane: Mother to Padra Fet and Beltone, humans on Malcassairo who, once reunited, took off in the rocket ship to Utopia. Whether they themselves or their descendants were turned into the Toclafane by the Master is unknown. (3.11) (Played by DEBORAH MACLAREN)

Shafe Cane, Padra Fet: Human spotted by the Doctor, Martha Jones and Captain Jack Harkness fleeing from the Futurekind on Malcassairo. They initially held off the Futurekind, then fled with Padra to the humans' Silo base. Padra was reunited with his mother and brother and later took off in the rocket to Utopia. Whether they themselves or their descendants were turned into the Toclafane by the Master is unknown. (3.11) (Played by RENE ZAGGER)

Shakespeare, William: Elizabethan playwright, generally perceived as England's greatest ever writer but, when the Doctor and Martha Jones met him in 1599, he was still coming to terms with the death of his son, Hamnet. He arrived on stage after a performance of *Love's Labour's Lost*, and announced he was planning a sequel, *Love's Labour's Won*. The Carrionite Lilith was in the audience and used her powers to get him to say it would be performed the next evening. He then joined forces with the Doctor and Martha Jones, who worked out that he was being manipulated by the Carrionites. Shakespeare tried to stop his play being performed, because the final words, written while under the Carrionites' spell, would open a portal to the Deep Darkness and enable a Millennium of Blood to start on Earth. With a little help from Martha, Shakespeare was able to create a new ending for the play, using the words against the Carrionites own spellcasting and exiling them back into their prison forever. Shakespeare was immune to the Doctor's psychic paper and quickly worked out he and Martha were from the future. (3.2) (Played by DEAN LENNOX KELLY)

Shareen: A good friend of Rose Tyler's. 'Don't argue with the designated driver' was one of her pearls of wisdom. (1.2) She and Rose often used to go shopping, just to look at local boys. (1.3) Rose tried to tell her mum that she had stayed at Shareen's for the night, not realising that her first journey with the Doctor had in fact kept her away from home for twelve months. (1.4) The only time Rose and Shareen fought was over a man. (2.3)

Shaun: Object of desire for Martha Jones's friend Vicky, who didn't reciprocate Vicky's feelings. (3.13)

Sheffield: City where the Doctor planned to take Rose Tyler to see Ian Dury and the Blockheads perform in 1979. (2.2) The Grand Central Ravine was named after the Ancient British city of Sheffield, not York. Rose Tyler didn't know this when asked by the Anne Droid in *The Weakest Link* aboard the Game Station. (1.12)

Shining World of the Seven Systems: Gallifrey, the Doctor's home planet, was often referred to in this manner. (3.12)

Shipton, Sally: When flirting with Billy Shipton, Sally Sparrow accidentally referred to herself as this. In fact, Billy did end up marrying a girl called Sally, and he showed Sally Sparrow a photo of them on their wedding day. (3.10)

Shiver and Shake: Two lead characters in a British weekly comic during the 1970s. Shiver was a ghost, Shake an elephant. The Doctor likened his and Rose's partnership to theirs, implying how well they worked as a team in the Torchwood Institute Lever Room as they prepared to destroy the invading Cybermen and Daleks. (2.13)

Shonara: Girlfriend of Leo Jones, and mother of his baby, Keisha. She was presumably at home with Keisha on the night of Leo's 21st birthday party, but she was safely with Leo and Keisha in Brighton when the Master began rounding up the rest of the Jones family. (3.1, 3.12) (Played by CHANNON JACOBS)

Shipton, Billy: The Detective Inspector in charge of investigating the mysterious disappearances at Wester Drumlins. Attracted immediately to Sally Sparrow, he cancelled his evening plans and instead took her to the pound which was filled with abandoned cars from the house, as well as the TARDIS. The two flirted and, when Sally left, he promised to call her. Billy then noticed the Weeping Angels surrounding the TARDIS and was despatched by one of them to 1969. There he met the Doctor and Martha Jones who explained that they needed him to get a message to Sally Sparrow, but it was going to

take a while. (Played by MICHAEL OBIORA) The next time Billy saw Sally, nearly 40 years had passed for him, but barely an hour for her. During the intervening years, Billy had started to work in publishing, and then moved into video and finally DVD publishing. It was he who had put all the hidden Easter egg messages onto DVDs for the Doctor, and he told Sally to look at the list she had of the 17 DVDs they appeared on; she later worked out that it was a list of her own DVD collection. He showed her a photo of his wife, also called Sally, and they gently flirted again. Sally stayed with Billy until the rain stopped and Billy passed away. (3.10) (Played by LOUIS MAHONEY)

Short-range teleport: Part of the Clockwork Robots' inbuilt technology, enabling them to move short distances in space and, when the time-window technology aboard the SS *Madame de Pompadour* was activated, across the centuries as well. (2.4)

Shuttles: Shuttle 4 and Shuttle 6 were amongst those returning the surviving dignitaries home after the events aboard Platform One. (1.2)

Sierpinski sequence: Trying to override Dev Ashton's attempts to eject an escape pod, Riley Vashtee opted to use a Sierpinski sequence, a series of mathematical fractals that were self-replicating and in theory ought to have kept the computer-controlled locks busy for hours. Ashton then destroyed the controls, and the escape pod was jettisoned from the SS *Pentallian* towards the living sun with Vashtee and Martha Jones inside it. (3.7)

Sierpinski, Waclaw: Polish mathematician who created a series of mathematical fractals. Aboard the SS *Pentallian*, Riley Vashtee tried to use a Sierpinski sequence to stop Dev Ashton jettisoning the escape pod he and Martha Jones were trapped inside. (3.7)

Sight, the: Colloquial name for Gwyneth's extrasensory skills that enabled her to communicate with the Gelth. (1.3)

'Signalman, The': Cited by the Doctor as one of the Charles Dickens' canon that he'd read. He reckoned it was the best short story ever written. (1.3)

Silent Realm: A term used by the Doctor to describe the Void, through which the TARDIS passed to arrive on 'Pete's World'. (2.5)

Silo: The base where the human refugees lived, waiting for Professor Yana to power up the rocket which would take them to Utopia. It was guarded day and night by armed guards and had electrified fences to keep the Futurekind out. (3.11)

Silver Devastation: Area in the Isop Galaxy where the Face of Boe lived when he visited Platform One to see the final destruction of Earth, the planet his ancestors were from. (1.2) At the start of his life as the human Professor Yana, the Master was found as a naked, orphaned child on the coast of the Silver Devastation. (3.11)

Simmonds, Jake: Member of the Preachers, a renegade group on 'Pete's World' trying to overthrow society's dependence on Cybus Industries, convinced they were up to no good. After the deaths of Ricky Smith and Mrs Moore, Jake was left as the only member of the Preachers and joined the Doctor's final assault on the Cyber-conversion factory in Battersea Power Station. After defeating the Cybermen, he and Mickey Smith headed to France to see what the situation was there. (2.5, 2.6) When the Cybermen made their way through the Void to the real world, Jake and armed troopers were sent after them by Pete Tyler, but Jake was eventually returned to 'Pete's World' for good when the Void was sealed off by the Doctor. (2.13) (Played by ANDREW HAYDEN-SMITH)

Simmons: Sadistic engineer working for Henry Van Statten, charged with torturing the 'Metaltron' until it spoke. After the Doctor revealed it was in fact a Dalek, Van Statten demanded Simmons torture it further, to make it speak directly to Van Statten. Instead, the Dalek used its sucker to envelop Simmons' head, suffocating him and draining him of life. (1.6) (Played by NIGEL WHITMEY)

Singer: Nightclub chanteuse singing 'It Had to be You' in the drinking den that the Doctor went into shortly before an air raid began. Until that point, he had been unaware of exactly when the TARDIS had landed. (1.9) (Played by KATE HARVEY)

Singh, Dr Rajesh: Torchwood Institute scientist who was in charge of ascertaining the purpose of the Sphere, but had had no luck. Once the Cybermen invaded, the Sphere activated, and four Daleks – the Cult of Skaro – emerged. Needing information, the Daleks drew it from Singh's brain, desiccating him in the process. (2.12, 2.13) (Played by RAJI JAMES)

Single Molecular Transcription: A system that replaced microprocessors on Earth in 2019. (1.7)

Sinister Woman: An employee of Harry Saxon who worked alongside Francine Jones to try and trap the Doctor. Francine wanted to keep her daughter Martha safe from the Doctor, so allowed the Sinister Woman to listen in when they talked on their mobiles. She was present when Martha spoke to Francine from aboard the SS *Pentallian*, and tried to triangulate Martha's position. (3.7) She was still working alongside Francine, aided by a number of other minions, when Martha returned to Earth after Election Day and Saxon had become the British Prime Minister. The minions had brought Clive Jones back home, but he blew the plan by warning Martha to stay away. The Sinister Woman then had the whole Jones family arrested and incarcerated and ordered her armed guards to open fire on Martha's car when she arrived at her parents' house. (3.12) (Played by ELIZE DU TOIT)

Sisters of Plenitude: A superfluity of Catkind nuns who ran the Hospital on New Earth. Amongst their number were Matron Casp, Sisters Jatt and Corvin and Novice Hame. (2.1) After their secret experiments on human clones were exposed, the Sisterhood was presumably disbanded, and Hame sought penance for her sins by devoting her life to looking after the ailing Face of Boe. (3.3)

Skaro: Home world to the Daleks and destroyed during the Last Great Time War. One of the Cult of Skaro's aims was to turn Earth into New Skaro. (3.5)

Skasas Paradigm: A legendary mathematical problem, the solution to which would supply the ability to harness the basic energies that made up the universe and become gods – hence it's colloquial name, the God Maker. The Krillitanes on Earth at Deffry Vale High School, the Chosen Few, sought to enhance the intellect of the children there and have them solve the Paradigm for them. (2.3)

Skeleton Crew: The crew of the *Black Gold* – living skeletons who, according to Captain Kaliko, were cheaper than real people. They turned on their captain at the behest of the first mate, Swabb, in reality an OilCorp spy, but were all lost when the OilCorp rigs attacked the ship. (TIQ)

Skinner, Colin: Fiction-writing friend of Ursula Blake and founder member of LINDA. He and Bridget formed a close friendship, and he was devastated when she vanished, although Victor Kennedy told him that they could track her down together through some old phone numbers. In fact, Bridget had been absorbed

by Kennedy in his true form as the Abzorbaloff, and Skinner then suffered the same fate, although he remained conscious inside the Abzorbaloff. When he combined with his fellow victims to bloat the Abzorbaloff until he exploded, Skinner died. (2.10) (Played by SIMON GREENALL)

Skintank: The Doctor suggested placing Cassandra's consciousness in one of these rather than in Chip, as her old body and brain had expired. (2.1)

Skylab: Listing things of importance that happened in 1979, the Doctor told Rose Tyler that this space station fell back to Earth, nearly taking his thumb with it. (2.2)

Slabs: Solid leather, animated by rudimentary intelligence, these drones always worked in pairs, and were therefore useful for whoever owned them. A Plasmavore hiding on Earth from Judoon justice sculpted a pair of Slabs into resembling human despatch riders so they could blend into the background at the Royal Hope Hospital, where the Plasmavore was staying. The Doctor destroyed one Slab with an overdose of Roentgen radiation from the hospital's X-ray machine, whilst the other was vaporised by the Judoon. (3.1) (Played by MAT DORMAN, MICHAEL WILLIAMS)

Slade: Midlands rock group whose festive song 'Merry Xmas Everybody!', a number one in 1973, was heard on the radio in Clancy's Garage when Mickey Smith heard the TARDIS landing in the Powell Estate. (2.X) It was also being played a year later at the disco to celebrate the non-wedding of Donna Noble and Lance Bennett. (3.X)

Sleep: Coming in varying strengths, this was one of the Mood Patches available in Pharmacytown in the Undercity of New New York. Martha Jones was given a patch when kidnapped by Milo and Cheen to stop her struggling. (3.3)

Slipstream Engine: The method of propulsion the Family Slitheen used in the spaceship they put into a slingshot orbit and brought back down to Earth to crash into Big Ben. (1.4, 1.5)

SLITHEEN, THE FAMILY: A crime syndicate from the planet Raxacoricofallapatorius. Having been based in Britain for some months, they infiltrated the police, military forces, even Parliament by killing people of large stature and wearing their skins as suits, fitting themselves in by use of a slipstream compression field generator worn around their necks. They planned to instigate a third – nuclear – world war, by faking an alien incursion on British soil. With the world in panic, they persuaded the UN to allow nuclear weapons to be launched at supposed 'massive weapons of destruction'. Their plan was then to sell the resultant radioactive slag that had once been Earth to the highest bidder, to be used as fuel for interstellar spaceships. The Doctor managed, with Mickey Smith's help, to locate launch codes for sub-Harpoon missiles and so destroyed 10 Downing Street with the Family Slitheen inside. Jocrassa Fel Fotch Pasameer-Day Slitheen, and all the other Family members – except Blon Fel Fotch Pasameer-Day Slitheen, posing as MI5 operative Margaret Blaine – were killed in the explosion. (1.4, 1.5) Blon Fel Fotch ended up in Cardiff as Lord Mayor, hoping to use initially a nuclear accident, and then the energy from the Doctor's TARDIS to force open the Rift in space and time that coursed through the city. She could then escape from Earth. The power in the heart of the TARDIS reverted Blon Fel Fotch Pasameer-Day Slitheen to an egg, which the Doctor took home to be given a second chance. (1.11) The Doctor identified another member of the Family Slitheen as having been captured by a Graske on the planet Griffoth. (AotG) (Played by ELIZABETH FOST, PAUL KASEY, ALAN RUSCOE)

Slitheen, Blon Fel Fotch Pasameer-Day: One of the Family Slitheen, she murdered MI5 operative Margaret Blaine and used her identity to infiltrate the British Government while everyone's attention was diverted by the Big Ben incident. She was responsible for the death of the Prime Minister. (1.4, 1.5) She was the only Slitheen to escape the bombing of 10 Downing Street by activating a short-range teleport device concealed in her earrings and brooch. She ended up on the Isle of Dogs in East London, and later made her way to Cardiff where she became the Mayor, pushing through the construction of the Blaidd Drwg nuclear facility. The scale model of the facility was built upon the back of a tribophysical waveform macro-kinetic extrapolator. Not having the power to use it herself, she was hoping that a nuclear meltdown would supply what she needed to open the space and time Rift running through Cardiff and power up the extrapolator. As it turned out, the arrival of the TARDIS and Captain Jack's wiring up of the extrapolator to the TARDIS console supplied the very power she needed. Despite the Doctor's best attempts to get Blon to recognise the error of her ways, she still tried to kill Rose Tyler to ensure the Doctor took her away from Earth. Instead, the extrapolator's power, mixed with that of the Rift and of the TARDIS itself, opened up the heart of the TARDIS. Blon gazed into the pure energies of the Time Vortex and was reverted back to an egg. The Doctor took the egg back to Raxacoricofallapatorius in the hope that, reborn, Blon might take a different path. (1.11) (Played by ANNETTE BADLAND)

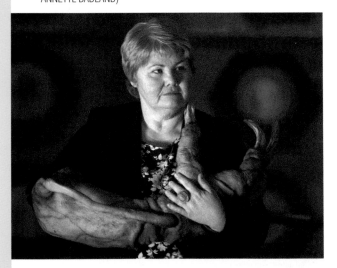

Slitheen, Jocrassa Fel Fotch Pasameer-Day: Leader of the Family Slitheen, he posed as Joseph Green, the Acting Prime Minister of Britain during the Big Ben incident. He then killed a roomful of UNIT experts, military officers and academics gathered to investigate the supposed alien incursion. However, he was killed when the Doctor arranged for a missile to obliterate 10 Downing Street with Jocrassa Fel Fotch and the rest of his family still inside. (1.4, 1.5) (Played by DAVID VERREY)

Slitheen, Sip Fel Fotch Pasameer-Day: One of the Family Slitheen, he posed as Assistant Police Commissioner Strickland, investigating Jackie Tyler's claims to have met the Doctor. However, he was killed when, after revealing his true nature to Jackie and her daughter's ex-boyfriend Mickey Smith, they discovered the Slitheen weakness for vinegar and showered him with it, causing him to burst. (1.4, 1.5) (Played by STEVE SPEIRS)

Smith, Delia: British television cook, who first appeared regularly on TV in the 1980s, whom the Doctor referred to as one of the greatest chefs on Earth. (TIQ)

Smith, Jackson: Mickey Smith's father who, before leaving him in the care of Rita-Anne and heading to Spain, worked at a key-cutter's on Clifton Parade. On 'Pete's World', Ricky Smith told the same story. (2.5)

Smith, John: Regular alias used by the Doctor when on Earth, sometimes just plain 'Mr', sometimes as a 'doctor', either medical or scientific. Arriving amidst the London Blitz on 21st January 1941, he elected to be Doctor John Smith from the Ministry of Asteriods. (1.9) He used it again to pose as a physics teacher at Deffry Vale High School. (2.3) When getting himself admitted as a patient at the Royal Hope Hospital, to investigate the plasma coils that had been placed around the outside of the building, he became a patient called John Smith. (3.1) In Elizabethan England, Martha Jones jokingly continued to call him 'Mr Smith'. (3.2) After turning himself human in an attempt to escape from the Family of Blood, the Doctor actually became a man called John Smith, from Nottingham, who was a history teacher in 1913, at Farringham School for Boys. There he met and fell in love with Nurse Joan Redfern and they even had a glimpse of a future life together involving marriage, children and grandchildren, ending with John's death from old age, in 1963. However, the vision could never come true as John had to turn himself back into the Doctor to defeat the Family of Blood, and thus broke Joan's heart. (3.8, 3.9)

Smith, Pauline: Mickey Smith's mother, a victim of the Reapers as they broke into the world after Rose Tyler saved her dad's life and created a breach

SMITH, SARAH JANE: A journalist who claimed to be writing a piece for the *Sunday Times* about Deffry Vale High School and the amazing performance of its students since the arrival of Hector Finch as Headmaster. In truth, she was investigating for the same reasons as the Doctor, Rose Tyler and Mickey Smith – UFO sightings three months previously. Some years before, she had travelled with the Doctor, eventually leaving him abruptly when he had been summoned back to his home planet. He later left her a gift of K-9 Mark III, but that had not been enough for Sarah, who had found it difficult to go back to a normal life. After initial hostility between her and Rose, the two came to be friends, although Sarah tried to warn Rose of the dangers of believing that she would travel with the Doctor for ever. (2.3) (Played by ELISABETH SLADEN)

in time, but presumably restored to life when Pete Tyler healed the wound. (1.8) (Played by MONIQUE ENNIS) When Mickey was older, she walked out on him and his father, and eventually Mickey was brought up by his grandmother, Rita-Anne. (2.5) However, Mickey was still in semi-regular contact with her, so, when Rose thought Mickey had died at the hands of the Nestene Consciousness, she commented that she'd have to tell her of her son's fate. (1.1) On 'Pete's World', Ricky Smith's mother did all the same things that Pauline had done. (2.5, 2.6)

Smith, Ricky: Mickey Smith's counterpart on 'Pete's World'. Physically identical to Mickey, Ricky's life had taken much the same path. His father, Jackson, had left him in the care of his grandmother, Rita-Anne, when he went to Spain, and his mother had also left. Where their lives diverged was in that Rita-Anne was still alive, and Ricky was London's Most Wanted… for unpaid parking tickets. After Thin Jimmy's capture, Ricky became de facto leader of the Preachers and grudgingly accepted that they had to take Mickey with them. Together they tried to escape the pursuing Cybermen near Bridge Street but

Ricky was killed, leaving Mickey to overcome the hostility of Jake Simmonds, the remaining member of the Preachers, who reckoned Mickey could never replace Ricky. (2.5, 2.6) (Played by NOEL CLARKE)

Smith, Sydney: In the fiction the Doctor created for John Smith, John believed his father was a watchmaker, from Nottingham. (3.8)

Smith, Verity: In the fiction the Doctor created for John Smith, John believed his mother had been a nurse. (3.8)

Smythe: Schoolboy at Farringham School for Boys in 1913, who took part in the war games there, manning the Vickers Gun. (3.8)

Sneed and Company: Cardiff-based firm of undertakers in the 1860s, situated at 7 Temperance Court, Llandaff. It was blown up when the possessed maid Gwyneth lit a match to destroy the gaseous Gelth that occupied the premises. (1.3)

Sneed, Gabriel: Undertaker that the Doctor and Rose Tyler met in Cardiff in 1869. His work had been disrupted by what appeared to be ghosts inhabiting the bodies of the recently deceased and making them walk. In fact, this was an alien species who called themselves the Gelth. They sought bodies to inhabit as they crossed to Earth via a Rift, before beginning their intended conquest of the planet. One of the bodies they inhabited was Sneed's, killing him in the process. (1.3) (Played by ALAN DAVID)

Snell, Mr: Teacher at Farringham School for Boys who Mr Rocastle told to contact the police before the Family of Blood attacked. (3.9)

Mickey Smith

I once saved the universe with a big yellow truck.

Son of Pauline and Jackson Smith, Rose Tyler's on-off boyfriend Mickey initially found himself drawn into the Doctor's world when he was just a young boy, at a point when he hadn't even knowingly met him yet. Attacked by the Reapers in a playground in 1987, this version of Mickey sought refuge in a nearby church. (1.8) He was instinctively drawn to one of the women there for protection – a woman he could always trust, and would never, ever forget: Rose Tyler...

Perhaps it was partly Mickey's need for protection that attracted him to Rose in later life. When he was six, his mother had abandoned him, with his father disappearing to Spain not long after, leaving Mickey in the care of his blind grandmother, Rita-Anne. Following her death some years later, Mickey left school in order to become a car mechanic, and moved into a flat on the Powell Estate.

Five years later, in 2005, Mickey encountered the Doctor when he was captured and replicated by the Nestene Consciousness. He was later rescued from its lair under the London Eye, and abandoned on Earth when Rose chose to explore the universe with the Doctor in his TARDIS. (1.1) Mickey didn't date anyone else in Rose's absence, and waited an entire year for her to return. During this time, he was believed by Jackie Tyler to have been responsible for her daughter's disappearance, and was taken in for questioning by police five times. As a result, he became increasingly withdrawn from society, and started researching the Doctor on the internet and in history books, uncovering details of his past visits to Earth, and his previous involvement with UNIT. His fascination then led to him maintaining the late Clive Finch's website, Doctor Who? (1.4)

When the Doctor and Rose did eventually return to Earth in 2006, Mickey was quickly snubbed by them both, with the Doctor nicknaming him 'Ricky' and 'Mickey the Idiot' in numerous attempts to frustrate him. Although initially hesitant to support the Doctor's cause, Mickey was able to use his advanced computer skills to hack into the Royal Navy and UNIT computer systems during the Slitheens' fraudulent invasion of Earth, and hijacked a missile, using it to destroy the Slitheens inside Downing Street. It was after this initial display of courage that the Doctor invited Mickey to travel with him as a companion, but the offer was declined. (1.5) He would later use his computer knowledge to track the Sycorax ship at Christmas, (2.X) to investigate the strange occurrences around Deffry Vale High School, (2.3T, 2.3) and to uncover the deactivation code for the emotional inhibitor inside every Cyberman on 'Pete's World'. (2.6)

Although he claimed that he was making a fresh start for himself with Trisha Delaney, Mickey found himself remaining consistently faithful to Rose. (1.11) In her absence, Mickey took the opportunity instead to keep Jackie company, visiting her every Sunday for dinner, (2.X) and helping out with odd jobs around the flat. (2.10) He also continued his work as a garage mechanic at Clancy's, and considered himself to be the Doctor and Rose's 'Man in Havana', carrying out their surveillance and technical support from afar. In reality, he gradually realised, he was their 'Tin Dog'.

Mickey officially joined Rose and the Doctor aboard the TARDIS following their encounter with the Krillitanes, (2.3) travelling first to a 51st-century spaceship, the SS *Madame de Pompadour*, (2.4) before crashlanding on a parallel version of Earth in the present day. (2.5) Mickey later chose to stay behind on 'Pete's World' in order to look after 'his' grandmother following the death of her real grandson, and Mickey's alter-ego, Ricky Smith. (2.6) He then assisted Pete Tyler and Jake Simmonds in their mission to liberate the world from the remaining Cybermen scattered across the globe, but this attempt was frustrated when the Cybermen used Torchwood technology to travel across the Void and into Rose Tyler's universe. Mickey followed them, masquerading as Samuel in the Torchwood Institute, (2.12) and was reunited with the Doctor and Rose in the events leading up to the Battle of Canary Wharf. He was then safely transported back to 'Pete's World' before the Doctor sealed the breach between the universes forever. When the Doctor last saw him, he was living with Pete Tyler and his adopted family, Jackie and Rose Tyler. (2.13)

(Played by NOEL CLARKE, CASEY DYER)

Socialist Worker: Posters advertising this newspaper, decrying Margaret Thatcher as Prime Minister of Great Britain and Northern Ireland, were on the wall close to where Rose Tyler watched her father's death, near Jordan Road outside the Brandon Estate. (1.8)

Soft Cell: Eighties pop-synth duo. Their cover version of 'Tainted Love' was played on Cassandra's 'iPod' (in truth, a huge jukebox) at the reception aboard Platform One in the Manchester Suite. (1.2)

Sol 3: Name by which Earth was referred to by the Spacelane Traffic Advisors when warning interstellar travellers to stay away after the Toclafane had arrived – Sol 3 was considered to be entering its Terminal Extinction and was therefore closed. (3.13)

Solace: Mountain range on the continent of Wild Endeavour, on the planet Gallifrey. The domed citadel of the Time Lords used to be situated between it and the mountain Solitude. It was destroyed along with the rest of Gallifrey at the end of the Last Great Time War. (3.12)

Solar flares: The Controller of the Game Station used these to mask her conversation with the Doctor. She continued to give him the Daleks' coordinates after the solar flares had ended, and was exterminated as a result. (1.12)

Soldier: On 'Pete's World', Mickey encountered this soldier at a roadblock when he went in search of his grandmother's house. (2.5) (Played by ANDREW UFONDO)

Solitude: Mountain range on the continent of Wild Endeavour on the planet Gallifrey. The domed citadel of the Time Lords used to be situated between it and the mountain Solace. It was destroyed along with the rest of Gallifrey at the end of the Last Great Time War. (3.12)

Solomon: The Hooverville in Manhattan's Central Park was run by former soldier Solomon. He ruled with strength but compassion and often led by example – he went with the Doctor, Martha Jones and a young Hooverville inhabitant, Frank, into the sewers, to earn a dollar from Mr Diagoras for a day's work. Solomon soon discovered that terrifying inhuman events were occurring under the streets of Manhattan but, after Frank was lost to the Pig Slaves, he returned to Hooverville to prepare his people for battle. When the Doctor returned to Hooverville with a rescued Frank, Solomon tried to reason with the pursuing Daleks, but Dalek Caan exterminated him. (3.4, 3.5) (Played by HUGH QUARSHIE)

Son of Mine: Malicious and malevolent member of the Family of Blood, who saw the death and destruction they wrought as sport. He took on the body of schoolboy Jeremy Baines and infiltrated the school, hoping to sniff out the Doctor, whose body he wanted to inhabit and so live forever. Not realising the Doctor had made himself wholly human, the Family followed him to the village dance, hoping to expose him. Son of Mine murdered the doorman and had both Martha Jones and Joan Redfern threatened with execution unless the Doctor turned back. But the person they were dealing with believed himself to be John Smith, a teacher at the school and couldn't understand what they wanted. Son of Mine then led an attack on the school using the Scarecrows he had created using molecular fringe animation. Not realising he wasn't dealing with Baines, Rocastle, the Headmaster, challenged Son of Mine, who then murdered the bursar, Mr Phillips, to demonstrate he meant business. After failing to get the Doctor to change, Son of Mine decided to flush him out by bombing the village from the spaceship. John Smith then arrived, offering up the fob watch which contained the Doctor's life essence, but Son of Mine discovered firstly that it was empty and was just a watch again, and secondly that the Doctor had already reasserted himself and had tricked the Family. He overloaded the ship's systems and Son of Mine led his Family out just before it blew up. The Doctor then captured him and trapped him, immobile, within one of his Scarecrow's forms and left Son of Mine watching over one of England's fields for eternity. (3.8, 3.9) (Played by HARRY LLOYD)

Sonic blaster: Captain Jack Harkness had one of these multi-grade guns, which the Doctor recognised as being of 51st-century construction. It was manufactured in the weapon factories of Villengard and operated on a digital basis, meaning it could reverse the damage it did. Its one weakness was that it was battery-powered. (1.10)

Sonic screwdriver: Gallifreyan technological device carried by the Doctor, which has been used in an amazing variety of ways. It has unlocked doors (not deadlocks though). It has scanned people to determine a species or identify medical flaws. It has increased or decreased the power levels of other objects. With numerous settings, easily controlled at the flick of a thumb, it has been used by Time Lord and humans alike. The Doctor lost one sonic screwdriver after destroying a Slab with Roentgen radiation (the sonic burnt out), but he quickly replaced it. Just as he would be lost without his TARDIS or companions, the Doctor would be lost without his sonic screwdriver.

'Sound of Thunder, A': Sci-fi short story by Ray Bradbury in which a time traveller crushes a butterfly in prehistoric times and finds his world changed when he returns to the future. Martha Jones asked the Doctor if it was safe to travel through Elizabethan England in case she did something similar. (3.2)

South Africa: Country that Hutchinson, House Captain at Farringham School for Boys, heard that his father might be moving to. Timothy Latimer's uncle had been there, in Johannesburg, on a six-month posting and loved it. (3.8) A lightning strike in South Africa brought down a Toclafane once, and Martha Jones had gained access to the readings, so that a similar electrical pulse could be generated to stop another one. (3.13)

Southampton: Hampshire city with famous docks, from which the RMS *Titanic* sailed for New York. A local family, the Daniels, were supposed to be aboard but were apparently stopped from travelling by their friend, the Doctor. (1.1)

Southwark: Region of South London. The Powell Estate where Jackie and Rose Tyler lived was part of Southwark. (1.1) The Carrionites were based there, in Allhallows Street, close to the Globe Theatre. (3.2)

Southwark Cathedral: 13th-century London cathedral, and the first Gothic church in the capital, it was a place where Londoners fled for safety during the Blitz of the Second World War. Amongst those Londoners was a young Richard Lazarus, and the positioning of his LazLabs building in full view of his beloved cathedral was not accidental. After Lazarus had been changed by his GMD, he took refuge in the cathedral, but went on an attempted killing spree once more. The Doctor used the church organ, boosted by his sonic screwdriver, to create a hypersonic wave that disorientated the Lazarus Creature, which fell to its death on the cathedral floor, the professor's transformation reversed. (3.6)

Spacelane 77: Closed due to solar flares ranged at 5.9 according to Channel ☺+1 (1.7)

Space pig: A common-or-garden Earth pig, which was augmented by Slitheen technology, dressed in a spacesuit and sent into space in a ship, the trajectory of which guaranteed it would come crashing down in Central London. The resultant panic enabled the Family Slitheen to take control of the British Government. The space pig was taken to Albion Hospital, where Toshiko Sato and the Doctor tried to help it. Terrified, it ran squealing down a corridor towards a nervous Army soldier, who shot it dead. (1.4) (Played by JIMMY VEE)

Spain: European country where Jackson Smith went after leaving his son, Mickey, with Rita-Anne. On 'Pete's World', the same circumstances had led to Ricky Smith living with his version of Rita-Anne. (2.5) Donna Noble was on a scuba-diving holiday in Spain when the Cybermen and Daleks came through the Void, so remained unaware of the invasion and the Battle of Canary Wharf. (3.X)

were actually a two-way conversation between the Doctor and herself about the Weeping Angels — lethal assassins that could send people into the past if they weren't being watched. The Angels attacked, but she and Larry made their way to the TARDIS, which dematerialised around them — leaving the Weeping Angels trapped. A year later, Larry and Sally had set up a shop together, but still the mystery remained — why had she been the one the Doctor had contacted? Then she saw the Doctor and Martha, who had no idea who she was. Sally gave him all her notes, realising that she was setting off the chain of events leading to what had already happened. Sally was then able to resume her normal life, hopefully with Larry Nightingale tagging along. (3.10) (Played by CAREY MULLIGAN)

Spears, Britney: American singer, whose song 'Toxic' was played in the Manchester Suite aboard Platform One by Lady Cassandra's jukebox. (1.2)

Sparrow and Nightingale: When Kathy Nightingale and Sally Sparrow first went to Wester Drumlins, Kathy suggested they should form a detective agency called Sparrow and Nightingale, which Sally thought was 'a bit ITV'. A year later, Sally had opened an antiquarian book and rare DVD store with Kathy's brother, Larry, and that was the name they chose for it. (3.10)

Sparrow, Sally: Amateur photographer with an eye for things old and decrepit, she snuck into Wester Drumlins, an old deserted house in London, to take some photos. She was astonished to find that behind some wallpaper was a message for her, apparently written in 1969 by someone called the Doctor, warning her about the Weeping Angels. Sally came back the next day with her mate, Kathy Nightingale, but their exploration was interrupted by the arrival of a man with a letter for Sally. Just as the man identified himself to Sally as Kathy's grandson, Kathy herself vanished. Looking for Kathy, Sally found a key in the hand of one of the Weeping Angel statues. The letter purported to be from Kathy, who said she had been transported to 1920. Kathy's brother had some DVDs with a bizarre one-way conversation from a man calling himself the Doctor. He told her that this half-message had been hidden on 17 DVDs, and gave her a list of their titles. Deciding to report Kathy's disappearance to the police, Sally met DI Billy Shipton, the officer in charge of investigating a series of disappearances from Wester Drumlins. Billy showed her a number of cars, all of which had been abandoned at the old house, their owners vanished, alongside an old-fashioned police box. As she left, she wondered whether the key she had found might fit the police box but, when she returned to the car pound, she discovered that Billy had now vanished too, only to call her moments later from hospital, 40 years older and dying. Sally realised that the discs containing the one-way conversation were in fact the 17 DVDs that she owned. With Kathy's Doctor-obsessed brother, Larry, she returned to Wester Drumlins and discovered that the messages

Spencer, Lady Diana: When Pete Tyler got Jackie's name wrong in their wedding vows, Jackie suggested they carry on, citing a similar incident at Lady Di's wedding where she had got Prince Charles's name wrong a year earlier. (1.8)

Sphere Chamber: Area in the Torchwood Tower where the Sphere, or Void Ship, was stored, overseen by Dr Singh. It later became the location for the initial battle between the Cybermen, Daleks and Jake Simmonds' forces. (2.12, 2.13)

Spiders: Robotic creatures employed by Cassandra aboard Platform One to monitor the other guests and then sabotage the space station, thus contriving a hostage situation, apparently masterminded by Cassandra's other robotic slaves, the Adherents of the Repeated Meme. (1.2) Cassandra used robot spiders again, when hidden away on New Earth, to observe the Doctor and Rose's arrival there. (2.1)

Spike Rooms: Satellite Five had a number of these on its many Floors. They were areas where journalists could link, via technological implants in their foreheads, into the network of news channels and, at the speed of thought, process news to be broadcast throughout the Earth Empire. (1.7) A century later, by when the space station had become the Game Station, many of the Spike Rooms had become either storage rooms or been converted into studios. (1.12, 1.13)

Spinning Wheel, the: South East London pub where Jackie Tyler arranged to meet Tina the Cleaner to take part in a pub quiz. (2.10)

Spion Kop: A battleground in Africa, during the Boer War. Joan Redfern's husband Oliver died there. (3.8)

Spock, Mr: Character from the science fiction TV series *Star Trek*, played by Leonard Nimoy. Rose suggests to the Doctor that much of his technology is 'not very Spock' and not what she had expected of him. She later introduces the Doctor to Captain Jack Harkness, having told Jack the Doctor's name is Spock. (1.9)

Spray Painter: A young lad on the Powell Estate who the Doctor finds spray-painting the words 'BAD WOLF' on the side of the TARDIS, and is later made to clean it off again. (1.4, 1.5). (Played by COREY DOABE)

Squawk: Caw's son – the metal bird was given to Martha disguised as a brooch, with which Caw and Baltazar could track the TARDIS's journeys as it searched out the datachips required to locate the *Infinite*. Squawk grew up to be a living metal bird just like his cunning father and, over three years trapped on Volag-Noc, was trained by the Doctor to work for him instead. When the *Infinite* was destroyed and Baltazar trapped on the decaying asteroid, Squawk, as the Doctor had instructed, collected Baltazar and returned him to Volag-Noc to be incarcerated there. (TIQ) (Voiced by TOBY LONGWORTH)

St Christopher's Church: Location of the wedding between Stuart Hoskins and Sarah Clark. As an old building, it was the final refuge of the survivors on Earth hiding from the Reapers as they broke into the world after Rose Tyler saved her dad's life and created a breach in time. (1.8)

St Mary's Church: Chiswick church situated in Haven Road, where Donna Noble and Lance Bennett were getting married when Donna vanished. (3.X)

Stage 1 Disinfection: Anyone entering the Wards in the Hospital on New

Earth had to go through disinfection in the elevators before they could approach the patients. (2.1)

Stage Manager: A worker at the Taliesin Lodge where Charles Dickens was reading *A Christmas Carol*, it was his job to get Dickens on stage to begin his reading. (1.3) (Played by WAYNE CATER)

Stalin, Josef: Leader of the Communist Party of the Soviet Union, who had seen his country through to victory against Nazi Germany during the Second World War. He was reviled by the West however, which saw communism as a major threat to world peace. The Doctor cited Stalin's Russia as being where he would have expected to see the police abducting people in the night, as opposed to London's Muswell Hill in 1953. Stalin was actually no longer in charge of Russia when the Doctor made the comment, having died some months earlier, power having ceded to Nikita Khrushchev. (2.7)

Stan: A mate of Mickey Smith's who might have put him and Rose up after the first attack by the Roboform Santas. (2.X)

'Starman': Top ten hit for David Bowie in 1972. When the Doctor was trying to sneak quietly away from the Tylers' flat on the Powell Estate, the song was being played by one of their neighbours. (1.4)

Stars in their Eyes: One of the programmes broadcast from the Game Station. Losing contestants would be blinded. (1.12)

Statue of Liberty: The TARDIS landed at the base of this New York landmark on 1 November 1930. (3.4, 3.5)

Steino-magnetic tool: A tool the Doctor used to construct a portable scanner to help him find the Isolus Podship. (2.11)

Stet radiation: Below the Silo base on Malcassairo, stet radiation was

Steward [1]: Blue-skinned Crespallion official aboard Platform One charged with overseeing Earthdeath. He was killed when Cassandra's robot spiders sabotaged the Control computer, resulting in the sunshields outside his office lowering and vaporising him. (1.2) (Played by SIMON DAY)

Steward [2]: Leader of the staff at Torchwood House, working to Sir Robert and Lady Isobel MacLeish. He was taken by surprise when the Brethren of St Catherine arrived and held them all prisoner, but was freed by Rose Tyler and the Doctor. He believed the Werewolf had been killed but in fact became its first victim. (2.2) (Played by RON DONACHIE)

Stewart, Jackie: British 20th-century racing-car driver. Rodrick believed he wrote the novel *Lucky* when asked by the Anne Droid in *The Weakest Link* aboard the Game Station. (1.12)

Stoker, Mr: Consultant at the Royal Hope Hospital who was in charge of medical students including Martha Jones on the day that the hospital was transported to the Moon by the Judoon platoon. Observing Earth in the sky, he wondered if he'd ever see his daughter again, currently at university, or see his planned retirement in Florida. He didn't, since the Plasmavore disguised as Florence Finnegan drained his blood from his body as a screen against the Judoon's scanners. (3.1) (Played by ROY MARSDEN)

Stone, Jimmy: Friend of Rose Tyler's. It was because she moved in with him for a few months that she left school before sitting her A Levels. Having deprived her of £800 and broken her heart, he later ended up in prison and then started work as a door-to-door salesman.

Strand: Street in London that links the West End to the City of London, along which the Olympic Torch-bearer headed east, towards Stratford. (2.11)

Strategy 9: Code used by the humans on Sanctuary Base 6 to enable a lockdown, during which the humans could gather in a sealed area, and then open all the airlocks, sucking everything else (i.e. the possessed Ood) out into space. (2.9)

Stratford: Area of East London, from which children had been disappearing in 2012. (2.11)

Stratford Olympic Park: Specially built stadium readied for the 2012 Olympic Games in East London. Eighty thousand people filled the stadium waiting for the Olympic Torch to arrive and start the games. When Chloe Webber needed to keep the Isolus which inhabited her body happy, she drew the stadium and everyone within it promptly vanished. The Doctor was able to send the Isolus home from the stadium, and the missing people all reappeared safe and sound. (2.11)

being used to power the rocket's drives. Utterly lethal to humans (though it left clothing intact), when the Futurekind's Wiry Woman turned the power off, Guard Jate was instantly vaporised by it. (3.11)

Steve: A journalist friend of Suki Macrae Cantrell's aboard Satellite Five. (1.7)

Steven, Uncle: Guest at the wedding of his nephew Stuart Hoskins and Sarah Clark. He hadn't arrived, nor had his wife Lynn. (1.8)

Steve-o: One of Mickey Smith's co-workers at Clancy's Garage. (2.X) (Played by PAUL ZEPH GOULD)

Stevie: Party guest at the Tyler household on 'Pete's World', when they were celebrating Jackie Tyler's birthday. Pete Tyler asked him about his work at Torchwood. (2.5)

Streete, Peter: Architect of the Globe Theatre who, under Carrionite influence, designed it as a tetradecagon, 14 being an important number in the spellcasting of the Carrionites. After his work was completed, the Carrionites broke his mind and he was abandoned in Bedlam. The Doctor used his Time Lord abilities to clear Streete's neural pathways so he had a moment of clarity and could explain what had happened to him. This drew the attention of the Carrionites and Mother Doomfinger arrived and killed Streete with a massive coronary to stop him speaking further. (3.2) (Played by MATT KING)

Streets, The: His 2002 single 'Don't Mug Yourself' broke through onto Pete Tyler's car radio in 1987 as the time breach occurred, as a result of Rose Tyler saving her father's life earlier. This disturbed Rose as she recognised the song and knew something was wrong. (1.8)

Strickland, Assistant Commissioner: The senior police officer who visited Jackie Tyler after she informed the authorities of the Doctor's presence. In fact, Strickland was Sip Fel Fotch Pasameer-Day Slitheen, a disguised member of the Family Slitheen, the real Strickland having been murdered previously. Revealing himself as a Slitheen, Strickland attacked Jackie and Mickey Smith in Mickey's flat. The Doctor, Rose Tyler and Harriet Jones assembled enough clues about the Slitheen's physical make-up for the Doctor to deduce their weakness – Jackie threw various kinds of vinegar over Sip Fel Fotch, causing him to burst, covering them with the remains of his body. (1.4, 1.5) (Played by STEVE SPEIRS)

Strood: Housemate alongside Crosbie and Lynda in the *Big Brother* house that the Doctor was transported in. He refused to go with the Doctor and Lynda when they escaped and may have been exterminated when the Daleks invaded the Game Station. (1.12) (Played by JAMIE BRADLEY)

Sub-Harpoon: Type of missile used by the Doctor and Mickey Smith to destroy 10 Downing Street after the Family Slitheen had occupied it and tried to start World War Three. (1.5)

Sudoko #509: Puzzle book attempted by Dr Singh while waiting for something to happen to the Sphere. He rather gave the impression he'd already solved the puzzles in the previous 508 books. (2.12)

Suki: Friend of Rose Tyler and Mickey Smith's. She worked in a hospital and had told Rose there were jobs going in the canteen there. (1.1)

Sullivan, Ed: American TV star, whose entertainment series was famous for showcasing early rock 'n' roll stars, such as Elvis Presley, who performed his single 'Hound Dog' on 28 October 1956 watched by 60 million people. The Doctor was taking Rose Tyler to see this live when they ended up in London in 1953. (2.7)

Sumatra: Indonesian island where the Doctor was washed up after surviving the eruption of Krakatoa. (1.1)

Sun: Colloquial name for the star which illuminates Rose Tyler's home solar system. (1.2) A living sun was found to exist in the Torajii system, which the crew of the SS *Pentallian* had fusion-scooped living matter out of. It fought back by possessing members of the crew and letting them burn people. The crew were finally able to return the stolen material and the survivors went on their way, now aware of the possibility of living suns. (3.7)

Sunday Mirror: British tabloid newspaper, which Vivien Rook was working for when she was murdered by the Toclafane. (3.12)

Sunday Times: Sarah Jane Smith claimed to be writing a piece for this newspaper about Hector Finch and his amazing teaching methods at Deffry Vale High School. In fact, this was a ruse to get inside the school and investigate. (2.3)

Sunfilters: The protective screens around Platform One, which stopped the interior frying due to its closeness to the expanding Sun. The sunfilters could be lowered either separately or in unison. (1.2)

Sunita [1]: One of Sarah Clark's expected guests at her wedding, who hadn't shown up. (1.8)

Sunita [2]: Older child at the wedding reception for Donna Noble and Lance Bennett's non-wedding. Donna asked her to make herself useful after the attack by the Roboform Santas. (3.X)

Surgeons: Two white-coated figures who kept Lady Cassandra moisturised whilst aboard Platform One. (1.2) (Played by VON PEARCE, JOHN COLLINS)

Surgery: One of the areas within the Hospital on New Earth run by the Sisters of Plenitude. (2.1)

Susan: Villager at the dance in Farringham when the Family of Blood attacked, killing Mr Chambers and demanding the Doctor hand himself over to them. (3.9)

Suzie: One of Sarah Clark's friends, she greeted the car as Sarah arrived along with Bev. They informed Sarah that many of the guests had not arrived. (1.8) (Played by RHIAN JAMES)

Swabb: First mate aboard Captain Kaliko's ship, the *Black Gold*. Although just an animated skeleton, he was secretly working for OilCorp, which had promised him a new body if he betrayed Kaliko. He decided to take Martha Jones's body but, as a result of Kaliko and the Doctor's actions, Swabb was knocked overboard and last heard of swearing his revenge from the planet Bouken's sandy surface. (TIQ) (Voiced by TOM FARRELLY).

Swales, Julia: Intern at the Royal Hope Hospital and good friend to

Martha Jones. Julia dealt less well with being transported to the Moon than her colleague, although she was the last person to succumb to the oxygen deprivation. She was fine, however, once the hospital was returned to Earth. (3.1) (Played by VINEETA VISHI)

Sycorax: The name both of a race of long-lived scavengers and of their home world – an asteroid (their planet's Sycoraxic name translated as 'Fire Trap'). The Sycorax were feared throughout the galaxy, and legend had it they would be one of three races still in existence at the end of the universe, along with humanity. Found in the JX82 system, 'Fire Trap' had long since been destroyed when they arrived in the skies above Earth, their armada ready and waiting in orbit around the 'Jewel of Star Crafell'. Proficient in both martial artistry and chemical and biological manipulation, the Sycorax were eventually forced to flee Earth after the death of their Leader. The departing ship was destroyed, killing all aboard, when Harriet Jones gave the order to enable the Torchwood Institute to use stolen alien tech to blow the ship up. It was reduced to a fine ash that floated back to Earth, and most people assumed this was snow. (2.X) When in Elizabethan England, the Doctor found a skull in the Globe Theatre's prop store which reminded him of a Sycorax helmet. William Shakespeare liked the word, and later used it for a character in his play *The Tempest*. (3.2)

Sycorax Leader: Bullish commander of the Sycorax force that attempted to invade Earth. Onboard the Sycorax spaceship, the Doctor challenged him to a sword duel, and won. Instead of accepting his defeat, he tried to attack the Doctor again, who operated a control on the ship which left the Leader plunging to his doom thousands of feet below. (2.X) (Played by SEAN GILDER)

Sycoraxic: Language spoken by the Sycorax. The Sycoraxic word 'gatzaa' translated as both 'human' and 'cattle'. (2.X)

'Tainted Love': Song covered by the 1980s pop duo Soft Cell, played on Cassandra's iPod (in truth, a huge jukebox) at the reception aboard Platform One in the Manchester Suite. (1.2)

Taj Mahal: Major landmark in Agra, which the 'ghosts' (really Cybermen) materialised around and later were drawn back into the Void from. (2.12, 2.13)

Take That: British boy band due to perform at the opening ceremony for the 2012 Olympic Games at Stratford. Former member Robbie Williams was expected to rejoin them for the event. (2.11)

Taliesin Lodge: Cardiff auditorium holding a charity event in aid of a children's hospital where Charles Dickens read from *A Christmas Carol* on Christmas Eve 1869. (1.3)

Tallulah: Singer of 'Heaven and Hell', centrepiece of the New York Revue, on stage at the Laurenzi theatre in 1930s New York. Tallulah needed the job because, without it, she reckoned she'd end up living in Hooverville. She joined the Doctor in his investigation of the sewers beneath the theatre because her lover, Laszlo, had gone missing. When she discovered he had been turned into a Pig Slave, she stood by him. After facing the Daleks in Hooverville, she and Martha Jones went to investigate the Empire State Building and met up with the Doctor and Laszlo there. After the Daleks were defeated, Laszlo opted to live in Hooverville, hoping to continue his romance with Tallulah. (3.4, 3.5) (Played by MIRANDA RAISON)

The TARDIS

It's the TARDIS. MY TARDIS. Best ship in the universe...

TARDIS is an acronym for Time And Relative Dimension In Space. The TARDIS is capable of travelling anywhere in time and space, harnessing the power of the Time Vortex to voyage across the universe. Although technically a spaceship, it hasn't done much flying, instead dematerialising in one location, before reappearing in another, almost instantaneously. The Doctor once claimed that he had failed his test to fly a TARDIS – though he also sometimes said that he had been travelling in the TARDIS for 900 years or more. He never looked back...

Equipped with a chameleon circuit, a fully functional TARDIS can change its appearance to blend in with any environment and uses low-level perception filters to shift attention away from itself. The Doctor's TARDIS, however, became stuck in the form of a 1950s Police Public Call Box on a visit to London, and remained that way from then on. Dimensionally transcendental, the TARDIS is bigger on the inside than the outside, containing an entire world of time energy within its walls, all processed through the ship's central control console. The extent of its interior dimensions is unknown, though it does have at least an attic and a wardrobe, and probably a myriad of other rooms.

Grown by the Time Lords on Gallifrey, the TARDIS is an organic craft, linked to the Doctor and his companions by a telepathic field. It translates languages automatically inside their heads, but failed during the Doctor's regeneration, perhaps indicating that the Doctor himself was a key component of the TARDIS's circuitry. When the TARDIS died

after falling through the Void into a parallel universe, the Doctor was able to use his own internal energies to resuscitate the TARDIS by sacrificing ten years of his own life.

Following the Time War and the destruction of Gallifrey, the TARDIS had to find a new source of power, and started drawing energy from the universe around it. Having discovered the Rift running through Cardiff, the Doctor has returned there on a number of occasions, allowing the TARDIS to soak up the temporal radiation and refuel itself. This power is then stored in the heart of the TARDIS, and trapped beneath the central console, emerging only in instances of severe peril. On such occasions, the TARDIS console has split itself apart, enabling its soul to communicate directly with its occupants. It looked inside the minds of both Blon Fel Fotch Pasameer-Day Slitheen and Rose Tyler, interpreting their thoughts, and affording them limited control over the Time Vortex as a result.

Although nothing, theoretically, is able to penetrate a TARDIS, the Doctor's vessel has in fact been violated on a number of occasions. When the Reapers were descending upon Earth in 1987, the strength of the wound in time resulted in the TARDIS interior being thrown out of its exterior entirely. (1.8) A transmat beam managed to break through the TARDIS defences and transported the Doctor, Rose Tyler and Captain Jack Harkness to the Game Station following their trip to Kyoto in 1336. (1.12) Donna Noble found herself aboard the ship on her wedding day, the Huon particles inside her having magnetised with those in the heart of the TARDIS. (3.X) On another occasion, a ship called the *Titanic* crashed through the TARDIS walls, because the Doctor hadn't reactivated the ship's force fields. (3.13) On other occasions, the Doctor has caused the TARDIS to materialise around individuals, (1.13, 3.X) or to leave them behind entirely. (3.10)

The TARDIS's unique properties have enabled it to hack into flight computers and track objects through the Vortex or from planet to planet; read datachip technology; tow other vessels to safety; defy the gravity of a black hole; protect its occupants from the depths of space; perform atmospheric excitations; convert a Time Lord into a human; project images of the Doctor, both as security programs and between realities (though that required energy from a supernova); and sustain the chaos of a temporal

paradox. In times of emergency, the TARDIS can switch itself to emergency power in order to avoid detection, and it is programmed to lock onto the nearest centre of gravity when drifting aimlessly through space. It can be secured from the outside using a conventional Yale key, or deadlocked from with the control room itself.

The Doctor has used his sonic screwdriver from outside to initiate emergency programs on the console, and also, once, to fuse the ship's coordinates, locking them permanently between locations. The console includes basic flight controls, such as the dimensional stabiliser, the vector tracker and the vortex loop, together with the gravitic anomalyser, the helmic regulator and a handbrake. It also features a scanner and trim phone, and has incorporated an extrapolator to serve as a fully functional force field, which the Doctor has used to nudge the TARDIS minor distances upon materialisation. The Doctor also keeps a medical kit within the ship, and oxygen masks are fitted in the ship's roof, as is the chameleon arch.

The Doctor aside, several other beings have been inside the TARDIS: Rose Tyler, Mickey Smith, Jackie Tyler, Adam Mitchell, Captain Jack Harkness, Blon Fel Fotch Pasameer-Day Slitheen, Cassandra, Sarah Jane Smith, Ida Scott, Donna Noble, Martha Jones, Sally Sparrow, Larry Nightingale, the Master, Lucy Saxon, and a Dalek.

Tanya: Young former UNIT officer, in the service of the Master aboard the *Valiant*. He used her as a masseuse. (3.13) (Played by EMILY MOORE)

Taunton: Devonshire town. The Doctor mused that the psychic energy he had observed in Elizabethan England would require a generator the size of Taunton. (3.2)

Taurean, HMS: Royal Navy Trafalgar Class submarine, which, after hacking into the UNIT computer systems, Mickey Smith discovered was situated ten miles off the coast of Plymouth. It carried a Sub-Harpoon UGM 84A missile, which the Doctor then used to destroy 10 Downing Street and the Family Slitheen members still inside. (1.5)

Taxi Driver: A 1976 movie, starring Robert De Niro. Mickey Smith impersonated De Niro's character Travis Bickle aboard the SS *Madame de Pompadour*. (2.4)

Taxi driver: Picked up Donna Noble and the Doctor, preparing to drive them to Chiswick, until he realised they didn't have any money, at which point he turfed them out. (3.X) (Played by GLEN WILSON)

Tebb Street: Road in Hull where Kathy Wainwright lived when she wrote the letter to Sally Sparrow, detailing her life from 1920 through to 1987. She lived at number 43. (3.10)

Teenaged Mum: A victim of the Reapers as they broke into the world after Rose Tyler saved her dad's life and created a breach in time. (1.8) (Played by ZOË MARIE MORRIS)

Telescope: Designed by Sir George MacLeish and Prince Albert in the Observatory atop Torchwood House which, when linked to the Koh-I-Noor diamond, created a beam of moonlight powerful enough to destroy the Haemovariform. (2.2)

Teletubbies: BBC children's programme, created by Ragdoll Productions. The Master watched this on a TV set and pointed out to a Toclafane sphere that the Teletubbies were wonderful because they had televisions in their stomachs. (3.12)

Television channels: Satellite Five broadcast over 600 channels, including Channel McB, Channel ☺+1 and Bad WolfTV. (1.7)

Tempest, The: A play by William Shakespeare. The Doctor used the phrase 'Brave new world' to Martha Jones when they first arrived in Elizabethan England. He later mentioned that a skull from the Globe Theatre's prop stores reminded him of a Sycorax – Shakespeare liked the word and considered using it, which he later did, naming the mother of a character in *The Tempest* as Sycorax. (3.2)

Tennessee: Home state in America of 18-year-old Frank, one of the inhabitants of Manhattan's Hooverville. (3.4, 3.5)

Terry: Soldier based at Albion Hospital and part of the search for the augmented pig that the Slitheen had launched into space, ensuring the subsequent crash back to Earth would cause a huge distraction and enable them to take over the British Government. (1.4)

Tesco: British chain of grocery supermarkets. Rose Tyler observed caustically that there wasn't one on Sanctuary Base 6. (2.9)

Texas: American state where some of the citizens of Manhattan's Hooverville were from. (3.4) Lady Cassandra said that her father had been born there. (1.2)

Thames Flood Barrier: Consisting of four huge steel gates, the Thames Barrier was built during the 1970s and 1980s because London is prone to flooding. The Doctor, Donna Noble and Lance Bennett travelled beneath it, where a secret Torchwood Institute base had been built next to the flood chamber. Torchwood had drilled a hole through to the Earth's core, revealing the Secret Heart, a Racnoss Webstar, around which Earth had formed over four billion years earlier. When the Empress of the Racnoss enabled her trapped children to break free, the Doctor used small bombs to blow up the walls of the flood chamber, drawing water from the Thames down into the chamber and then down the tunnel. This drowned the surviving Racnoss children. Escaping the destruction, the Doctor and Donna climbed on top of one of the four barrier gates, only to find that the entire Thames had been drained of water. (3.X)

Thatcher, Margaret: Listing things of importance that happened in 1979, the Doctor told Rose Tyler that Thatcher became Britain's first female Prime Minister. (2.2) She was still Prime Minister at the time of Pete Tyler's death in a hit-and-run accident in November 1987. (1.8)

Thaw, Lady Sylvia: Benefactor of Richard Lazarus's GMD, and representative of Harry Saxon, who had put a lot of money into the project's research and development. She believed that she and Lazarus were more than just business partners and was shocked at how rapidly, once he had rejuvenated himself, he dismissed her love. She became the first victim of the Lazarus Creature that he became as it drew the life force from her. (3.6) (Played by THELMA BARLOW)

Thay, Dalek: Former Commandant of Station Alpha, later one of the Cult of Skaro, who brought the Genesis Ark to Earth in the Void ship, after the Time War ended. He was the first Dalek to confront and exterminate the Cybermen in Torchwood Tower. (2.12, 2.13). After fleeing the Battle of Canary Wharf via an emergency temporal shift, along with the rest of the Cult, Thay ended up in Manhattan in 1930. Thay donated three segments of his Dalekanium-laced polycarbide armour to act as a conductor for the gamma radiation needed

to activate their new Dalek-Human army. Thay stayed with the Dalek Sec Hybrid during the attack on Hooverville, observing his leader's un-Dalek-like reactions to the slaughter, and later exterminated him once Sec was chained to Thay's casing. When the Dalek-Human army turned on their creators, Thay was the first to be destroyed on the stage of the Laurenzi theatre. (3.4, 3.5) (Operated by DAN BARRATT, BARNABY EDWARDS (2.12, 2.13), NICHOLAS PEGG (3.4, 3.5), voiced by NICHOLAS BRIGGS)

'The Angels have the phone box': A line from the DVD Easter eggs featuring the Doctor's conversation that Larry Nightingale had printed on a T-shirt. (3.10)

'The skies are made of diamonds': A phrase used by Creet's dead mother about why Utopia was going to be a good place for humanity to end up. One of the Toclafane repeated the phrase to Martha Jones on Earth, and she realised that the Toclafane were the telepathically linked survivors from Utopia, who had trapped themselves inside the spheres. (3.11, 3.13)

Thin Jimmy: Former leader of the Preachers, he was arrested shortly before Mickey Smith met Jake Simmonds and Mrs Moore. His arrest left Ricky Smith as London's Most Wanted… and thus leader of the Preachers on 'Pete's World'. (2.5)

This Is Spinal Tap: The Doctor quoted this movie when he opted to 'turn this up to 11', meaning the volume of the organ in Southwark Cathedral he used to destroy the Lazarus Creature. (3.6)

This Is Your Life: Iconic television series that started in America in 1952, in which celebrities were joined by old friends and family to celebrate their lives and achievements – an Australian version also existed, and both Britain and New Zealand have versions running still. The Doctor suggested that when he found Mickey Smith and Harriet Jones aboard the Sycorax ship, it was like an episode of the programme. (2.X)

Thomas, Dylan: The Doctor quoted a line by this poet – 'Rage, rage against the dying of the light' – which Shakespeare thought he might nick, but the Doctor told him that he couldn't. (3.2)

Thrace: Lady Cassandra O'Brien once attended a drinks party in honour of the Ambassador of Thrace, when a dying man approached her and told her she was beautiful. She remembers this as being the last time anyone told her that. In truth, the dying man was herself, transferred into the dying body of Chip. (2.1)

Thwaites: Schoolboy at Farringham School for Boys in 1913 who knew the drill before the Family of Blood attacked. (3.9)

TOCLAFANE: On Gallifrey, 'Toclafane' was the name given to imaginary evils to frighten children. The Master used the name for the last humans at the end of the universe in the year 100,000,000,000,000 who he discovered had, upon reaching Utopia, degenerated into cannibals, similar to the Futurekind on Malcassairo and experimented on themselves, reducing themselves to nothing more than telepathic shrunken heads, with the instincts and emotional responses of children and armed with knives and lasers. The Master planned to use them to subjugate Earth and be the army in his New Time Lord Empire. The Doctor realised that Toclafane was not their real name because of the Gallifrey connection, and was horrified to work out who they really were. The Master was using the Doctor's TARDIS to power a Paradox Machine which enabled six billion Toclafane to come to 21st-century Earth and slaughter their progenitors but, when Captain Jack Harkness destroyed the Paradox Machine, the Toclafane were instantly propelled back to their own future, trapped on Utopia for what little time remained in the existence of the universe. (3.12, 3.13) (Voiced by ZOË THORNE, GERARD LOGAN, JOHNNIE LYNE-PIRKIS)

Tide of Blood: The moment when the portal between the Deep Darkness and the Globe Theatre was to be opened by William Shakespeare's words, influenced by the Carrionites' spellcasting. (3.2)

Tight Fit: British pop group who had a number one hit with their cover of 'The Lion Sleeps Tonight' – which Mr Crane played loudly to cover the screams as Morris and the other homeless people were given the Ultimate Upgrade on 'Pete's World'. (2.5)

Time Agency: Mysterious pan-galactic group who recruited from worlds across the universe those who showed a particular aptitude for undercover espionage work involving time travel. Captain Jack Harkness was an agent, the first chosen from his home on the Boeshane Peninsula, but left years later after the Agency stole two years of his memories. (1.9, 1.10, 3.13)

Time Lords: Ancient and powerful race of beings from the planet Gallifrey. they tended to observe events in the universe rather than becoming involved, teaching in their Academy the importance of calm detachment. They were, however, known to have acted in wars during the Dark Times, and unwittingly instigated the Last Great Time War against the Daleks by trying to go back in time to avert, or at least significantly alter, their creation. Aeons later, Gallifrey and the entire race of Time Lords were destroyed in the War. There were two exceptions: the Doctor, whose actions eventually brought about the end of the War, and the Master, who fled and turned himself temporarily human to escape the Daleks. (1.2, 1.6, 1.12, 1.13, 2.3, 2.13, 3.X, 3.3, 3.11, 3.12, 3.13)

Time of Manifestation: The moment when the Wire would have access to the millions of people watching the Queen's Coronation in 1953 and be able to absorb their faces. (2.7)

Time War, the Last Great: The Eternals witnessed it, and fled our universe, never to return. The Forest of Cheem were terrified and saddened by it. The Time War raged across the whole of time and space, which, it has been said, saw the universe convulse. It has been speculated that the Time War was initially provoked by the Time Lords during the genesis of the Daleks, when the

Doctor was sent on a mission to alter or prevent the Daleks' conception. Many great civilisations were lost during the War – the Nestenes' home planet was obliterated, the Gelth Confederacy lost their physical forms, Arcadia fell, as did Perganon and Ascinta, and one turning point came when the Dalek Emperor took control of the Cruciform. The legendary final battle between the Daleks and the Time Lords led to the final devastation of both civilisations in a single second, something witnessed and quite possibly instigated by the Doctor, after he had tried everything else he could to stop the War. However, although the Time Lords were obliterated, factions of Daleks survived. The Emperor and his crippled ship fell back through time and ended up hiding invisibly on the edge of Earth's solar system for centuries before revealing itself, with a new army, during the time of the Fourth Earth Empire. One solitary Dalek fell through time to Earth in the 1960s, landing on Ascension Island, whilst the Emperor's personally selected Cult of Skaro fled into the Void, taking with them a Time Lord prison ship named the Genesis Ark, containing millions of imprisoned Daleks. The Doctor and the Master were the only surviving Time Lords and, after the destruction of the Emperor, his ship and three of the Cult of Skaro, Dalek Caan is the only known Dalek survivor. (1.1, 1.2, 1.3, 1.6, 1.12, 1.13, 2.3, 2.9, 2.12, 2.13, 3.X, 3.3, 3.4, 3.5, 3.11, 3.12, 3.13)

Time Windows: Technology aboard the 51st-century ship, the SS *Madame de Pompadour*. These enabled the Clockwork Robots to observe the lifetime of the real Madame de Pompadour. Whether they were originally part of the ship or were added by the Clockwork Robots to aid their task is unknown. (2.4)

Tina the Cleaner: Friend of Jackie Tyler's. She lived on the Powell Estate, and had taken in a lodger: a medical student who owned a stethoscope, which Jackie 'borrowed' to check on the Doctor's health. (2.X) Elton Pope watched her and Jackie chatting outside a laundrette. (2.10) (Played by CATHERINE CORNFORTH)

Titanic, RMS: Royal Merchant Ship *Titanic* set sail from Southampton Docks bound for New York on 10 April 1912. Four days later, it struck an iceberg and sank, claiming the lives of over 1,480 passengers and crew. (1.1) The Doctor implied to Jabe Ceth Ceth Jafe that he was aboard the ship when it went down, and he was left clinging to an iceberg for three days. (1.2) After saying goodbye

to Martha Jones in 2008, the Doctor took the TARDIS into space, whereupon it was crashed into by a vessel bearing the name *Titanic*. (3.13)

'To Be a Pilgrim': Hymn sung by the choir at Farringham School for Boys. (3.8, 3.9)

Tom: Boy playing football on his front lawn with Dale Hicks when Dale vanished in front of him. (2.11) (Played by JACK PALMER)

Tom's Dad: Concerned neighbour in Dame Kelly Holmes Close. Dale Hicks vanished while playing with his son, so he was anxious to know what the authorities were doing to solve the problem. (2.11) (Played by TIM FARADAY)

Top Rank: Venue in Sheffield where the Doctor planned to take Rosc Tyler to see Ian Dury and the Blockheads perform in November 1979. (2.2)

Top Shop: Cardiff clothes store where Captain Jack Harkness told the Zu-Zana android that he'd bought his clothes from during the *What Not to Wear* programme, broadcast from the Game Station. (1.12)

Torajii Alpha: Primary planet in the Torajii system, and where SS *Pentallian* crewmember Erina Lissak originated from. (3.7P)

Torajii System: Quadrant of space patrolled by the cargo ship SS *Pentallian*, home to a sentient sun and half a universe away from Earth. (3.7)

Torchwood Estate: Grounds upon which Torchwood House was built. Prince Albert was very fond of his visits, according to his widow, Queen Victoria. (2.2)

Torchwood Operative: When the editor of *The Examiner* contacted the Torchwood Institute to say she was being sold a story about them, this man came and collected the reporter from her office and took him back to Torchwood Tower. (2.12T) (Played by DAFYDD EMYR)

Torchwood Tower: The Torchwood Institute referred to One Canada Square, at the heart of the Canary Wharf business district in East London, as Torchwood Tower. Torchwood was actually responsible for having One Canada Square constructed because of the radar blackspot that the breach into the Void created, 600 feet above sea level. After the destruction of Torchwood, the building was presumably returned to local businesses to use. On 'Pete's World', the Torchwood Institute used the same building but had already been brought down by Pete Tyler's people. Trapped on 'Pete's World', Rose Tyler probably took over that version of Torchwood, determined to use the technology there to protect her new home. (2.12, 2.13)

Torchwood Worker: The woman who passed a Jiffy bag full of information about the Torchwood Institute to reporter Atif in a park. (2.12T) (Played by CATHERINE HARRIS)

Touchdown Institute: Broff thought that the Great Colbalt Pyramid was built over the remains of this when asked by the Anne Droid in *The Weakest Link* aboard the Game Station. He was wrong – it was the Torchwood Institute. (1.12)

Tower of London: Landmark on the north bank of the Thames. UNIT had a Mission Control base beneath it. (2.X)

'Toxic': Song made popular by Britney Spears. When Earthdeath occurred, the observers aboard Platform One listened to this song, as Lady Cassandra O'Brien told them 'Toxic' was a traditional Earth ballad. (1.2)

Trammps, The: American group who sang 'Disco Inferno', a song quoted by Lady Cassandra O'Brien when she revealed everyone would burn to death aboard Platform One as she teleported away. (1.2)

Transgenic Laboratory: Huge complex the Daleks built with the last of their technology beneath the sewers at the foot of the Empire State Building in 1930s New York. In it, they planned the Final Experiment, which would see the combining of Dalek and human DNA to create a massive Dalek-Human army. After the Daleks were defeated, the Doctor used their technology to find a way of halting Pig Slave Laszlo's degeneration. (3.4, 3.5)

Tribophysical waveform macro-kinetic extrapolator: Technology obtained by Blon Fel Fotch Pasameer-Day Slitheen in an airlock sale. When ridden, rather like a pan-dimensional surfboard, it created a force field around the rider, enabling them to ride the energy from a vast explosion. The Slitheen's plan was initially to combine the energy from a nuclear explosion with that of the Rift running through Cardiff, though she eventually attempted to use Rift energy combined with leaking TARDIS power. She hid the extrapolator beneath a scale model of the Blaidd Drwg power plant. (1.11) Captain Jack Harkness kept it and later used it to create a force field around the TARDIS to keep the Daleks at bay. (1.13) The Doctor later integrated it into the TARDIS systems completely and used it to shunt his craft away from the Empress of the Racnoss. (3.X)

Trine-E: One of the two robots, the other being Zu-Zana, who would take a human and decide how to make them look more fashionable for their TV show *What Not to Wear*. They would end the show, broadcast across Earth from the Game Station, by physically reconstructing their 'victims' with buzzsaws and lasers if they weren't satisfied. Captain Jack Harkness found himself in their show and destroyed the two robots with his Compact Laser Deluxe. (1.12) (Voiced by TRINNY WOODALL, played by ALAN RUSCOE)

Triton: Home world to the 40th-century scourge of the galaxy, Baltazar, who was the planet's Corsair King. (TIQ)

Troy: Legendary city in Turkey. The Doctor told Rose Tyler he had witnessed the fall of Troy, around 1183 BC (1.3) History teacher Mr Parsons was bemused because one of his students had been able to give him the exact height of the Trojan walls. (2.3)

Twelfth Night: A play by William Shakespeare. The lodgings house Shakespeare was in when he met the Doctor and Martha Jones was the Elephant Inn, which he later used in *Twelfth Night*. (3.2)

Twenty-second century: Where the Doctor took Rose Tyler during her first trip in the TARDIS, although they didn't leave the ship to visit it. (1.2)

Tyler, Jacqueline Andrea Suzette [1]: Mother of Rose Tyler, fiercely protective of her daughter, she was left a widow after her husband Pete was killed on the day of their friends Stuart and Sarah Hoskins' wedding, when Rose was six months old. (1.8) Jackie and Rose lived in Bucknall House on the Powell Estate in South East London, from where Jackie ran her mobile hairdressing business. Born on 1 February 1967, she was a big fan of Cliff Richard, (2.7) Il Divo (2.10) and *EastEnders*. (2.12) After she was caught up in the Auton invasion, (1.1) Jackie feared Rose was missing or dead at the hands of her boyfriend Mickey Smith, as she didn't return for a year. (1.4) When she did, and explained where she had been and who the Doctor was, Jackie begged her not to carry on travelling with him. This was after Jackie and Mickey had been attacked by a member of the Family Slitheen, and she realised the Doctor was prepared to sacrifice both himself and Rose to save the world. (1.5) She felt the Doctor was a dangerous influence. But she realised she was fighting a losing battle and, when the Doctor tricked Rose into going back home, she helped Rose get the TARDIS to take her back to him. (1.13) The next time she and Mickey, who were now close friends due to their mistrust of the Doctor, saw Rose she came home with the newly regenerated Doctor, who helped them foil the Sycorax invasion. Impressed by this new Doctor, Jackie had them all over to Christmas dinner (2.X) and was far more relaxed when Rose next went off travelling with the Time Lord. (2.1) She saw her daughter again when she and the Doctor returned from their first visit to the parallel Earth, 'Pete's World', to explain that Mickey was living there now, (2.6) and she got a phone call from Rose while she was flirting with Elton Pope. Jackie told Elton she would give her life for Rose and the Doctor. Soon afterwards, she explained to her daughter how Elton had been trying to use her to get to them. (2.10). When the TARDIS next materialised at the Powell Estate, Jackie was convinced she was being visited by the ghost of her father, Grandad Prentice, which turned out to be a Cyberman. As a result of this ghostly vision, Jackie found herself being taken in the TARDIS to the Torchwood Institute where, due to a mix-up, the Doctor let everyone there believe she was Rose. (2.12) After escaping the Cybermen, Jackie met the rich and successful 'Pete's World' version of her husband, and they began to bond, although Jackie's assurance that there hadn't seen anyone since him was a tad disrespectful to the legion of men she had, if not dated, certainly had the odd coffee with: Billy Croot, Jim, Howard, Rodrigo, Elton, and even a sailor. After the Doctor sent the Daleks and Cybermen back into the Void, he needed to seal off the breach between the two worlds, which left Jackie, Rose and Mickey in 'Pete's World' for ever. Jackie and Pete rekindled their romance and, after a few months, she fell pregnant with a new child. (2.13) (Played by CAMILLE CODURI)

Tyler, Jacqueline Andrea Suzette [2]:
Wife of businessman Pete Tyler on a parallel Earth, 'Pete's World', where she didn't have a daughter called Rose. Instead, Rose was the name of her Yorkshire Terrier. Their marriage was rocky, and Pete moved out. On her 40th birthday, the Cybermen invaded Jackie's party, killing many of the guests, or taking them to the Cyber-conversion factory in Battersea Power Station to receive the Ultimate Upgrade and become Cyberforms. Jackie Tyler was converted, but recognised Pete when he tried to rescue her and revealed his presence to the other Cybermen. (2.5, 2.6) (Played by CAMILLE CODURI, Cyberform version voiced by NICHOLAS BRIGGS)

The Torchwood Institute

If it's alien, it's ours…!

Founded by Queen Victoria in 1879 following her encounter with a Lupine-Wavelength-Haemovariform, the Torchwood Institute was set up with the express intention of keeping Britain great and fighting the alien hordes, including the Doctor. Independent from the Government and the United Nations, by 2007 the Institute was based in Torchwood Tower, scavenging alien technology in order to protect and advance the British Empire. Torchwood was responsible for destroying the Sycorax ship on Christmas Day, using technology from a Jathaa Sun-Glider. They later abducted a journalist who was investigating their link with the 'ghosts', (2.12T) and it was because of their experiments that Cybermen from 'Pete's World' were able to cross the Void and invade. (2.12)

Led by Yvonne Hartman, Torchwood's operatives included Dr Rajesh Singh and Adeola Oshodi, and all of them received a basic level of psychic training. Captain Jack Harkness also joined Torchwood Cardiff during the 20th century, following his return to Earth from the year 200,100. In addition to research into the Ghost Field, Torchwood investigated strange lights over Deffry Vale, shortly after the Krillitanes infiltrated Deffry Vale High School. (2.3T, 2.3) They were also the sole proprietors of HC Clements, where Donna Noble was working as a secretary when she met Lance Bennett. (3.X)

Although a top-secret organisation, Torchwood was known to individuals such as Harriet Jones, Detective Inspector Bishop, and Victor Kennedy somehow obtained their files on the Doctor and Rose Tyler.

Following the destruction of their London base in the Battle of Canary Wharf, Torchwood became more accessible. Journalist Vivien Rook was able to contact them directly with her concerns about Mr Saxon and the Archangel network in 2008, and Huw Edwards referred to them on-air following the Olympic spectators' disappearance in 2012. (2.11)

Following the destruction of the old regime, Torchwood Cardiff was then restructured by Captain Jack Harkness in the Doctor's honour, alongside four other operatives, including Toshiko Sato. (1.4) The Master sent the Cardiff team to the Himalayas shortly after his election as Prime Minister, and Jack was unable to contact them. (3.12)

Jack later refused the Doctor's invitation to travel aboard the TARDIS again, and returned to his work at Torchwood Cardiff instead. (3.13) The Great Cobalt Pyramid would later be built on the remains of the Torchwood Institute (1.12) and, in the far future, the crew of Sanctuary Base 6 were all representatives of the Torchwood Archive. (2.8, 2.9)

On 'Pete's World', an alternative version of Torchwood operated more publicly, and published studies into male fertility and global life spans via the Cybus mobile phone network. (2.5) One of Pete Tyler's friends, Stevie, worked for this version of the Institute before the People's Republic discovered their past misdeeds and claimed control. (2.12) Using Torchwood technology to travel across the Void, Pete Tyler, Mickey Smith and Jake Simmonds then followed the Cybermen into our universe, before returning with Rose and Jackie Tyler. Stranded on 'Pete's World', Rose joined her father at the newly reformed Torchwood, defending the Earth against alien threats. (2.13)

Tyler, Peter Alan [1]: Rose Tyler's father was born on 15 September 1954, and died on 7 November 1987, on his way to the wedding of Stuart Hoskins and Sarah Clark. He was hit by a car after picking up from their flat in Bucknall House a vase he and wife Jackie (the Maid of Honour) were presenting to the couple. Rose Tyler grew up hearing great stories about how Pete was a successful self-made man and a great husband. The truth, as Rose found out when the Doctor took her back to the day he died, was less romantic. Pete was a womaniser, his marriage to Jackie was rocky and all his money-making schemes, including his Vitex health drinks, were failures. But Rose wanted to see her dad, and saved his life, so he could go to the wedding as if everything was normal. This caused a tear in the fabric of time, allowing antibody-like wraiths, the Reapers, to spill into the world of 1987, wiping people out of time and feeding off the resultant chronal energy. Trapped with Jackie and Rose in a church, with the Doctor seemingly killed by the Reapers, Pete worked out the truth when he kept seeing a car driving in the area then vanishing. He left the church, and walked in front of the car. He died with Rose, who he now understood to be his baby daughter grown up, cradling him. Although the location of Pete's death, as well as the exact time, had been altered, his death was enough to heal the breach in time, the Reapers vanished and the missing people were all returned. (1.8) (Played by SHAUN DINGWALL)

Tyler, Peter Alan [2]: On 'Pete's World' (named by the Doctor in his honour), Pete Tyler was still alive in 2007, was still married to Jackie and was a hugely successful businessman thanks to his Vitex drinks. His company having been bought out by Cybus Industries, Pete was a very rich man, but his marriage was crumbling and he didn't trust Cybus' owner, John Lumic. In fact, Pete was secretly feeding sensitive information to an underground resistance movement, the Preachers, under the codename Gemini. When Cybus unleashed the results of its Ultimate Upgrade project, the Cybermen, Pete was forced into fighting back after Jackie was converted. He met Rose and together they worked alongside the Doctor to destroy the Cybermen. (2.5, 2.6) The few surviving Cybermen gained sympathy across the world when it became known they had once been living people, and the Cybermen were able to regroup and then cross the Void into Rose's home world. Pete was able to send Jake Simmonds from the Preachers and other armed fighters through the Void after the Cybermen, only to get caught up in a war between the Cybermen and the Daleks. Reunited with Rose and her mother, Pete helped stop the invasion. He returned to 'Pete's World' when the Doctor sealed the Void for ever, taking Jackie, Mickey Smith and Rose with him. He and Jackie decided to make a go of life together, even though neither one was the other's 'real' partner. After three months, Jackie fell pregnant. (2.13) (Played by SHAUN DINGWALL)

Rose Tyler

Can I just say – travelling with you, I love it!

The daughter of Peter and Jackie Tyler, Rose grew up with her mother on the Powell Estate in South East London, her father having been killed in a car accident when she was six months old. She left school to live with Jimmy Stone, who subsequently broke her heart and left her £800 in debt, and then moved back in with Jackie, resumed an old relationship with a local boy, Mickey Smith, and found a job at Henrik's department store, where she was working as a shop assistant when the Doctor first met her.

After the two of them had defeated the Nestene Consciousness, she was invited aboard the TARDIS. During her travels in the TARDIS, Rose met Charles Dickens in Cardiff and was made a Dame by Queen Victoria in Scotland. She saw the war-torn London of 1941 and the post-war capital of 1953. She and the Doctor took a trip to the 2012 Olympics in Britain's near future and visited a spaceship some 3,000 years after her own time, chatted to a famous French aristocrat more than 250 years before Rose was born and had a narrow escape from Japan's 14th-century capital, Kyoto. She also saw what would become of television in the 200,001st century and a future for the human race of that era badly at odds with the Doctor's enthusiastic description of a Great and Bountiful Empire.

At the very start of their travels together, the Doctor had hoped to impress her with the prospect of watching the world end from the safety of an orbiting space station some five billion years in the future. They later made a return trip to that era, and visited the New Earth

Rose had encountered a Dalek for the first time in 2012, in an underground museum in Utah. Unaware of its true nature, Rose felt sympathy for the imprisoned creature, and inadvertently allowed it to absorb her DNA, enabling it to regenerate. As the Dalek killed the inhabitants of the base, Rose used her connection with the Dalek to end the slaughter, ordering it to commit suicide in the process. Some time later, the TARDIS crew were transported onto the Game Station in the year 200,100, shortly before it came under attack from a huge Dalek fleet. The Doctor sent Rose home in the TARDIS, condemning himself to death alone. Desperate to return to his side, Rose forced open the ship's console hoping to communicate with the heart of the TARDIS. Instead, she absorbed the Time Vortex itself, granting her mastery over the whole of time and space, and allowing her to return to the Game Station. She confronted the Dalek Emperor and divided its fleet into atoms. The power, though, was killing her, and the Doctor absorbed it from her, sacrificing his own life.

This was the first time that Rose 'lost' the Doctor – the Vortex energy triggered his regeneration, and Rose found herself with an apparent stranger. The second time also involved the Daleks. As the Cult of Skaro and the Cybermen from the parallel Earth battled at Canary Wharf, the Doctor devised a plan that would seal both species in the Void. As Rose helped activate the Levers that opened the breach and sucked the Daleks and the Cybermen into the Void, she fell towards the opening, but was saved by Pete Tyler. She was transported to 'Pete's World', where she joined her mother and Mickey. Rose now had her whole family around her, with Pete and Jackie reunited and expecting a baby. But the breach was now closed and she could never see the Doctor again.

(1.1–2.13) (Played by BILLIE PIPER, JULIA JOYCE)

that the human race had gone on to establish. On each of these trips, she encountered a selection of alien races of all shapes, sizes and colours, her early wariness quickly evolving into appreciation for the different wonders the Doctor could show her – on one visit to an unnamed alien world, as they watched a new unfamiliar species wheeling in the sky, the Doctor asked her how long she would stay with him. Her answer was: for ever. However, many of the aliens that Rose and the Doctor encountered were less than friendly, among them the Gelth, Raxacoricofallapatorians, the Jagrafess, Roboform Santas, Sycorax, a Werewolf, Krillitanes, Clockwork Robots, the Wire, the Beast and the Abzorbaloff. They also endured bodily possession by the self-proclaimed last human, Lady Cassandra O'Brien.

Early in their adventures, the Doctor and Rose returned to the Powell Estate to find they had been absent for a whole year, and a distraught Jackie had thought her daughter missing or dead. Jackie pleaded with Rose not to resume her travels, but this had no effect. Rose did though stay in touch with her mother, either by phone – the Doctor had upgraded her mobile so she could call from any time and anywhere – or on frequent return visits. Rose also persuaded the Doctor to take her back to 1987, as she wanted to be with her father as he died. She couldn't resist saving Pete's life, creating a wound in time and letting in the Reapers, which rampaged across the planet until her dad sacrificed himself for the sake of the world.

Travelling later to a parallel Earth, Rose discovered a world where Pete Tyler was still alive, and had become a successful businessman, and Rose had never been born – instead, the parallel Jackie doted upon a terrier named Rose. It was only after Jackie had been converted into Cyberform that Rose revealed her true identity to Pete, but was shunned. Much later, the Doctor and Rose met this Pete again, when the 'Pete's World' Cybermen attacked Rose's Earth. The breach that they used also let through the Daleks.

Ultimate Upgrade: The official name for the Cyber-conversion process on 'Pete's World', whereby a human brain was soaked in chemicals, placed in a metallic head shell, connected to the steel body via Cynaps and had its natural emotional responses suppressed by an artificial inhibitor. On crossing the Void into the real Earth, the Cybermen carried out the same process on human captives there. (2.5, 2.6, 2.12, 2.13)

'Un-Break My Heart': English-language song by Diane Warren, covered in Spanish under the title 'Regresa A Mi' by Il Divo and played to Elton Pope by Jackie Tyler as she tried to seduce him. (2.10)

Undercity: Lower region of New New York, untouched and unaware of the devastation in the Overcity, powered by the Face of Boe to stop it falling into the ocean. The Undercity had become a series of small towns, like Pharmacytown, where the remaining inhabitants of New New York could go for supplies. (3.3)

UNIT: A special military-scientific elite force, made up of forces from across the world, specialising in threats to security of an extraterrestrial nature. A collection of UNIT specialists arrived from Geneva to attend a briefing at 10 Downing Street over the Big Ben incident, including Colonel Muriel Frost. They, along with various academics and soldiers, were killed by the Slitheen, who had electrified their ID cards. (1.4, 1.5) When the Sycorax spaceship intercepted the Guinevere One

space probe and began to broadcast to Earth, Prime Minister Harriet Jones joined UNIT's Major Blake in the organisation's secret Mission Control base beneath the Tower of London to supervise the situation. Blake was murdered by the Sycorax when the UNIT officer, the PM and Professor Daniel Llewellyn were taken aboard the alien's vessel. (2.X) UNIT were

memory of his experiences. (AotG) (Played by BEN HOLLAND)

Utah: America's 45th State, on the western side of the continent. Surrounded by desert plains, it was an ideal location for Henry Van Statten to build his underground base. (1.6)

Utopia: Legendary location where the last members of the human race planned to assemble, 100,000,000,000,000 years in the future. It was out towards the Wildlands of space, beyond the Condensate Wilderness but close to the Dark Matter Reefs. Those trapped on Malcassairo were dependent on a rocket which Professor Yana was trying to launch. With help from the Doctor and Captain Jack Harkness, the rocket took off, taking the humans to Utopia where, ultimately, they or their descendents would become the Toclafane. Later, the Master and Lucy Saxon were able to travel to Utopia to discover it was everything the humans had hoped it wouldn't be. There were no diamonds in the skies – indeed, as the universe around them began to decay, the humans on Utopia had destroyed the world, leaving it dark and cold, with only the furnaces with which they defiled their own bodies to light the darkness. (3.11, 3.13)

also given authority over the British military by US President Winters after the first appearance of the Toclafane, and were initially responsible for security aboard the *Valiant*, though they were dismissed by the President as he prepared to greet the Toclafane. (3.12) In an abandoned UNIT base in North London, Martha Jones claimed, was the last of the phials of liquid needed to arm the gun she was allegedly preparing to kill the Master with. (3.13) Under the Doctor's guidance, Mickey Smith was able to access UNIT computer systems (1.5, 2.X), and a web page about UNIT was seen by the Doctor when he accessed a mobile phone to search for HC Clements. (3.X)

Units Ten/Six/Five and Ten/Six/Six: Two Cybermen sent to investigate the Sphere Room in Torchwood Tower. They encountered Dalek Thay in the corridor, who shot them down. (2.13) (Voiced by NICHOLAS BRIGGS)

Universal Roaming: The method by which the Doctor ensured both Rose Tyler's and Martha Jones's mobile phones could work anywhere in time and space. (1.2, 3.7)

University of Edinburgh: Posing as Dr James McCrimmon, the Doctor told Queen Victoria he had studied in Edinburgh under Dr Joseph Bell. (2.2)

University of Mars: Adam Mitchell pretended he was a student visiting from the University of Mars, to explain away his lack of an Info Chip to the Nurse aboard Satellite Five. (1.7)

Untempered Schism: A rip in the fabric of space and time, through which eternity and the Time Vortex could be observed. Looking into it as Novices about to enter the Academy on Gallifrey, young Time Lords would have different responses. It sent the Master insane, it made the Doctor flee, others it would inspire. It was destroyed along with the rest of Gallifrey at the end of the Last Great Time War. (3.12)

Urchin: A London boy kidnapped by the Graske at Christmas 1883, and replaced with a Changeling. He was eventually returned home with no

Utopia Project: A human cadre, the Science Foundation, postulated the concept of Utopia and formulated the Utopia Project thousands of years before Professor Yana got the rocket launched away from Malcassairo and towards Utopia. (3.11)

V

Valiant: UNIT aircraft carrier, which Harry Saxon helped design. It did not sail on the seas but flew in the skies above Earth. It was decided that Earth would greet the Toclafane there, thus not in any one

country's territory. After the Toclafane invaded, the Master made the *Valiant* his base of operations for the next year, keeping Francine, Clive and Tish Jones prisoners there, working for him. Captain Jack Harkness was chained up below decks, Lucy Saxon became one of a harem of girls the Master kept onboard, and the Doctor, physically reduced to a shrunken, 900-year-old Time Lord, was held in a birdcage. The TARDIS was also stored there, cannibalised by the Master to create the Paradox Machine. After the Master had been defeated, Lucy Saxon shot him dead on the bridge. (3.12, 3.13)

Van Cassadyne energy: The main component of a Delta Wave. Trapped on the Game Station, facing half a million Daleks, the Doctor opted to use the Station's resources as a huge transmitter, creating a Delta Wave which would fry anything in its path. The Emperor foresaw this eventuality and reminded the Doctor that, should he use the Delta Wave, he would indeed wipe out the Daleks, but before that, it would kill everything between them, including the population of Earth. In the end, faced with the choice, the Doctor resigned himself to failing, and the Wave was never activated. (1.13)

Van Statten, Henry: The internet-owning American billionaire, whose intelligence was matched only by his arrogance and self-obsession. Although his main business was his Geocomtex Corporation he was an avid collector of all and any extraterrestrial artefacts. If he found a way to exploit them commercially through Geocomtex, he would. He kept his artefacts in an exhibit room, inside a bunker 53 storeys below Utah. He owned something he called a 'Metaltron', which he knew was alive but, no matter how much he had it tortured, he could not get it to respond. When the Doctor and Rose Tyler arrived, it did finally, and the Doctor realised he

was facing a Dalek. The Dalek freed itself and went on a murderous rampage, wiping out virtually all Van Statten's security and staff, but he refused to run the risk of damaging the prize of his collection. Eventually, face to face with it, Van Statten revealed how terrified he was, but the Dalek spared him after a plea from Rose. After the Dalek was destroyed, Van Statten suffered a fate which had previously befallen so many of his staff – his subordinate Goddard had him mind-wiped and dumped on the streets somewhere, to live the remainder of his life as a brainless junkie. (1.6) (Played by COREY JOHNSON)

Vashtee, Riley: One of the crew aboard the SS *Pentallian*, he was horrified to learn that Korwin McDonnell had destroyed the engineering equipment, setting the cargo ship on a collision course with a nearby sun. He and Martha Jones headed for the auxiliary controls at the front of the ship, trying to get through the locked doors in time, answering trivia questions that the crew had set as passwords. Along the way, however, they were intercepted by a sun-possessed crewmate, Dev Ashton and, to escape him, they hid in an escape pod. Ashton jettisoned the pod, sending it towards the sun. Inside, Vashtee and Martha discussed their impending deaths, and he revealed that his father was dead and he'd run away from his mother six years before because she hadn't wanted him to sign up for work on a cargo ship. Vashtee and Martha were saved when the Doctor remagnetised the ship and the pod. Once back aboard, Vashtee made it to auxiliary with Orin Scannell, and they vented the scooped-up fuel from the sun, managing to get the ship back on course. Sad to say goodbye to Martha, Vashtee remained with Scannell aboard the *Pentallian*, awaiting rescue by the authorities. (3.7) (Played by WILLIAM ASH)

Veronica of Reykjavik: Prestigious florist on 'Pete's World'. Jackie Tyler had flowers for her birthday party delivered from her. (2.5)

Versailles: Suburb of Paris, France – and home to the legendary Palace, or Hall of Mirrors as it was known. In 1745, Jeanne-Antoinette Poisson, aka Madame de Pompadour, aka Reinette, was moved in as the King's consort. In 1758, a party at Versailles was interrupted when Clockwork Robots from the 51st century attacked, intending to remove Reinette's brain for use in the repair of their spaceship, which was named after her. The Doctor cut off their link to the future, the Robots deactivated and everyone at the Palace was saved. (2.4)

Vespa: Italian-design motorised scooter, first on the market in 1946. The Doctor had a pink Vespa parked in the TARDIS, which he and Rose used to get around North London in 1953. After defeating the alien criminal calling itself the Wire, the Doctor gave the scooter to young Tommy Connolly, telling him he was too young to ride it yet. (2.7)

Vault, the: Geocomtex's secret underground base, beneath the Utah desert, which would double as a bunker in the event of a nuclear strike above ground had over fifty storeys of research, development and security and, below that, was the Vault, containing Henry van Statten's exhibit room, where he kept his alien artefacts. Also in this Vault was the 'Cage' – the containment area where the 'Metaltron' was tortured. Van Statten attempted to seal the Vault off at Level 46 (his office) when the Dalek tried to fight its way out. (1.6)

Vel Consadine: Civilisation which had the concept of evil represented by a horned beast in its culture. (2.9)

Veltino: The extinct race that had once inhabited the planet Krop Tor, giving it its name, which translated from their language as 'the bitter pill'. (2.8)

Venezuela: South American country. On 'Pete's World', the diamond-studded ear pods given to Jackie Tyler as a gift from John Lumic were able to pick up signals from as far afield as Venezuela. (2.5)

Venom Grubs: Inhabitants of a number of planets in the Isop Galaxy. Mindless, lethal giant arthropods, Blon Fel Fotch Pasameer-Day Slitheen's father used to threaten to feed her to them when she was young. (1.11)

Venus: Planet in Earth's solar system, next in line to the Sun. The Doctor carried a toothbrush filled with Venusian toothpaste, and he gave it to Martha Jones when they stayed in Elizabethan England. (3.2)

Vicar [1]: Officiated at St Christopher's Church for the wedding of Stuart Hoskins and Sarah Clark. He became a victim of the Reapers as they broke into the world after Rose Tyler saved her dad's life and created a breach in time. (1.8) (Played by LEE GRIFFITHS)

Vicar [2]: Was about to perform the marriage service at St Mary's Church in Chiswick between Donna Noble and Lance Bennett when Donna vanished. During the resultant pandemonium, another wedding got delayed, and the Vicar ended up calling the police to try and sort out the bedlam around him. (3.X) (Played by TREVOR GEORGES)

Vicar [3]: Gave the Remembrance Day service attended by an old Tim Latimer, the Doctor and Martha Jones. She read from Binyon's 'For the Fallen'. (3.9) (Played by SOPHIE TURNER)

Vicky: A friend of Martha Jones. She obsessed about a guy, Shaun, she was in love with. He never looked twice at her, but she put her own life on hold while she focused on him. Martha told her to move on and get out — and likened herself to Vicky over her feelings toward the Doctor. She and the Doctor parted company as best of friends. (3.13)

Victoria, Queen Alexandrina: Queen of Great Britain and Ireland, Empress of India, the Doctor and Rose Tyler encountered her at a period of her life when she lived mainly at Balmoral Castle in Scotland, to which she was heading when they met. She had been travelling by train until the Brethren of St Catherine blocked the line with a tree, so was now travelling by coach. Together, they all travelled to Torchwood House to stay the night as guests of her late husband's friend's son, Sir Robert MacLeish. MacLeish senior and Prince Albert had built a vast telescope in the Observatory atop the House which, it transpired, had been designed as a trap for the Haemovariform that had existed in the area for over 300 years. Victoria faced this werewolf bravely, but may or may not have been cut by its claws. The Host virus was passed by blood, and Victoria was later diagnosed with haemophilia, a hereditary illness which her forebears were not known to suffer from. She was grateful to the Doctor and Rose for destroying the Haemovariform but, after honouring them both, she exiled them from the British Empire's shores. When Lady Isobel MacLeish confessed she no longer wished to live at Torchwood House, Victoria decided to keep the place herself and set up the Torchwood Institute to defend the British Empire against further alien threats. (2.2) (Played by PAULINE COLLINS) A web page about Queen Victoria was seen by the Doctor when he accessed a mobile phone with his sonic screwdriver to search for HC Clements. (3.X)

Vietnam: Listing things of importance that happened in 1979, the Doctor told Rose Tyler that China invaded Vietnam. (2.2)

Vikram: Guest at the wedding between Donna Noble and Lance Bennett. He had a mobile phone. (3.X)

Vile, Doctor: False personality adopted by the Doctor, pretending to be a galactic pirate and responsible for stirring up the war between Earth and the Mantasphids. The Empire then sent out a message across the galaxy, demanding his apprehension. (TIQ)

Villengard: Captain Jack Harkness had a digital sonic blaster, manufactured in the weapons factories of Villengard. The Doctor suggested that he had caused an accident in Villengard's main reactor, destroying the weapons factories completely and planting a banana grove in its place. (1.10)

Vinegar: See *Acetic acid*

Viscum album: The proper name for European mistletoe, such as that which the Brethren of St Catherine wore to protect themselves from the Haemovariform they had brought to Torchwood House in 1879. Sir George MacLeish had varnished his library with the oil from *viscum album* to keep the werewolf out. (2.2)

Vitex: One of Pete Tyler's get-rich-quick schemes had involved selling a health drink called Vitex. It failed. (1.8) In 'Pete's World', that version of Pete Tyler made millions out of Vitex (especially the Cherry-Lite flavour) and became a minor celebrity because of his adverts, culminating in the phrase 'Trust me on this' entering popular culture. Cybus Industries bought up Pete's Vitex company, making him even richer. (2.5, 2.6)

Void, the: The space between the dimensions separating billions of divergent realities and parallel worlds (including 'Pete's World'). (2.5) It contained absolutely nothing: no light, dark, direction, time or sense of reality. The Cybermen had moved from 'Pete's World' and across the Void over a long period of time to break into Rose Tyler's reality. A Void ship containing Daleks had escaped into the Void with the Genesis Ark, then pushed itself back into the world, though with part of it still locked into the Void. They were using the breaches caused by both the Cybermen and Torchwood to ease themselves through. When they did, they emerged and began a war with the Cybermen. Because everything that had ever crossed the Void was contaminated with an almost undetectable substance he called Void stuff, when the Doctor reopened the Void fully, everything contaminated was instantly sucked back in through the Wall. Once all the Daleks and Cybermen were back inside the Void, the Doctor sealed it for ever, trapping them into an eternity of nothing. Rose Tyler had also been almost drawn in, since she had passed through the Void, but was saved by the 'Pete's World' version of her father, who transported her to his home. Rose was sealed off from the Doctor, presumably for ever. (2.12, 2.13)

Void ship: A spheroid, 20 feet in diameter, which could be seen but not properly touched. No matter how hard anyone looked at it, it was if it wasn't quite there. It gave off no sensory information that either humans or computers could read, and yet it was actually there. A Torchwood team led by Dr Rajesh Singh had studied it, but even a new spectrometer brought in by Torchwood's R&D team couldn't get a reading off it. Once the Cybermen had broken through the Lever Room, the Sphere, which the Doctor identified as a Void ship, began to operate and become 'real'. But the Cyber Leader in the Lever Room informed the Doctor it wasn't their technology – indeed, it had nothing to do with Cybermen at all. All parties were astonished to see four Daleks – the Cult of Skaro – emerge from within, bringing with them the Genesis Ark. (2.12, 2.13)

Void stuff: Particles of matter which clung to anything that had passed through the Void. It was only visible through 3D glasses. The Daleks and Cybermen had had relatively lengthy excursions through the Void and were therefore coated in it. As a result, they were easily sucked back into the Void when it was fully opened by the Doctor. So would Rose Tyler have been, but she was saved by the 'Pete's World' version of her father, who transported her to his home. Rose was sealed off in 'Pete's World', where she had to remain without the Doctor, presumably for ever. (2.12, 2.13)

Volag-Noc: Ice-covered planet that housed under its surface a galactic prison, run by the robotic Governor Locke and his Warders during the 40th century. Amongst the inmates were Baltazar, Gurney, Kaliko and, later, the

Doctor. A regular visitor to Volag-Noc was Mergrass, who would do deals between the prisoners and other inmates or outside sources. Gurney used a device he bought from Mergrass to usurp Locke from his role as Governor. Gurney imprisoned Locke in Cell 8447, but the Doctor freed him. Disturbed by Gurney's inhibitors, Locke tried to kill all the inmates but the Doctor stopped him and later reprogrammed him to run a fairer prison, before having Baltazar returned to the planet for incarceration. (TIQ)

Vomit-O-Matic: Installed at no extra cost to Adam Mitchell when he had the Type Two chip inserted into his head. As soon as the doors in his forehead whirred open and he saw his own brain, Adam threw up, but the Nurse told him the nano-termites now implanted into his throat had frozen the waste created by his gag reflex. (1.7)

'Voodoo Child': Single by Rogue Traders, which was played by the Master aboard the *Valiant* as the Toclafane began their descent. Lucy Saxon danced along to it, too. (3.12)

Vortex Loop: Essential component of the TARDIS console. (AotG)

Vortex Manipulator: Wrist device supplied to Time Agents. Captain Jack Harkness owned one – he used it to teleport himself from Albion Hospital back to his ship. It had a holographic projector in it, could scan for alien tech and was capable of providing medical readouts. After the battle against the Emperor Daleks' forces on the Game Station, Jack was exterminated but brought back to life by Rose Tyler. He tried to use the Vortex Manipulator to get back to 21st-century Earth, hoping he could track the Doctor down there but, due to the damage caused by the Daleks, it fried and he was transported to 1869, the device now burnt out. When trapped on Malcassairo, the Master having stolen the TARDIS, the Doctor used his sonic screwdriver to temporarily reboot the Vortex Manipulator's time-travelling abilities, initially to get them to 21st-century London and later as a spatial teleporter. This took Martha Jones off the *Valiant* and down to the surface of Earth. Later still, it transported the Master and the Doctor back and forth from the *Valiant*. When Captain Jack parted ways with the Doctor once again, the Doctor undid his earlier repair work, leaving the Vortex Manipulator incapable of teleport, either in time or space. (1.9, 1.10, 1.13, 3.11, 3.12, 3.13)

Vossaheen, Princess:
Rose Tyler did not know the surname of this royal figure during *The Weakest Link* aboard the Game Station. (1.12)

Vulcan salute: From the television series *Star Trek*. The Doctor showed Chloe Webber that he could do a Vulcan salute to charm her – but it failed and Chloe was more frightened than ever because she didn't understand the Isolus that was inhabiting her body. She later returned the salute as a way of telling the Doctor that she was willing to talk to him. (2.11)

Wagner, Mr: A Krillitane who had taken human form and was working at Deffry Vale High School as a mathematics teacher. He was killed when K-9 heated up the drums of Krillitane Oil in the school kitchen and blew Wagner, the school and himself to pieces. (2.3) (Played by EUGENE WASHINGTON)

Wainwright, Ben: Young farmer who was the first person Kathy Nightingale met when she was transported from the London of 2007 to the Hull of 1920. Clearly attracted to Kathy, he pursued her and eventually they got married (although she lied about her age). They had three children together, two boys and a girl called Sally, but Ben died of influenza in 1962. (3.10) (Played by THOMAS NELSTROP)

Wainwright, Katherine: See *Nightingale, Katherine Costello*

Wainwright, Malcolm: Kathy Wainwright's grandson. She asked him to find Sally Sparrow at Wester Drumlins at exactly the moment she knew she was going to be sent back in time by the Weeping Angels. Although Kathy was now dead, Malcolm did as bidden and gave Sally a letter from Kathy explaining what had happened to her and asking her to contact her brother Larry. (3.10) (Played by RICHARD CANT)

Wainwright, Sally: Daughter of Ben and Kathy Wainwright, named in honour of Kathy's old friend Sally Sparrow. She had two older brothers. (3.10)

Walford: Fictional setting for the BBC TV soap opera *EastEnders*. The Doctor refers to Walford while crossing the cavern beneath Krop Tor. (2.8) Peggy Mitchell runs the show's Queen Vic pub, as seen on Jackie Tyler's television. (2.12)

Walker, Captain: Torchwood operative put in command of the mission to Krop Tor by Torchwood Archivist McMillan. It was believed that the power source detected beneath Krop Tor would be enough to power the entire Earth Empire. The only clue she could offer Walker was a book of maps, hieroglyphs, writings and drawings found by the destroyed Gedes Expedition. Walker took a ship to the K 37 Gem 5 black hole and used the gravity funnel linking it to Krop Tor as a route down. Things went wrong, however, and Walker was killed in the descent, leaving Zachary Cross Flane as acting captain. (2.8T) (Played by JASON MAY)

Wall Street Crash: The 1929 event which wiped out much of America's financial prosperity, after years of a business boom, driving the country into its Depression Era, which lasted until 1933. (3.4, 3.5)

Walterley Street, SE15: South London street running alongside St Christopher's Church. Mickey Smith ran along it from the playground after his mother Pauline had been destroyed by the Reapers. (1.8)

Ward, Shayne: British pop singer who, by 2012, had released a greatest hits CD, according to posters next to the TARDIS when it arrived in Stratford. (2.11)

Ward 26: Area in the Hospital on New Earth shared between the Face of Boe, the Duke of Manhattan and others in the upper echelons of the New New York social elite. (2.1)

Warders: Robotic prison guards under the ice planet of Volag-Noc. Wired into a central network, they automatically obeyed the Governor. (TIQ) (Voiced by DAN MORGAN)

Warp-shunt technology: The means of transport used by the Nestene Consciousness to flee the devastation of the Time War and reach planet Earth. (1.1)

Wash Inn: South East London launderette where Jackie Tyler met Elton Pope. (2.10)

Washington Public Archive: A photo on this website of the John F Kennedy assassination on 22 November 1963 clearly shows the Ninth Doctor watching from the crowds. (1.1)

Waterton Street, SE15: Street on which Mickey Smith had been brought up by his late grandmother, Rita-Anne until she tripped on a loose piece of stair-carpet and died. On 'Pete's World', Ricky Smith had continued to live there, as Rita-Anne was still alive. (2.5)

Watson, Thomas: Young electrical designer, assistant to Alexander Graham Bell and recipient of the very first telephone call. (1.8)

Watts, Den: Fictional character from the BBC soap opera *EastEnders*, whose ghost had returned to plague current publican Peggy Mitchell. (2.12)

Weakest Link, The: One of the many 'games' being played on the Game Station and broadcast throughout Earth – a general knowledge quiz show,

chaired by the Anne Droid – and played by Rose Tyler against the likes of Rodrick, Broff, Agorax, Fitch and Collcon. Like all the games, losing appeared to be instantly fatal, although in fact being shot by the Anne Droid involved being transported to the Dalek mothership and turned into part of the growing Dalek army created by the Emperor. (1.12)

Weatherman: As part of his television weather forecast, this presenter gave predictions of ghostly materialisations. (2.12) (Played by PAUL FIELDS)

Webber, Chloe: A 12-year-old girl who lived with her mother Trish on Dame Kelly Holmes Close. Chloe had encountered a lonely alien, an Isolus, which had merged with her, creating two intelligences in the one

body. Using Chloe's natural artistic bent, the Isolus gave her the power to draw things that would then take on a life of their own, while the object or person she had drawn disappeared from reality. Chloe was the cause of the disappearances of other kids – she had drawn them to be friends for the Isolus. She also created the Scribble Creature that attacked Rose outside a car garage, and a full-sized drawing of her late, violent father, which later threatened her and her mum. Eventually the Isolus was coaxed out of Chloe when Rose found a way to release its space capsule and, using the heat from the Olympic Torch being carried past the road, was able to get the Isolus back to the rest of its family. With the Isolus gone, Chloe and her mother Trish carried on with their lives after bonding more strongly than before and defeating the last vestiges of the ionic-powered image of Chloe's dad. (2.11) (Played by ABISOLA AGBAJE)

Webber, Mr: Trish's abusive husband who had died a year before in a car crash but who Chloe kept on having nightmares about. After Chloe absorbed the Isolus into herself and gained the ability to manipulate the drawings she created, she accidentally brought a drawing of Mr Webber to life and, even though the Isolus was gone, the residual ionic energy Chloe had used continued to animate it until she and her mum bonded again by singing 'Kookaburra' and the image of Mr Webber vanished for ever. (2.11) (Voiced by PAUL McFADDEN)

Webber, Trish: Resident of 53 Dame Kelly Holmes Close and mother of Chloe, a little girl who was having social problems, locking herself in her room to draw. Chloe had in fact been in communion with a lonely alien called the Isolus who just wanted companionship. Trish helped the Doctor and Rose Tyler find a way to free the Isolus, but not before they'd been threatened by a huge drawing Chloe had done of her violent father, who had died a year earlier. (2.11) (Played by NINA SOSANYA)

Webstar: The distinctive ships of the Racnoss. One of these, the Secret Heart, was trapped at the centre of Earth. Another, filled with television screens monitoring broadcasts across the planet, was piloted by the Empress of the Racnoss. She fired energy beams from it, trying to destroy Earth. It was eventually blown up by shells from a British army tank, just as the Empress returned to it. (3.X)

Wellgrove Hospice: The hospital where Sally Sparrow encountered the dying Billy Shipton. He knew he was destined to die the night he met her again, and she stayed there with him until the end. (3.10)

Wembley Stadium: Venue in North London. Rose Tyler saw ABBA perform there in November 1979. (AotG) The Stadium hosted the Olympic Games in 1948, which the Doctor enjoyed so much he watched it twice. (2.11)

Werewolf: The form chosen by the Lupine-Wavelength-Haemovariform that crashed to Earth in Scotland in 1560. Its current Host was placed on the Torchwood Estate and allowed

WEEPING ANGELS: Time-sensitive alien killers, as old as the universe, who thrived on chronon energy. They would send their victims back in time just by touching them, to live their lives in a different time zone, and the Angels would feed on the potential time energy created by the vanished people's preordained lives being disturbed. Often called Lonely Assassins, because they could never touch anything without sending it back in time, they could only move and attack if they weren't being observed (because if they were seen, they immediately became quantum-locked and froze into solid rock). Just blinking enabled them to cross vast distances towards their victims. The Doctor used an unwitting Sally Sparrow to trap them – when Sally and her friend Larry accessed the TARDIS, the Weeping Angels gathered around it, hoping to feed off its energy, but the Doctor had preset a dematerialisation sequence, meaning it vanished from around Sally and Larry, who were unhurt because, taken off-guard, the Weeping Angels were all looking at each other when the TARDIS dematerialised. All four were frozen for eternity, unable to close their eyes, and unable not to see one another. (3.10) (Played by AGA BLONSKA, ELEN THOMAS)

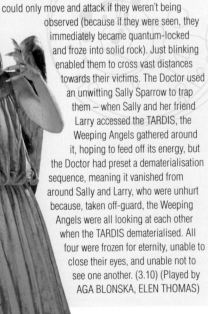

to transform, rampaging through Torchwood House, killing a number of people including the Steward, the footmen and male staff of the House, Captain Reynolds and Sir Robert MacLeish, before being destroyed in a trap made of focused moonlight set in motion some years before by Sir Robert's father and Prince Albert. (2.2)

Wester Drumlins: Old ramshackle house where the four Weeping Angels gathered. They had zapped the Doctor and Martha Jones back to 1969, but were after the TARDIS and needed Sally Sparrow to lead them to it after she took the key from them. The TARDIS was in a police car pound, surrounded by vehicles belonging to people who had gone to Wester Drumlins and never been heard from again – all sent back in time by the Weeping Angels. Larry Nightingale described Wester Drumlins as looking like Scooby-Doo's house. (3.10)

Western Mail: Cardiff newspaper on the front page of which the Doctor saw a photograph of Margaret Blaine and realised he had to investigate the Slitheen's activities. (1.11)

Westminster Abbey: Queen Elizabeth II was crowned there in 1953, watched by millions of people live on television, during which the Wire planned to steal all their faces. (2.7)

WH Smith: British chain of stationers and booksellers. Donna Noble knew she was still on Earth when she saw one in the London street the TARDIS had taken her and the Doctor to. (3.X)

What Not To Wear: One of the competitive programmes being transmitted from the Game Station around Earth. Two robots, Trine-E and Zu-Zana, would take humans and decide how to make them look more fashionable. However, they would then end the show by physically reconstructing their 'victims' with buzzsaws and lasers if they weren't satisfied. Captain Jack Harkness found himself in their show. (1.12)

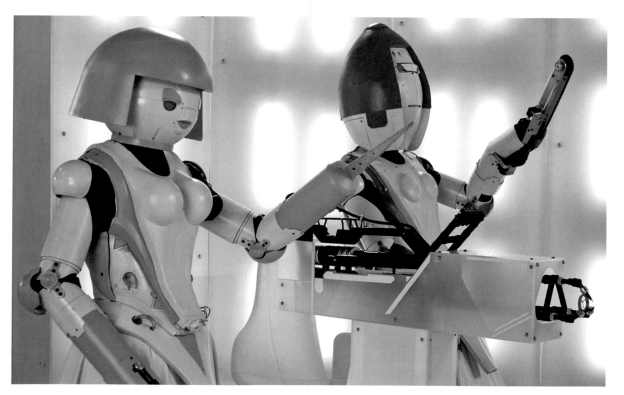

What's My Line?: BBC Television quiz show in which people would mime their job before a celebrity panel who would then guess their occupation. It ran from 1951 to 1963 and was playing on a television in Mr Magpie's shop when the Wire first appeared to him. (2.7)

White House: The Executive Office of the President of the United States of America. The President was due to address the American nation live from the White House on the evening of the Big Ben incident. (1.4)

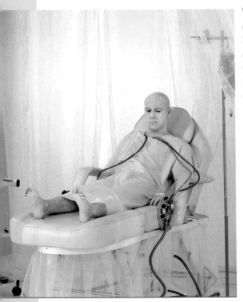

White People: A number of the humans who lived on New Earth came in extreme colours, including red and white. In the Hospital on New Earth, a White Man was cured by the Sisters of Plenitude of Pallidome Pancrosis. (2.1) (Played by PAUL ZEPH GOULD) The Doctor encountered another White Man in the New New York Motorway, when he jumped into his car from Brannigan's, claiming to be part of the Motorway Foot Patrol. Whitey was very annoyed that Junction 5 had been closed for three years. (3.3) (Played by SIMON PEARSALL)

Wicks: Schoolboy at Farringham School for Boys in 1913, who took part in the war games there, manning the Vickers Gun. (3.8)

Widdecombe, Ann: Conservative MP, who endorsed Harry Saxon's campaign to become Prime Minister. (3.12)

Wiggins: Young lad in Elizabethan England who tried to seduce Lilith, believing her to be a young, beautiful human. When Lilith introduced Wiggins to her parents, Mother Doomfinger and Mother Bloodtide, they literally tore him to shreds. (3.1) (Played by SAM MARKS)

Wild Endeavour: A continent on Gallifrey, the Doctor's home world, where the Time Lord citadel had sat, in the mountains of Solace and Solitude, beneath a glass dome. It was destroyed, along with the rest of Gallifrey, at the end of the Last Great Time War. (3.12)

Wildlands: An area of space, most likely unexplored, towards the edge of the known universe. Utopia wasn't quite as far as the Wildlands, nor the Dark Matter Reefs. (3.11)

Williams: Schoolboy at Farringham School for Boys in 1913, who was put in charge of arranging sandbags before the Family of Blood attacked. (3.9)

Williams, Robbie: British singer and former member of boy band Take That, who was due to rejoin his former band mates to perform at the opening ceremony for the 2012 Olympic Games at Stratford. (2.11)

Wilson, HP: Chief electrical officer at the Henrik's store where Rose Tyler worked. He was found dead by the Doctor, presumably at the hands of the Autons. (1.1)

Winters, Arthur Coleman: President of the United States of America and Representative of the United Nations to the Toclafane. He welcomed them to Earth aboard the aircraft carrier *Valiant*, but the Toclafane were interested only in the Master and, on live television, disintegrated Winters. (3.12) (Played by COLIN STINTON)

Wipeout: One of the programmes broadcast from the Game Station. Losing contestants were, oddly enough, wiped out. (1.12)

Wire, the: Criminal mastermind from the planet Hermethica, who led a gang that could transform themselves into plasmic energy. Sentenced to death, the Wire escaped and beamed itself through space, when it was drawn into a television set in Magpie's Electricals, a shop run by Mr Magpie. It used its plasmic powers to drain the life energy from its victims as they watched television, leaving them faceless, mindless husks, their basic consciousness (and faces) left trapped inside the television sets. The Wire planned to unleash its full potential via the Alexandra Palace transmitter mast as the nation sat down to watch Queen Elizabeth II's Coronation and physically renew itself, but the Doctor re-routed the Wire's broadcast frequency and used the mast to transmit the Wire onto a Betamax videotape, which he intended to record over later. (2.7T, 2.7) (Played by MAUREEN LIPMAN)

Wiry Woman: One of the Futurekind, who had evaded the normally rigorous guards and gained access to the Silo base on Malcassairo. She sabotaged the base's power systems, which killed a guard called Jate. The Doctor and Captain Jack were able to override her sabotage and the rocket eventually took off, after the Wiry Woman had been gunned down by other guards. (3.11) (Played by ABIGAIL CANTON)

Woman: Occupant of the slave house in Bexley, South London. She listened to Martha's story and was later on the streets saying the Doctor's name, along with the rest of mankind. (3.13) (Played by NATASHA ALEXANDER)

Woman Wept: A planet visited by the Doctor and Rose Tyler. It was named this because one of its continents, if viewed from space, resembled a women bent over in distress. They visited a deserted beach that seemed to be 1,000 miles long. (1.11)

Wombles, the: Fictional creatures who, in the books of Elizabeth Beresford, lived on Wimbledon Common, picking up the litter humans left behind and turning it to good use. One of the Wombles was the French cook, Madame Cholet. The Doctor referred to her as one of the greatest chefs on Earth. (TIQ)

Woolwich: South East London location of the warehouse where Elton Pope witnessed the Doctor and Rose Tyler engaging the Hoix. (2.10)

Workmen: After handing the Foreman over to the Daleks, Mr Diagoras, charged with overseeing the construction of the upper floors of the Empire State Building by the Cult of Skaro, ordered his workers to keep working until everything was completed that night. One worker (played by JOE MONTANA) protested that at that height, and late at night, they would most likely freeze and fall to their deaths instead of successfully fixing the Dalekanium slats to the mooring mast. Diagoras pointed out that he could always find other men to do the job, so the reluctant worker and a mate (played by STEWART ALEXANDER) found themselves doing the job after all. (3.4)

World War Five: The Doctor tells Rose Tyler he witnessed this war from sometime in Earth's future. (1.3)

Wristwatch: The Master had rigged his watch up so he could remotely activate the black hole converters within the warheads of his rockets. He threatened to set them off on Earth but the Doctor reminded him that he would die along with the planet. The Master surrendered the watch. (3.13)

XYZ

X-Factor, The: According to Lance Bennett, Donna Noble talked excitedly about this reality TV show. (3.X)

Yellen, Jack: Wrote the lyrics for 'Happy Days Are Here Again', one of the show tunes used as part of the New York Revue at the Laurenzi theatre in 1930s New York. (3.4)

Yew Tree Ball: Major Paris social event held on 25 February 1745, at which the young Jeanne-Antoinette Poisson hoped to catch the eye of King Louis with the intention of becoming his new mistress. (2.4)

York: The Grand Central Ravine was named after the Ancient British city of Sheffield, not York. Rose Tyler didn't know this when asked by the Anne Droid in *The Weakest Link* aboard the Game Station. (1.12)

'You Are Not Alone': The last words spoken by the Face of Boe, out loud rather than telepathically. He had waited until the end of his life to say them specifically to the Doctor, not just as a message but as a warning about Professor Yana. (3.3)

You've Been Framed: Long-running ITV series to which members of the public sent their home videos and got a financial reward if these were shown. Rhodri, the videographer at Donna Noble's wedding, had thought of sending his footage of the bride disappearing to the show. (3.X)

Young Woman: Passerby in the street in 1883 at Christmas, when a young street urchin was kidnapped by the Graske. (AotG) (Played by CATHERINE OLDING)

'Zadok The Priest': Anthem especially written by Handel for the Coronation of George II and used at all subsequent British Coronations during the anointing ceremony, including that of Queen Elizabeth II, watched by millions in 1953, when the Wire was scheming to steal their life energies in order to renew itself. (2.7)

Zaffic: An icy beef-flavoured drink Rose Tyler purchased aboard Satellite Five. (1.7)

Zed, Tobias: Virginal (according to the Beast) scientist aboard Sanctuary Base 6, his specialised field was archaeology but he was having difficulty understanding the strange hieroglyphs and inscriptions found on the objects scattered across the surface of Krop Tor after the drilling began. However, the more he studied, the more his mind drew the attention of the Beast, imprisoned deep below the planet. Transferring some of its consciousness into Toby, it used him as a tool to disrupt the Base's mission and ultimately led to the Doctor heading down to confront it. The Beast split its consciousness between Toby and the Ood – whether Toby was always aware of what he did is unknown. Eventually, realising that the Doctor would sacrifice Rose Tyler and the other human

survivors (including Toby) aboard an escape shuttle, the Beast placed all of its consciousness into Toby. Realising that Toby was dangerous, Rose Tyler ejected him into space and both he and the Beast were destroyed in the event horizon of the black hole. (2.8, 2.9) (Played by WILL THORP)

Zeus plugs: The Doctor needed these to close down the Time Windows aboard the SS *Madame de Pompadour*, but couldn't find them – then remembered he'd last had them in the 18th century, when he was using them as castanets at a party. (2.4)

Zone One: The Master's new name for Britain after the Toclafane had helped him take over Earth. (3.13)

Zovirax: Medicinal product on Earth, used to cover cold sores. An advertising campaign used the image of a leather-clad despatch biker with a black helmet, which caused Martha Jones to suggest the similar-looking Slabs came from the planet Zovirax. (3.1)

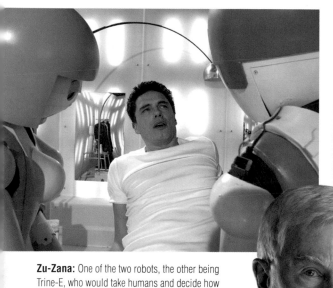

Zu-Zana: One of the two robots, the other being Trine-E, who would take humans and decide how to make them look more fashionable for their TV show *What Not to Wear*. However, they would then end the show, being broadcast across Earth from the Game Station, by physically reconstructing their 'victims' with buzzsaws and lasers if they weren't satisfied. Captain Jack Harkness found himself in their show and destroyed both robots with his Compact Laser Deluxe. (1.12) (Voiced by SUSANNAH CONSTANTINE, played by PAUL KASEY)

Zybamen: What Jackie Tyler called the Cybermen at first. (2.12)

PROFESSOR YANA: The personality imposed upon the Master's body which integrated him, in human form, into events at the end of the universe. Yana had been an orphaned child, found naked on the coast of the Silver Devastation following a storm, with no possessions other than a broken fob watch – actually the receptacle that stored the Master's true consciousness. All his life, Yana had experienced headaches and heard the constant sound of pounding drums. He'd spent his time travelling between refugee ships, before eventually settling on the planet Malcassairo to work as a scientist, having assumed the archaic title of Professor for himself in the process. A genius across a variety of fields, he oversaw the development of the Utopia project for 17 years, with the help of his friend anChantho, and was willing to sacrifice his own life to ensure the survival of the human race when his Footprint Impeller System finally became active. It was during a conversation with Martha Jones that Yana discovered the truth about time travel, and was encouraged by her curiosity to open his fob watch, at which point the Master reasserted himself, effectively destroying both Professor Yana and his work. (3.11) (Played by DEREK JACOBI)

Key to References

Throughout this book, information pertaining to a specific episode is followed by a bracketed numerical: '(3.2)' after the entry for Lilith indicates that Lilith was in 'The Shakespeare Code'. A '(T)' after the number refers to the relevant *Tardisode*: '(2.8T)' in the entry for 'Chenna' indicates that the entry relates to the *Tardisode* for 'The Impossible Planet'. As well as the *Tardisode*, this book also incorporates references from *The Infinite Quest*, *Attack of the Graske* and 2005's *Children in Need* mini-episode.